ONLINE TEACHING AT ITS BEST

Merging Instructional Design with Teaching and Learning Research

Linda B. Nilson
Ludwika A. Goodson

JOSSEY-BASS
A Wiley Imprint
www.josseybass.com

Published by Jossey-Bass

A Wiley Brand

One Montgomery Street, Suite 1000, San Francisco, CA 94104–4594—www.josseybass.com

Jossey-Bass books and products are available through most bookstores. To contact Jossey-Bass directly call our Customer Care Department within the U.S. at 800-956-7739, outside the U.S. at 317-572-3986, or fax 317-572-4002.

Wiley publishes in a variety of print and electronic formats and by print-on-demand. Some material included with standard print versions of this book may not be included in e-books or in print-on-demand. If this book refers to media such as a CD or DVD that is not included in the version you purchased, you may download this material at http://booksupport.wiley.com. For more information about Wiley products, visit www.wiley.com.

Library of Congress Cataloging-in-Publication Data

Names: Nilson, Linda Burzotta, author. | Goodson, Ludwika A., 1947- author.
Title: Online teaching at its best / Linda B. Nilson, Ludwika A. Goodson.
Description: San Francisco, CA : Jossey-Bass, 2017. | Includes index.
Identifiers: LCCN 2017042134 (print) | LCCN 2017025733 (ebook) | ISBN
    9781119242314 (pdf) | ISBN 9781119242307 (epub) | ISBN 9781119242291 (pbk.)
Subjects: LCSH: Web-based instruction.
Classification: LCC LB1044.87 (print) | LCC LB1044.87 .N55 2017 (ebook) | DDC
    371.33/44678--dc23
LC record available at https://lccn.loc.gov/2017042134

Cover design by Wiley
Cover images © Thomas E. Fagan/EyeEm/Getty Images
Printed in the United States of America

FIRST EDITION

PB Printing   SKY10020149_073020

CONTENTS

To Emma, Abby, and Sophia—all future online students—and Leslie J. Briggs, former professor of instructional systems design at Florida State University, who asked the burning question: "What do models of teaching have to do with models of instructional design?"

Linda B. Nilson is director emerita of the Office of Teaching Effectiveness and Innovation at Clemson University and author of *Teaching at Its Best: A Research-Based Resource for College Instructors* (Jossey-Bass), now in its fourth edition. She also wrote *The Graphic Syllabus and the Outcomes Map: Communicating Your Course* (Anker/Jossey-Bass, 2007), *Creating Self-Regulated Learners: Strategies to Strengthen Students' Self-Awareness and Learning Skills* (Stylus, 2013), and *Specifications Grading: Restoring Rigor, Motivating Students, and Saving Faculty Time* (Stylus, 2015). Her next book, *Avoiding Crickets: Strategies for Creating Engaging Discussions*, coauthored with Jennifer Herman, will be published by Stylus.

In addition, Nilson coedited *Enhancing Learning with Laptops in the Classroom* (Jossey-Bass, 2005) and volumes 25 through 28 of *To Improve the Academy: Resources for Faculty, Instructional, and Organizational Development* (Anker/Jossey-Bass, 2007–2010), which is the major publication of the Professional and Organizational Development (POD) Network in Higher Education.

Nilson's career as a full-time faculty development director has spanned over twenty-five years. She has published many articles and book chapters and has given over 450 keynotes, webinars, and live workshops at conferences, colleges, and universities both nationally and internationally on dozens of topics related to college teaching and scholarly productivity. She has also taught graduate seminars on college teaching.

Before coming to Clemson University, she directed teaching centers at Vanderbilt University and the University of California, Riverside, and was a sociology professor at UCLA, where she entered the area of educational development. After distinguishing herself as an excellent instructor, her department selected her to establish and supervise its teaching assistant training program. In sociology, her research focused on occupations and work, social stratification, political sociology, and disaster behavior.

Nilson has held leadership positions in the POD Network, Toastmasters International, Mensa, and the Southern Regional Faculty and Instructional Development Consortium. She was a National Science Foundation Fellow at the University of Wisconsin, Madison, where she received her Ph.D. and M.S. degrees in sociology. She completed her undergraduate work at the University of California, Berkeley.

• • •

Ludwika A. Goodson is Associate Director for Faculty Development at the Center for the Enhancement of Learning and Teaching at Purdue University Fort Wayne. Her career spans thirty years in instructional design, the last seventeen focusing on online teaching in higher education. Within this scope of work, she has created online course templates, conducted seminars on teaching with technology, and supported initiatives to advance the scholarship of teaching and learning.

After teaching at Iowa State University, Goodson enrolled in the educational technology program at Sir George Williams University in Montreal, Canada. Thereafter, she launched her instructional design career at Florida State University, where she and Dee Andrews wrote "A Comparative Analysis of Models of Instructional Design," most recently reprinted in the third edition of *Instructional Technology: Past, Present, and Future*, edited by Gary J. Anglin.

Soon after, Goodson formed her company, Instructional Systems Design, supervising instructional designers and media consultants in education and evaluation projects for a dozen different agencies over ten years. She then returned to Florida State to conduct research and develop curricula in the Educational Services Program and design online courses at the Office of Distributed and Distance Learning. Her later role at Georgia Southern University encompassed collaboration with faculty in both classroom and online courses and in faculty learning communities. At Embry-Riddle Aeronautical University's Worldwide Division, she produced online courses and taught an award-winning online course to prepare faculty for online teaching.

Goodson has served as an external evaluator for the National Science Foundation and science, technology, engineering, and mathematics faculty development projects and a contributor to the *Encyclopedia of Educational Technology* and *Real-Life Distance Learning: Case Studies in Research and Practice.* She participates in the Association for Educational Communications and Technology, SoTL Commons Conference, Georgia International Information Literacy Conference, and Professional and Organizational Development Network in Higher Education (POD) Conference, where she and Linda Nilson first met.

Goodson earned her M.A. degree in educational technology at Sir George Williams University. Her instructors included BBC and CBC producers and education specialists who showcased the power of learning with instructional media. She completed doctoral courses and preliminary exams in instructional design and development at Florida State, where her instructors included Robert Gagné and Leslie Briggs.

Why another book on online teaching? Because too many earlier books overfocus on technologies, give prescriptive advice based on anecdotal experiences and common sense, and fail to address much in the way of learning theory, cognitive processes, course design, motivation, or pedagogy. We intend to fill these gaps by concentrating in this book on best teaching practices, anchoring our advice in research, and emphasizing cognitive science, learning theory, course design frameworks, and motivational techniques.

■ HOW THIS BOOK IS ORGANIZED

This book is written largely for faculty members, especially those new to online teaching. From the point of view of other audiences reading this book—instructional designers; administrators at online institutions; faculty and educational developers working with online faculty; and faculty and students in curriculum and instruction, instructional design, and instructional systems design—this book is written from the faculty's perspective, in faculty language. We hold true to faculty's primary end, which is student learning, and their primary means, which is evidence-based pedagogy. We organize each of the chapters not around a technological tool—such as the discussion board, open educational resources, or video-recording software—but around a best teaching practice as applied to online courses.

With the technology available today, all such practices transcend the environment. In fact, some of them have little to do with technology at all except that they must be communicated online using technology. Chapter 1, which focuses on best teaching practices that research has identified thus far, drives this point home. We summarize those practices from different sources and integrate them into one list. We completely reject the idea that designing an online course begins with selecting the bells and whistles, as if anyone's goal is "to convince others that only the best technology and technical details" go into their online instruction, rather than the importance and applicability of what students will learn (Snelbecker, Miller, & Zheng, 2008, p. 6).

Chapter 2, on setting significant outcomes, is the starting point for course design. What do significant outcomes have to do with technology? The only connection is a back-handed one. Perhaps because technology has rendered facts and figures so readily available, we are compelled more than ever before to focus on "deeper and richer experiences of teaching and learning" (Barbezat, Zajonc, Palmer, & Bush, 2014, p. 3). Content is no longer enough. We have to establish a course on "functional relevance" (Snelbecker, Miller, & Zheng, 2006), as a "purposeful enterprise" (Gagné & Merrill, 2000; Richey, 1996; Smith & Ragan, 2005a, 2005b), and a means to "significant learning" (Fink, 2013). Students want to know, "So what?" They want to learn something they can't just look up on the web. They may apply new concepts and master new procedures, but how do these fit into the bigger picture of worthwhile human activity? How does their new knowledge solve real problems?

Chapter 2 proposes ways to integrate significant outcomes into online courses. Fortunately, the scholars cited in the previous paragraph address many ways. We also provide and compare examples of such outcomes in online courses that vary by discipline and learning objectives, such as creativity, problem solving, situated cognition, knowledge construction, and learning from errors. Then we illustrate how significant outcomes in turn shape course design.

Where this chapter leaves off, the next one begins, and it brings in technology only as a means to an end. Chapter 3, which explores how to design a coherent course, starts with formulating clear, assessable student learning outcomes, which furnish the foundation for any course in any environment. Coherence requires aligning every other aspect of a course—the content, learning activities, and assessments—with those outcomes. As the evidence tells us, it leads to better learning (Biggs, 2003; Dick, Carey, & Carey, 2015; Fink, 2013; Smith & Ragan, 2005a, 2005b; Wiggins & McTighe, 2011).

Since assessments should simply mirror outcomes, the process of developing assessments for cognitive outcomes is often straightforward. However, significant learning encompasses affective, ethical, self-regulatory, and social behavioral changes in students as well, and assessing these, whether online or face-to-face, presents genuine challenges. We offer advice in this area for the online environment.

Deciding which learning activities will most effectively and efficiently enable students to achieve the course outcomes presents another set of nonobvious decisions. While classroom faculty already have a few sources to turn to, such as Davis and Arend (2013) and Nilson (2016), online teaching methods often diverge from live ones. We lay out tools and options for what works well online. Many of these methods can transfer successfully from the live to the online context: discussion, PBL (problem-based learning), and for the sciences, POGIL (process-oriented guided inquiry learning) and PLTL (peer-led team learning) (Eberlein et al., 2008). We also explain how to use and adapt procedural templates for coherent online course design from the instructional systems literature (e.g., Dick et al., 2015; Smith & Ragan, 2005a, 2005b; Smith, 2014).

Finally, we address practical issues in developing an online course, some of which involve technology, such as these:

- Constructing a syllabus
- Following online copyright guidelines
- Managing files
- Incorporating video applications
- Using tools for online student activities
- Adding online guests
- Designing online and proctored assessment
- Providing feedback
- Upholding academic integrity
- Ensuring student privacy

In chapter 4, we flesh out the details of online teaching methods we recommended in chapter 3. We then turn to the cognitive scientific principles that we list in chapter 1. They tell us how the mind works and learns, so they should guide how we plan and implement our teaching whatever the environment.

As with coherent course design, classroom faculty can refer to several comprehensive sources for practical ways to implement learning principles from cognitive science (e.g., Ambrose, Bridges, DiPietro, Lovett, & Norman, 2010; Bransford, Brown, & Cocking, 1999; Nilson, 2016; Persellin & Daniels, 2014). We also know that when even a novice instructor implements just some of these principles, students attend classes at a higher rate, are more engaged, and learn twice as much as students in a lecture-based course taught by an experienced instructor (Deslauriers, Schelew, & Wieman, 2011).

However, online faculty have considerably fewer "actionable instructional tactics" (Williams, 2013) and little guidance on how to use technology for learning (Ehrman, 2013; Kreber & Kanuka, 2006), so most of this chapter focuses on applying cognitive scientific principles in online teaching. Specifically, we suggest strategies for organizing, presenting, and engaging students with online content that aim to:

- Minimize cognitive load
- Facilitate elaborative rehearsal
- Support active engagement
- Allow knowledge construction
- Provide optimally scheduled repetition
- Furnish multimodal learning experiences
- Supply timely feedback
- Add emotional elements to the course material
- Give students multiple opportunities for testing, self-testing, and retrieval practice

We can design a tightly aligned course and incorporate evidence-based learning experiences and still see very little learning if the students fail to invest sufficient time and effort. This is where motivation comes in, the focus of chapter 5. Consider its title: "Motivating Elements: Course Policies, Communications, Assessments, and More." It carries the optimistic news that faculty can weave doses of motivation into just about every course component. But they have to weave *multiple* motivating elements because different students respond differently to each one. Perhaps this explains why there are so many theories of motivation. The idea of one or two magic motivational bullets eludes us.

This chapter assembles the evidence about the role that motivation plays in determining how much effort students invest in a course and whether they complete it and achieve its outcomes. Student persistence has been an issue in all learning environments but especially online. We also review the research on how factors other than motivation influence student persistence (the convenience of the course pace, students' control over the sequence of learning, and the relevance of the content, to name a few), but their effects may be mediated by motivation.

The literature on classroom teaching identifies a list of feedback and grading policies, as well as types of communication, activities, assignments, and assessments that are designed to boost student motivation (e.g., Hoskins & Newstead, 2009; Nilson, 2016). So does the online teaching literature (e.g., Chyung, 2007; Robb, 2010; Robb & Stutton, 2014), but the overlap between the two lists is minimal. This just shows how bifurcated the teaching literature remains. We bring the two lists together to create a powerful collection of motivating factors and suggest ways to build these into online courses. We also link these factors to one or more of the many theories of motivation.

Chapter 6 turns to the social side of teaching and learning: developing interactivity, social connections, and community. This side represents one set of high-impact practices over which faculty have complete control: student-instructor, student-content, and student-student interaction. This chapter opens with a review of the literature on the effects of these interactions—specifically, how the quantity and the quality of each type influence student persistence, performance, course completion, and satisfaction.

Next we show how online technologies, used wisely, can foster interactivity, social connectedness, and community in online courses, starting with student-instructor interaction. Of the three types of interaction, this one makes the biggest difference in student success. Many channels are available, and we explain how to narrow the options to best serve the course goals and content. Some of these options are important to student motivation, while others facilitate proven teaching methods, such as scaffolding the material and providing students with early feedback. Student-content interaction encompasses various media representations, discussion formats, interactive technologies, carefully chosen social media, study aids, and connections with subject librarians. Meaningful student-student interactions can involve sharing, collaboration, peer review, or peer instruction on any of several whole-class or small-group communication platforms.

Finally, this chapter offers advice on practical student engagement and participation matters like these:

- Tracking attendance
- Explaining netiquette
- Requesting replies from students
- Obtaining student feedback about the course
- Dealing with disruptive students
- Preparing items and folders in advance
- Determining one's availability to students
- Using and responding to course statistics provided by the learning management system

The material in chapter 7 helps ensure that all students can participate equally in an online course. We address the three challenges faculty face in making a course accessible:

1. *Attitude.* Some faculty look on universal design as just another set of technical chores they have to do to stay out of trouble with instructional designers and the administration. We foster a positive attitude toward universal design, helping faculty appreciate the fact that it supports all students and ensures inclusion.
2. *Knowledge about tools and formats.* Faculty need to recognize which tools and formats (document and media) support accessibility and which do not.
3. *Knowledge about implementation.* Faculty need to learn exactly how to make their course materials accessible.

Most of the chapter focuses on the last challenge, acquainting instructors with the many tools now available to make their lives easier and providing instructions on how to use them. Here we name just a few:

- Using YouTube's closed captioning feature
- Adding "alt text" or "alt tags" to images
- Allowing the readability of tags and structure by correctly saving documents to PDF
- Working around tables and charts
- Using style sets to ensure the readability of text materials (available in Microsoft Word and most learning management systems)

In chapter 8, on creating a supportive culture for online teaching, we close with advice to college and university administrators on how to support their online faculty. After all, faculty do make the difference in what students learn (Condon, Iverson, Manduca, Ruiz, & Willett, 2015; Umbach & Wawrzynski, 2005), and only well-prepared, confident instructors can design and teach top-quality online courses that retain and gratify students.

Chapter 8 opens by explaining the difficulties and stresses that faculty experience when they teach online for the first time. For instance, they are accustomed to communicating with students face-to-face and expect a certain type of student participation and social dynamic between them and a class. In an online course, technology mediates all communication, participation, and social relationships, as well as faculty roles, responsibilities, and expectations.

The institution can facilitate the faculty's transition in two ways. First, it can publicize the pedagogical value of technology and online education (Jones, Lindner, Murphy, & Dooley, 2002; Lu, Todd, & Miller, 2011) most effectively by anchoring its claims in scholarly research, which this book provides. Second, it can create a supportive culture by ensuring that faculty and staff feel comfortable and confident using online technologies. Only a constellation of high-quality technical consulting and training can meet this need. Such training can also reduce faculty reluctance to change and skepticism about online pedagogy (Covington, Petherbridge, & Warren, 2005).

Make no mistake: considerable skepticism still exists among faculty, and technology administrators may overlook this because they tend to believe strongly in the efficacy of online education. The 2016 *Inside Higher Ed* Survey of Faculty Attitudes revealed that faculty have plenty of reservations about the effectiveness of online courses compared to their face-to-face classes (Straumshein, 2016). Over half doubt, some strongly, that online courses can achieve the same outcomes just as well as those achieved in live courses, and the experience of teaching online raises the portion of skeptical faculty to almost 60 percent. In contrast, 62 percent of the technology administrators say that online courses in general offer the same quality of instruction as live ones, and 88 percent believe this of online courses at their own institution.

Given their optimism and belief in technology, administrators may fail to appreciate the very different perceptions that faculty have of online learning. In many cases, these perceptions grow out of the difficult and disappointing experiences instructors have had teaching online. Indeed, because faculty do the actual frontline teaching, their perceptions cannot and should not be ignored.

If good teaching transcends the environment, it seems the training that faculty have been receiving gives too much attention to the technology and not enough to the teaching. With more emphasis on teaching in their training, faculty may indeed be able to design courses that achieve at least the same outcomes as the face-to-face versions (Brewer & Brewer, 2015). If they could, their skepticism may dissolve. Institutions then must support faculty through training not just in online technology but also in the most effective online pedagogy possible. This book aims to lay the foundation for this latter training.

■ THE AUDIENCES FOR THIS BOOK

We have developed *Online Teaching at Its Best: Merging Instructional Design with Teaching and Learning Research* to help and appeal to four readerships. Primary are faculty across disciplines and institutional types who need to begin designing and teaching an online course or would like to improve their current online offerings. The book uses the language and style that fit the teaching culture rather than the customary techie and instructional design cultures. We draw on cognitive science to explain how learning works and both instructional design research and the scholarship of teaching and learning to recommend research-based teaching methods for the online environment. Our emphasis on evidence-based practices makes this book the most scholarly of its kind available today.

An oversight or a deliberate avoidance of pedagogy in the minimum standards set by universities and organizations for online course design has left faculty with a prescription of what to do technologically and only minimal recommendations on the course elements to include. Unfortunately, this approach suggests that good teaching practices are less important than the technology. Given the standards often used in peer or external course reviews, faculty sometimes ask, "Is this what an online course is supposed to look like?" In sum, the typical standards are simply the minimum requirements for online course development, absent the teaching practices needed for effective learning.

Our secondary audience is undergraduate and graduate students in courses in education, curriculum and instruction, instructional design, and instructional systems design, as well as the faculty who teach them. We hope to ensure that when they graduate, they will begin their careers with a solid background in research-based course design, teaching, community building, motivational methods, and accessibility measures.

We also have two additional audiences in mind:

- Administrators and instructors at online institutions, such as the University of Phoenix, Kaplan University, Western Governors University, Nova Southeastern University, and Southern New Hampshire University, who are seriously interested in increasing student retention in their programs and supporting their online faculty.
- Faculty and educational developers at institutions that are expanding their online course offerings. In a national study of thirty-nine higher education institutions, 93 percent reported creating an online training activity for its faculty (Meyer & Murrell, 2014).

■ ACKNOWLEDGMENTS

First, we thank Lesley Iura, vice president and publisher (education) at Wiley, and Alison Knowles, former assistant editor at Jossey-Bass/Wiley, for putting their faith in us to produce a uniquely useful book for faculty on online teaching.

Ludwika: I acknowledge the support of my writing group and the following individuals who have shared their experiences and insights about their technology, online teaching, and faculty development journeys:

- Jeong-Il Cho, special education instructor of face-to-face classes
- Adam Dircksen, communication instructor of face-to-face and online classes
- Paul Edwards, chemistry instructor of face-to-face classes with online course components
- Anna Gibson, management instructor of face-to-face and online classes
- Regina Gordon, student and program manager
- Xiaokai Jia, instructional design and technology instructional consultant and designer
- Denise Jordan, nursing instructor of face-to-face and online classes
- John LaMaster, mathematics instructor of face-to-face and online classes
- Linda Lolkus, nutrition instructor of face-to-face and online classes

- Veronika Ospina-Kammerer, social work instructor of face-to-face and online classes
- Kathleen Surface, faculty information technology support–learning management system specialist
- Yvonne Zubovic, mathematical sciences instructor of face-to-face and online classes

Linda: I owe a lot of my inspiration and encouragement to the members of the fall 2015 and spring 2016 writing groups I led for Clemson faculty and graduate students while getting this book off the ground, as well as the spring 2017 writing group led by English lecturer and poet Mike Pulley. These fine colleagues pushed and held me accountable for making brisk progress. I am also grateful to my dear husband, Greg Bauernfeind, for always enthusiastically supporting my writing projects and speaking commitments and giving me the time to do them. He has shouldered more than his share of home-front tasks while helping me realize my dreams and potential.

LINDA B. NILSON
Anderson, South Carolina

LUDWIKA A. GOODSON
Fort Wayne, Indiana

■ REFERENCES

Ambrose, S. A., Bridges, M. W., DiPietro, M., Lovett, M. C., & Norman, M. K. (2010). *How learning works: Seven research-based principles for smart teaching.* San Francisco, CA: Jossey-Bass.

Barbezat, D., Zajonc, A., Palmer, P. J., & Bush, M. (2014). *Contemplative practices in higher education: Powerful methods to transform teaching and learning.* San Francisco, CA: Jossey-Bass.

Biggs, J. (2003, April). Aligning teaching and assessing to course objectives. *Teaching and Learning in Higher Education: New Trends and Innovations, 13*(17). Retrieved from https://www.dkit.ie/ga/system/files/Aligning_Reaching_and_Assessing_to_Course_Objectives_John_Biggs.pdf

Bransford, J. D., Brown, A. L., & Cocking, R. R. (1999). *How people learn: Brain, mind, experience, and school.* Washington, DC: National Academy Press.

Brewer, P. E., & Brewer, E. C. (2015). Pedagogical perspectives for the online education skeptic. *Journal on Excellence in College Teaching, 26*(1), 29–52.

Chyung, S. Y. (2007). Invisible motivation of online adult learners during contract learning. *Journal of Educators Online, 4*(1). Retrieved from http://www.thejeo.com/Volume4Number1/ChyungFinal.pdf

Condon, W., Iverson, E. R., Manduca, C. A., Ruiz, C., & Willett, G. (2015). *Faculty development and student learning: Assessing the connections.* Bloomington: Indiana University Press.

Covington, D., Peterbridge, D., & Warren, S. E. (2005, Spring). Best practices: A triangulated support approach in transitioning faculty to online teaching. *Online Journal of Distance Learning Administration, 8*(1). Retrieved from http://www.westga.edu/~distance/ojdla/spring81/covington81.htm

Davis, J. R., & Arend, D. D. (2013). *Facilitating seven ways of learning: A resource for more purposeful, effective, and enjoyable college teaching.* Sterling, VA: Stylus.

Deslauriers, L., Schelew, E., & Wieman, C. E. (2011). Improved learning in a large-enrollment physics class. *Science, 332*(6031), 862–864.

Dick, W., Carey, L., & Carey, J. O. (2015). *The systematic design of instruction* (8th ed.). Upper Saddle River, NJ: Pearson.

Eberlein, T., Kampmeier, J., Minderhout, V., Moog, R. S., Platt, T., Varma-Nelson, P., & White, H. B. (2008), Pedagogies of engagement in science. *Biochemistry and Molecular Biology Education, 36*, 262–273. doi:10.1002/bmb.20204

Ehrman, S. C. (2013, Winter). How technology matters to learning. *Liberal Education, 99*(1). Retrieved from https://www.aacu.org/publications-research/periodicals/how-technology-matters-learning

Fink, L. D. (2013). *Creating significant learning experiences: An integrated approach to designing college courses* (2nd ed.). San Francisco, CA: Jossey-Bass.

Gagné, R. M., & Merrill, M. D. (2000). Integrative goals for instructional design. In R. C. Richey (Ed.), *The legacy of Robert M. Gagné* (pp. 127–140). Syracuse, NY: Clearinghouse on Information Technology.

Hoskins, S. L., & Newstead, S. E. (2009). Encouraging student motivation. In H. Fry, S. Ketteridge, & S. Marshall (Eds.), *A handbook for teaching and learning in higher education: Enhancing academic practice* (3rd ed., pp. 27–39). London, UK: Routledge.

Jones, E. T., Lindner, J. R., Murphy, T. H., & Dooley, K. E. (2002). Faculty philosophical position toward distance education: Competency, value, and educational technology support. *Journal of Distance Learning Administration, 5*(1). Retrieved from http://www.westga.edu/~distance/ojdla/spring51/jones51.html

Kreber, C., & Kanuka, H. (2006). The scholarship of teaching and learning and the online classroom. *Canadian Journal of University Continuing Education, 32*(2), 109–131.

Lu, M.-Y., Todd, A. M., & Miller, M. T. (2011, Fall). Creating a supportive culture for online teaching: A case study of a faculty learning community. *Online Journal of Distance Learning Administration, 14*(3). Retrieved from http://scholarworks.sjsu.edu/cgi/viewcontent.cgi?article=1009&context=comm_pub

Meyer, K. A., & Murrell, V. S. (2014). A national study of training content and activities for faculty development for online teaching. *Journal of Asynchronous Learning Networks, 18*(1). Retrieved from http://files.eric.ed.gov/fulltext/EJ1030527.pdf

Nilson, L. B. (2016). *Teaching at its best: A research-based resource for college instructors* (4th ed.). San Francisco, CA: Jossey-Bass.

Persellin, D. C., & Daniels, M. B. (2014). *A concise guide to improving student learning: Six evidence-based principles and how to apply them.* Sterling, VA: Stylus.

Richey, R. C. (1996, November). R. M. Gagné's impact on instructional design theory and practice of the future. In *Proceedings of Selected Research and Development Presentations at the 1996 National Convention of the Association for Educational Communications and Technology,* Jacksonville, FL. Retrieved from http://files.eric.ed.gov/fulltext/ED397828.pdf

Robb, C. A. (2010). *The impact of motivational messages on student performance in community college online courses* (Order No. 3430898). ProQuest Dissertations & Theses Global. (87782240308). Retrieved from http://search.proquest.com.ezproxy.library.ipfw.edu/docview/778224030?accountid=11649

Robb, C. A., & Sutton, J. (2014). The importance of social presence and motivation in distance learning. *Journal of Technology, Management, and Applied Engineering, 31*(2), 2–10.

Smith, P. L., & Ragan, T. L. (2005a). *Instructional design* (3rd ed.). Hoboken, NJ: Wiley.

Smith, P. L., & Ragan, T. L. (2005b). *Instructional design* (3rd ed.) instructor companion site. Retrieved from http://bcs.wiley.com/he-bcs/Books?action=index&itemId=0471393533&itemTypeId=BKS&bcsId=2112

Smith, R. M. (2014). *Conquering the content: A blueprint for online course design and development* (2nd ed.). San Francisco, CA: Jossey-Bass.

Snelbecker, G. E., Miller, S. M., & Zheng, R. Z. (2008). Functional relevance and online instructional design. In R. Zheng & S. P. Ferris (Eds.), *Understanding online instructional modeling: Theories and practices* (pp. 1–17). Hershey, PA: IGI Global.

Straumsheim, C. (2016, October 24). Doubts about data: 2016 Survey of Faculty Attitudes on Technology. *Inside Higher Ed*. Retrieved from https://www.insidehighered.com/news/survey/doubts-about-data-2016-survey-faculty -attitudes-technology

Umbach, P., & Wawrzynski, M. (2005). Faculty do matter: The role of college faculty in student learning and engagement. *Research in Higher Education, 46*, 153–184.

Wiggins, G., & McTighe, J. (2011). *The understanding by design guide to creating high-quality units*. Alexandria, VA: ASCD.

Williams, J. J. (2013). *Applying cognitive science to online learning*. Paper presented at the Data Driven Education Workshop at Conference on Neural Information Processing Systems, Lake Tahoe, NV. Retrieved from http://dx.doi .org/10.2139/ssrn.2535549

CHAPTER 1

Teaching at Its Best, No Matter What the Environment

Abundant research shows that excellent teaching rests on the same principles across all platforms—classroom, online, or hybrid. But online education holds special challenges that stem from both students and instructors. Online faculty face challenges that classroom faculty do not. The demands or excitement of technology can easily distract online faculty and instructional designers from developing and integrating the best teaching practices in their courses. Different readerships for the body of teaching and learning research and that of instructional design exacerbate the challenge of keeping best teaching practices at the forefront. To identify these practices, we start with the face-to-face teaching literature and argue for its online applicability.

Any given instructional strategy can be supported by a number of contrasting technologies (old and new), just as any given technology might support different instructional strategies. But for any given instructional strategy, some technologies are better than others: Better to turn a screw with a screwdriver than a hammer—a dime may also do the trick, but a screwdriver is usually better.

—Arthur W. Chickering and Stephen C. Ehrmann (1996)

■ TEACHING QUALITY AS KEY

Like Chickering and Ehrmann (1996), we start from the premise that excellent teaching is excellent teaching—and, conversely, ineffective teaching is ineffective teaching—whether the environment is classroom based, online, or hybrid. Why? Because in terms of the mind, learning is learning. Being the oldest type, face-to-face teaching has led the way in defining best practices, so we examine these practices later in the chapter and consider how smoothly they can transfer to technology-based environments.

The evidence for our claim that excellent teaching transcends the environment abounds. Simonson and Schlosser (2009) cite many sources and examples showing that what matters most in student learning is good teaching, not the technology. Waterhouse (2005) notes that e-learning improves when pedagogy drives the technology. Smith (2014) echoes this same theme, as does Funk (2007), who contends that ineffective online instruction lowers students' odds of course completion. Similarly, after a review of nearly five hundred online courses, Xu and Jaggars (2013) suggest that improvements in online courses would better support student success. After reviewing the research, Simonson, Smaldino, and Zvacek (2015) conclude, "What we know about best practices in education is directly applicable to distance education" (p. 73). Among the most powerful ones across environments are opportunities for student collaboration, as well as self-reflection and self-monitoring (US Department of Education, 2010; Hattie, 2009).

In fact, when online faculty follow good teaching practices, their students can actually learn a little more than in a comparable face-to-face course (Broida, n.d.; Shachar & Neumann, 2010; US Department of Education, 2010). The gain is due at least in part to the greater time on task that online learning typically requires. For example, unlike in a classroom, unprepared students cannot remain invisible if they must participate in a discussion forum (Brewer & Brewer, 2015; Lineweaver, 2010). Online and hybrid learning can offer other advantages over face-to-face, such as the rich multimedia resources available, the always available community of learners in the course, the 24/7 access to content and instructions, and the reflection built into asynchronous discussion (Conrad & Donaldson, 2012; Harlen & Doubler, 2004; Hiltz & Goldman, 2005; Jaffe, Moir, Swanson, & Wheeler, 2006; Rabe-Hemp, Woolen & Humiston, 2009; Riel & Polin, 2004; Schwen & Hara, 2004; Vrasidas & Glass, 2004).

Still, the quality of the teaching makes all the difference. Based on their extensive review of research on online learning, Tallent-Runnels et al. (2006) conclude:

> Students' learning in the online environment is affected by the quality of online instruction. Not surprisingly, students in well-designed and well-implemented online courses learned significantly more, and more effectively, than those in online courses where teaching and learning activities were not carefully planned and where the delivery and accessibility were impeded by technology problems. (p. 116)

Online courses do present challenges that classroom courses do not. In the next section, we consider the amazing growth of online education in recent years, as well as the stubbornly lower completion rates of online versus face-to-face courses. Students, instructors, and institutions struggle with the completion challenge for online courses. The subsequent section addresses the challenges that faculty face in moving from exclusively classroom to online teaching. These go beyond the technological to encompass social and pedagogical as well.

▪ THE SPECIAL CHALLENGES OF ONLINE LEARNING

Perhaps college pedagogy has not yet had enough time to catch up with the rapid expansion of online learning. The annual reports of institutions throughout North America and beyond document acceleration in the growth of online programs and courses:

- According to Allen and Seamon's *Grade Level: Tracking Online Education in the United States* (2015), 70.7 percent of all currently active, degree-granting institutions that are open to the public have some distance offerings.

- In 2013, the number of students enrolled in a distance education course was 3,750,745 in public institutions, 770,219 in private nonprofit ones, and 736,415 in private for-profit ones.
- The number of students taking at least one online course grew at an annual rate greater than that of the overall higher education student body.
- A 2014 survey by the Instructional Technology Council similarly reports that student enrollment in online courses has continued to grow faster than overall enrollment at colleges and universities (Lokken & Mullins, 2015).
- Besides fully online classes, more educators are turning to hybrid learning, using online course materials and activities to replace forms of face-to-face class time (Johnson, Adams Becker, Estrada, & Freeman, 2015).

As the demand for online learning keeps growing, we also anticipate that more universities will begin adding online course design to their instructional design master's and doctoral programs. Yet in spite of the radical expansion of online courses, they encounter challenges from two sources: the students who take these courses and the faculty—both those teaching online courses and those who are not teaching them yet.

Challenges from the Students

Despite these impressive figures of student participation, student completion of online courses remains a problem. According to diverse sources, the overall retention rates for online courses are 10 to 20 percent below those for face-to-face courses. For example, according to US Department of Education data, the 55 percent average retention rate for first-time, full-time students in online courses was more than 20 percent lower than the national average retention rate of 77 percent in both traditional and online courses (Burnsed, 2010). Completion and retention data are available from the following reports:

- Variable completion rates, some equal to face-to-face classes, some lower, some higher, and differences in course completion rates by discipline (Atchley, Wingenbach, & Akers, 2013; Tallent-Runnels et al., 2006; US Department of Education, 2010)
- Noncompletion rates as high as 47 percent (Tirrell & Quick, 2012)
- Top-ranked online school retention rates ranging from 70 to 87 percent (Stone, 2014), and those at the top-twenty-five colleges hovering at 97 to 99 percent (Best Value Schools, 2014)
- No reports on completion rates for many institutions (US Department of Education, 2010)

Barshay (2015) summarizes the results of five recent studies, all of which found that community college students are less likely to do well in online courses than in the comparable traditional courses. The most recent study she describes shows that although the stronger California students tend to enroll in the online version of a community college course, they are 11 percent less likely to complete, pass, or get an A or a B, regardless of their economic and academic background. Admittedly, the gap has almost disappeared at the more elite institutions that accept the most motivated and best academically prepared students (Barshay, 2015).

Through these murky figures, it is still clear that many students need more than the convenience of online learning and more than an online collection of content, activities, assignments, and assessments. They need support and motivation to persist and succeed. An instructor's social presence, clear directions and expectations, relevant course materials, and engaging assignments help students learn and complete their courses (Boston et al., 2009; Ley & Gannon-Cook, 2014; Park & Choi, 2009; Sheridan & Kelly, 2010; York & Richardson, 2012).

Challenges from the Faculty

Although more and more faculty are teaching fully online or hybrid courses, many still have reservations about quality. According to the 2016 *Inside Higher Ed* Survey of Faculty Attitudes (Straumsheim, 2016), only 19 percent agree that for-credit online courses can achieve outcomes that are at least equivalent to those achieved in face-to-face courses, and 55 percent disagree or strongly disagree. Even faculty who teach online report doubt about their own courses, with 60 percent believing that student learning in online courses will fail to match that of their live counterparts. Only 4 to 6 percent think that online courses can exceed face-to-face instruction in rigorous student engagement, content delivery, and at-risk student success. These perceptions persist in spite of contrary findings reported in research studies. Perhaps the push for faculty to develop more and more online courses as quickly as possible leaves inadequate time to learn how best to use online technology, thereby keeping these doubts alive (Meyer & Murrell, 2014).

This same survey asked academic technology administrators similar questions and obtained considerably more positive opinions about the effectiveness of educational technology and online courses. For instance, 30 percent of the faculty believe that technology has not improved student learning outcomes at all, versus only 13 percent of the technology administrators. Similarly, 93 percent of the administrators believe that online courses provide the same or better quality of instruction than live ones, in contrast to 46 percent of the faculty, and only 4 percent of the faculty believe the quality of instruction to be better (Straumsheim, 2016).

Technology tools and ways to use them are the specialties of technology administrators, not faculty or teaching and learning scholars. It is not surprising that these technology administrators provide faculty training for online courses that emphasizes what and how to use the technology tools. Because of this focus, faculty are left to tackle their online courses with too little teaching guidance for using those tools to actively support learning. When this happens, online student learning fails to measure up to classroom learning. Most likely, if faculty obtained stronger student learning and outcomes achievement in their online courses, their doubts and reservations would disappear.

■ THE SPECIAL CHALLENGES THAT ONLINE FACULTY FACE

Many online faculty have not yet incorporated the best teaching practices throughout their courses. When building online materials and dealing with technical issues, they tend to give more attention to getting the technology right than getting the teaching right, even overlooking the strategies they already use in their traditional courses. In fact, in their online courses, they admit to inconsistently applying and often omitting one or more of the seven principles of good practice in undergraduate education (Zhang & Walls, 2009). These principles are (Chickering & Gamson, 1987):

- Encourage contact between students and faculty
- Develop reciprocity and cooperation among students
- Encourage active learning
- Give prompt feedback
- Emphasize time on task
- Communicate high expectations
- Respect diverse talents and ways of learning

It is not the faculty's fault. Left with little time and mental resources to move beyond the technology, faculty put pedagogy in the background. They focus on what an online course "is supposed to look like" to measure up to minimal technical standards, and too few institutions give them the pedagogical support to integrate best teaching practices with the technology tools they use. Aside from the fact that departments often leave faculty too little time to prepare strong courses, the standards that serve as guideposts for online course design tend to address minimum requirements and bypass both teaching pedagogy and online pedagogy (Hirumi, 2009). Technologies *can* fit well with the teaching methods that would work best for a course. However, the mix of technology training, the absence of pedagogy in online course design standards, and the high cognitive load in using the technology create a context in which faculty have trouble discerning the "best fit."

In earlier years, there were few empirical data on what constitutes good pedagogy online (Newlin & Wang, 2002). More recently, some research studies put good pedagogy into practice with positive results such as Barber, King, and Buchanan's (2015) application of problem-based learning in an online class community. But like many other studies, this research appears in a technical journal. The online learning literature informs technologists and instructional designers but offers little help to faculty, especially those beginning to teach online. Just as faculty tend to miss out on the type of research and strategies featured in technical publications, instructional designers tend to miss out on the college teaching and learning literature. This body of literature, often called the scholarship of teaching and learning (SoTL), provides a well-researched tool kit for faculty who teach. Instructional designers also have their own well-researched tool kit (e.g., Dick, Carey, & Carey, 2015; Gagné, Wager, Golas, & Keller, 2005; Smith & Ragan, 2005a, 2005b; Spector, Merrill, Elen, & Bishop, 2014). Yet these bodies of literature reside on separate sides of the canyon.

As an example, Smith and Ragan (2005a, 2005b) do a fine job of explaining instructional design theory and procedures, but they do not integrate SoTL evidence-based teaching practices from the higher education teaching and learning community, nor do they speak to the needs of those on the online frontline, the faculty who most often design and teach these courses. Similarly, the Dick et al. book (2015) on systematic design of instruction excellently covers instructional analysis, the types of assessments for different levels of learning, and formative evaluation, yet it limits pedagogy to constructivist strategies (e.g., Pelich & Pieper, 2010). Sponsored by the Association for Educational Communications and Technology (AECT), the fourth edition of the *Handbook of Research on Educational Communications and Technology* (Spector et al., 2014) includes more evidence-based pedagogy, including discipline-specific teaching strategies, but its primary audience is instructional designers and technologists.

SoTL-based pedagogy is also rare in other books on online teaching. For example, *The Perfect Online Course: Best Practices for Design and Teaching* (Orellana, Hudgins, & Simonson, 2009) provides a mosaic of research and framework perspectives in a collection of articles, only a few of which address any pedagogical issues. Dooley, Lindner, and Dooley (2005) and Jia (2012) take similar approaches. So do Stavredes and Herder (2014), whose guide for online course design limits instructional strategies to cognitive presence, teaching presence, and scaffolding. Unfortunately, none of the books on online learning provide faculty with a coherent picture of pedagogically based, high-quality online teaching.

By the same token, faculty, educational developers, and SoTL advocates seem unaware of the instructional design literature. Their research focuses on classroom teaching and learning. The technologies it integrates fit best into face-to-face settings (e.g., personal response systems and mobile learning) and hybrid courses (e.g., online quizzes and videos for the flipped classroom). Yet the instructional design literature addresses the conditions of learning in ways that are applicable to traditional as well as online courses and would complement, even extend, many of the findings in the SoTL literature. For example, instructional design research offers evidence-based recommendations about fostering learning with visuals, including what types of visuals to use, how to place text on them, how to sequence text or narration with them, and whether to use text or narration to explain them (e.g., Clark & Mayer, 2011; Mayer, 2014). Its findings dovetail neatly with those in cognitive psychology. Other aspects also are deeply connected. For example, teachers of science courses use inquiry methods that originated with Gagné, a scholar and leader in instructional design. Indeed, Gagné's conception of science processes and methods of learning furnish the foundation for science curricula and instruction (Finley, 1983; Iatradis, 1993; Mewhinney, 2009).

Without a bridge to connect SoTL pedagogy, instructional design, and online learning (see figure 1.1), it is no wonder that technology trumps pedagogy and that many faculty remain suspicious of online teaching. Yet when good practices lead course design, online learning can be more effective than classroom learning and can produce better learning outcomes (Elkilany, 2014; Guidera, 2003; US Department of Education, 2010). Placing teaching and learning, rather than the technology, at the center of online courses could shift faculty expectations and raise the status and value that faculty accord to online teaching—in other words:

> An effective transition to online learning requires two key types of support: *increasing the value of online learning by enhancing faculty understanding of the pedagogical value* of technology and increasing competence in online learning, including faculty knowledge of specific technology-based skills. (italics added; Lu, Todd, & Miller, 2011, ¶6)

This book interweaves the findings from the most valid teaching and learning research with those from the instructional design and online learning literature. We believe that this integrated approach will make the most sense to faculty and will enable them to make reasoned choices about how to use technology for teaching and transfer best pedagogical practices into designing, teaching, and assessing in their online courses. Their decisions will more closely reflect the broad-based principles for good practice in undergraduate education, which we examine in the next section, as well as research-backed ways to leverage those principles when using technology and designing online courses.

For this purpose, we draw on principles of undergraduate education such as these:

- Research-based principles for smart teaching (Ambrose, Bridges, DiPietro, Lovett, & Norman, 2010)
- Brain, mind, and school experiences (Bransford, Brown, & Cocking, 1999)
- Principles for good practice in undergraduate education (Chickering & Gamson, 1987)
- Evidence-based principles for improving student learning (Persellin & Daniels, 2014)

We look at ways to leverage technology for online courses—for example:

- Technology for implementing the principles of undergraduate education (Chickering & Ehrmann, 1996)
- The science of instruction for multimedia design (Clark & Mayer, 2011)

Figure 1.1   Bridging the Domains of Research and Applications

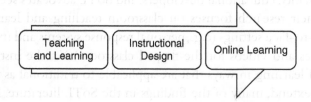

- Transactional distance theory for design of online instruction (Koslow, & Piña, 2015)
- Presentation design to facilitate online learning (Lumadue & Waller, 2014)
- Methods of technology-enabled learning (Moller, Robison, & Huett, 2012)
- Ways of establishing teacher presence in online courses (Shea, Vickers, & Hayes, 2010)

We also draw on bedrock principles of instructional design:

- Principles of instructional design (Gagné et al., 2005; Smith & Ragan, 2005a, 2005b)
- Systematic design of instruction (Dick et al., 2015)
- Instructional design for learning to solve problems (Jonassen, 2004)
- First principles of instruction (Merrill, 2002)
- Affective and cognitive instruction (Martin & Briggs, 1986)
- Theoretical foundations of learning environments (Jonassen & Land, 2012)
- Constructivist teaching (Pelech & Pieper, 2010)
- Instructional design knowledge base (Richey, Klein, & Tracey, 2011)

To these perspectives, we add factors associated with successful online courses (US Department of Education, 2010) and models of faculty development for online teaching (e.g., Meyer, 2014; Meyer & Murrell, 2014). We also hope to better acquaint instructional designers with the highest standards in classroom teaching and their potential for expression in the online environment. This knowledge should enable them to communicate better with the faculty to whom they consult.

■ TEACHING AND LEARNING ACROSS ENVIRONMENTS

To identify proven principles of teaching and learning, we have to turn first to the face-to-face teaching literature. We also feature a few of the parallels with instructional design. We began with the classic seven principles of good practice identified by Chickering and Gamson (1987) and based on a review of almost forty scholarly publications about student-faculty contact, reciprocity and cooperation, active learning, promptness of feedback, time on task, high expectations, and diverse talents and ways students learn. Nine years later, Chickering and Ehrmann (1996) explained how these seven principles can easily translate from the classroom to the online environment using various instructional technologies. Instructors have gradually integrated these principles into classroom practices and teaching with technology, including some online courses (Chickering & Gamson, 1999; Hathaway, 2014; Johnson, 2014; Koeckeritz, Malkiewicz, & Henderson, 2002; Lai & Savage, 2013; McCabe & Meuter, 2011; Newlin & Wang, 2002; Ritter & Lemke, 2000).

Based on research in education and educational psychology, Bransford et al. (1999) wrote a seminal work about how people learn, but they focused on memory issues in school children and did not propose learning principles. However, some the major points they made—for example, on the importance of learners practicing metacognition, structuring knowledge, and having valid prior knowledge on which to connect new knowledge—have been suggested as principles in later books about college-level teaching and learning.

The first of these later books, by Ambrose et al. (2010), lays out seven principles of learning with implications for effective teaching:

1. The amount of students' prior knowledge on a subject affects their learning and performance—the more prior knowledge, the easier and better the learning and the stronger the performance. However, inaccurate, inert, or insufficient prior knowledge can hinder learning and performance. *Teaching implications:* Instructors should find out what that prior knowledge is, remediate or activate it in students, have students self-assess their familiarity with it, and try to identify errors and misconceptions in that knowledge. Instructors should then address these misconceptions explicitly and find ways to discredit them.

2. The way students organize their prior knowledge also affects their learning and performance. *Teaching implications:* Instructors should help ensure that the organization of their students' knowledge is valid and rich with connections between important and meaningful features—major concepts, principles, and categories, for example.

3. Students' motivation determines how much effort and persistence they will put toward their learning. *Teaching implications:* Instructors should enhance the value of the material for students and create a supportive environment for learning. To enhance the value, they should show enthusiasm, reward students for achieving outcomes, and demonstrate the relevance of the material to real-world applications and students' current and future lives. To increase support for learning, they should do things like develop a course that aligns outcomes, learning activities, and assessments; incorporate early assessments that build student confidence; help students learn how to learn the material; clearly explain expectations for performance; and provide prompt feedback accordingly. Building in choice and reflection on the learning also increases both the value of the learning and the support for it.

4. Students develop mastery only when they can competently perform and integrate the component skills and apply them in the appropriate circumstances. *Teaching implications:* Instructors should decompose complex tasks into component skills, diagnose and provide practice for students in their weaker skills in different contexts, include the integration of skills in assessments, have students link contextual learning experiences to general principles, and give them practice in deciding where different skills and knowledge apply in various contexts.

5. Students need sufficient practice in meeting specific performance criteria at the desired level of competency, coupled with timely feedback targeted to improving performance on the specific criteria. *Teaching implications:* Instructors should start a course by assessing their students' performance level and adjusting the level of their practice to a reasonable level. Then instructors should make their performance goals, criteria, and standards explicit; scaffold complex tasks in decreasing detail over time; provide plenty of practice opportunities; supply models of strong and weak performances; incorporate instructor and peer feedback to groups as well as individuals; and have students explain how they use feedback in later work.

6. Students' learning is affected by the interactions of their level of social, emotional, and intellectual development with the climate of the course on the same dimensions. Faculty cannot influence the level of development that students bring into a course, but they do have control over the course climate. The more positive the climate, the more students are likely to learn. *Teaching implications:* Instructors should foster the safe expression of different points of views, answers to questions, and approaches to a problem, in part by posing questions and problems that are open to multiple respectable responses. In addition, instructors should choose inclusive content and examples, model inclusive behavior and language, personalize the class as much as possible, have students generate ground rules for interaction,

require them to provide evidence to back up their claims, encourage and model active listening, turn tensions and disagreements into learning opportunities, and obtain and respond to student feedback on class climate.

7. Students need to practice self-regulated learning before they can become self-directed learners. That is, they must plan, monitor, and evaluate their learning and modify their strategies accordingly to optimize their learning. *Teaching implications:* Instructors should provide opportunities for students to analyze assignments, assessment rubrics, and study examples of both excellent and poor products. Instructors should also model metacognition and have students reflect on and answer questions that direct them to self-assess and self-correct their work, assess their peers' work, assess their learning, and assess the effectiveness of their study strategies. Of course, these activities take on higher value when instructors explain at least a little about the ability of the brain to change with learning (brain plasticity) and the effort, self-awareness, and persistence that learning requires.

We can identify considerable overlap among these principles, especially principles 1, 2, 4, and 7, and Bransford et al.'s (1999) main points about learning. We can also see parallels with instructional design perspectives, which emphasize identifying student entry-level and prerequisite skills, relating outcomes to the structure and substance of students' mental models, ensuring student support and motivation, providing relevant practice and informative feedback, and varying the learning context to support retention and transfer (Dick et al., 2015; Gagné et al., 2005; Smith & Ragan, 2005a, 2005b).

While Chickering and Gamson's (1987) principles of good practice do not appear among Ambrose et al.'s (2010), some of the latter's principles do imply active learning, student-faculty contact, and student-student reciprocity and cooperation, and principle 5 mentions "prompt feedback," but only as one aspect of the best kind of feedback to give students. This scant overlap testifies to the progress we have made in understanding teaching and learning since the late 1980s.

Davis and Arend (2013) slice the pie somewhat differently, positing primary "ways of learning" for each of seven categories of learning outcomes and tying each category to particularly effective teaching methods (table 1.1).

According to Ambrose et al. (2010), students need practice in skills to acquire and refine them, whatever those skills may be. But Davis and Arend (2013) maintain that the context for the most effective practice will vary by the type of skill. If, for example, the skills involve precise procedures or psychomotor operations, the principles of behaviorism applied to practice exercises will most efficiently yield the best results. For another example, instructors can most effectively provide practice in exercising sound professional judgment and action in real-world-like situations, the kind that simulations, games, dramatic scenarios, and role plays afford.

Davis and Arend (2013) recommend flexibility in using their framework, however. They readily point out that feedback in any context borrows from behavioristic principles and would regard case studies, laboratories, and internships as suitable methods for teaching professional judgment. But they wisely alert us to the fact that case studies, simulations, service-learning, discussions, and group activities are ill suited to students who are acquiring procedural skills and basic disciplinary knowledge. By the same token, presentations, practice exercises, role plays, and labs will do much less to help students develop critical thinking skills or an open-minded awareness of multiple perspectives than will discussions, question-driven inquiries, and group work.

Although Ambrose et al. include teaching strategies and student activities to help instructors implement all seven of their best-practice principles, additional refinement proves its worth when it comes time

Table 1.1   Davis and Arend's (2013) Model of Learning Outcomes, Ways of Learning, and Teaching Methods

Intended Learning Outcomes: What Students Learn	Ways of Learning: Origins and Theory	Common Methods: What the Teacher Provides
Building skills Physical and procedural skills where accuracy, precision, and efficiency are important	*Behavioral learning* Behavioral psychology, operant conditioning	Tasks and procedures Practice exercises
Acquiring knowledge Basic information, concepts, and terminology in a discipline or field of study	*Cognitive learning* Cognitive psychology, attention, information processing, memory	Presentations Explanations
Developing critical, creative, and dialogical thinking Improved thinking and reasoning processes	*Learning through inquiry* Logic, critical, and creative thinking theory, classical philosophy	Question-driven inquiries Discussions
Cultivating problem-solving and decision-making abilities Mental strategies for finding solutions and making choices	*Learning with mental models* Gestalt psychology, problem solving, and decision theory	Problems Case studies Labs Projects
Exploring attitudes, feelings, and perspectives Awareness of attitudes, biases, and other perspectives; ability to collaborate	*Learning through groups and teams* Human communication theory; group counseling theory	Group activities Team projects
Practicing professional judgment Sound judgment and appropriate professional action in complex, context-dependent situations	*Learning through virtual realities* Psychodrama, sociodrama, gaming theory	Role playing Simulations Dramatic scenarios Games
Reflecting on experience Self-discovery and personal growth from real-world experience	*Experiential learning* Experiential learning, cognitive neuroscience, constructivism	Internships Service-learning Study abroad

Source: Davis, J. R., & Arend, B. D. (2013). *Facilitating seven ways of learning: A resource for more purposeful, effective, and enjoyable college teaching.* Sterling, VA: Stylus, p. 38. Reprinted with permission from the publisher.

to apply a given principle to a real course. Davis and Arend's model helps you determine what teaching strategies are best aligned to your specific outcomes. Similarly, Nilson (2013) refines Ambrose et al.'s principle of self-regulated learning by linking a wide range of planning, monitoring, and self-assessment activities and assignments to various course components and times during the term.

Davis and Arend's perspective and the instructional design literature overlap in several ways. Instructional designers also emphasize the wisdom of providing students with practice and using different strategies to teach different kinds of knowledge and skills. They similarly differentiate the effectiveness of different strategies for different purposes (e.g., Dick et al., 2015; Gagné et al., 2010; Jonassen, 2004, 2014; Smith & Ragan, 2005a, 2005b). However, they explicitly focus more on students' use of mental maps to acquire motor skills. Table 1.2 matches various intended learning outcomes with different conditions of

Table 1.2 Intended Learning Outcomes and Recommended Teaching Strategies

Intended Learning Outcomes	Recommended Teaching Strategies
Motor skills The student executes muscular movements with standards of speed, accuracy, force, and smoothness.	Introduce whole- and part-task routines. Explain and demonstrate. Supplement with visualization of performance and memory aids such as mnemonics. Guide retrieval and use of mental map for performance. Provide continued practice with informative feedback, and opportunity to adjust performance of part skills, connecting skills, and whole skills to desired proficiency level.
Verbal information The student articulates acquired knowledge such as labels or names, facts, and organized knowledge.	Introduce with emotional or novel information or event. Cue retrieval of related larger network. Elaborate relationship of new knowledge to larger network. Provide meaningful context. Segment content into learnable chunks. Represent new knowledge in structure, cases, logical relationships, memory aids. Arrange active, spaced practice and informative feedback in using new knowledge.
Conceptual understanding The student classifies a concept according to physical, sensory, or defined attributes.	Present concept with an inquiry approach or something interesting about the concept; add definition. Cue retrieval of component concepts or information. Progress from familiar to unfamiliar, simple to complex, best example to fuzzy example and nonexamples. Draw attention to distinguishing attributes and reasons for fit or nonfit (use questions and explanations). Point out common classification errors. Include concept maps, analogies, images (as appropriate). Arrange spaced practice and informative feedback in classifying examples and nonexamples.
Use of lower-order rules The student uses two or more concepts connected as a rule to solve simple routine problems.	Introduce rule with inquiry, a novel problem, or interesting use of rule. Preview what student will be able to do with the rule, as in future problem solving. Draw attention to related concepts in the rule. Guide learning with demonstration and application. Point out common errors to avoid, including misconceptions, overgeneralization, or undergeneralization. Arrange spaced practice and informative feedback in applying the rule. Provide varied situations for application to enhance transfer.
Use of higher-order rules The student uses two or more rules connected as a problem-solving strategy to solve more complex problems.	Provide authentic meaningful relevant task, goal-directed activity (multiple representations of problem and structure). Compare and relate to larger task or problem and role of strategic thinking in problem solving. Prompt recall of related previous experiences. Differentiate strategies for types of problems (logical, algorithmic, story, rule using, decision making, troubleshooting, diagnostic, case analysis, design, strategic performance, dilemma). Bridge from worked example(s) to problem task. Align practice with type of problem and strategy. Progress from simple to complex with varied new and relevant problems. Encourage reflection on solutions, provide feedback, and fade out coaching (scaffolding).

(Continued)

Table 1.2 (*Continued*)

Intended Learning Outcomes	Recommended Teaching Strategies
Cognitive strategies (self-regulated learning) The student will monitor, plan, and control personal ways of thinking and learning.	Introduce benefits of cognitive strategies. Prompt recall of ways of thinking and results. Explain strategy(ies) and purpose(s). Provide opportunities for inventing and practicing strategies, and experience results.
Attitude (dispositions) The student will voluntarily express a disposition to make a desired choice among alternatives.	Provide relevant choices, pros and cons, and their consequences. Relate to larger set of values. Stimulate empathy related to choices. Provide a respected model who advocates or shows the desired choice and positive results. Provide role-playing opportunities. Provide situations for making the choice and reinforcement for the desired choice.

learning (recommended teaching strategies) drawn from multiple instructional design resources, primarily Dick et al. (2015), Gagné et al. (2010), Martin and Briggs (1986), and Smith and Ragan (2005a, 2005b), with a few elaborations from Jonassen (2000) and Merrill (2002).

In the representation of learning outcomes and conditions, you can see that there are more similarities than differences with Davis and Arend's framework. Differences include some specifications of the mental models and the examples that Davis and Arend use, whereas instructional design conditions give a broad strategy that could include such examples. For example, simulations and dramatic scenarios can fit with conditions for problem solving. Davis and Arend also include *practicing professional judgment* and *reflecting on experience* as additional outcomes.

One more set of teaching and learning principles, one overlapping very little with those mentioned thus far, deserves recognition. In their concise, literature-packed volume, Persellin and Daniels (2014) derive six principles, the first three of which come from cognitive psychology and the fourth of which hails from multimedia research. After each principle, they list instructional applications:

1. Desirable difficulties enhance long-term retention. *Instructional applications:* Quizzes; opportunities for students to generate and apply material; spaced and interleaved practice sessions; occasions for students to work through confusion and frustration; challenging (but comprehensible) readings; extended wait time after posing questions; concept mapping.

2. Meaningful and spaced repetition enhances retention. *Instructional applications:* Regular and frequent quizzes; division of a skill into component parts and occasions for students to practice the weaker parts; encouraging students to study the material daily and to create their own review tools.

3. Emotional intensity and relevance deepen learning. *Instructional applications:* Personalized and positive classroom environment; dramatic, surprising, and humorous instructor behavior; opportunities for students to react to material emotionally; frequent, low-stakes feedback; oral presentation of emotional material; actions and words to increase student self-efficacy; hooks to capture student attention; games for reviewing material; storytelling; examples of the relevance of the material from current events, popular media, and students' lives both now and potentially in the future.

4. Multisensory learning deepens learning. *Instructional applications:* Assignments and activities in which students experience the materials in at least a few of the following ways: reading, seeing, drawing,

hearing, writing about, talking about, thinking about, acting out, reenacting, and touching; use of PowerPoint for images; students' reaction to controversial material in a human agree-disagree spectrum, integrated with debate; student presentations in the style of a micro-TED talk or PechaKucha (twenty slides each shown for twenty seconds) with emphasis on graphics, followed by discussion.

5. Small group work engages students. *Instructional applications:* Any of a wide variety of structured cooperative learning activities (e.g., think-pair-share, jigsaw, fishbowl, send a problem, numbered heads together); document sharing with collaborative editing; peer review of writing; team-based learning; problem-based learning; process-oriented guided-inquiry learning (POGIL).

6. Low-stakes formative assessment enhances retention. *Instructional applications:* Any of a wide variety of structured classroom assessment techniques (e.g., minute paper, muddiest point, and background knowledge probe); knowledge surveys (of students' confidence in their ability to perform tasks or answer questions on course material); lecture notes exchange between student pairs, followed by fill-ins and corrections; student-created flash cards; prelesson and postlesson quizzes; survey of student mis/preconceptions; student-generated test questions; extended wait time after posing questions; ConcepTests (multiple-choice items followed by a round of anonymous individual responses, then small-group discussion, and another round of anonymous individual responses using low-tech or high-tech response collection systems).

Principles 1, 3, and 4 are relatively new to the literature on teaching and learning principles. However, even in these, we see some overlap with Ambrose et al. (2010): the relevance of the material as a key motivator and the decomposition of complex skills into component parts, with practice opportunities for students in their weaker subskills. In addition, multisensory learning bears partial similarity to Chickering and Gamson's (1987) best practice of appealing to different ways of learning.

Persellin and Daniels's (2014) principles 2, 4, and 6 all pertain to practice. Principle 6 on formative assessment translates into the kind of practice with feedback that Ambrose et al. (2010) emphasize. Of the other principles, principle 2, on the best schedule for practice, hails from cognitive psychology and instructional design, which also draws on cognitive psychology. Principle 4, on the efficiency of multisensory practice, identifies learning factors not mentioned before in the face-to-face teaching literature and hails from instructional design.

Principle 5 makes the claim that group work engages students, which is not the same as improving retention or deepening learning, but it recalls Chickering and Gamson's (1987) best practice about ensuring cooperative interaction among students. Davis and Arend (2013) also mention group work but only as an especially effective method for broadening students' awareness and understanding of different perspectives and attitudes, which should further develop their social and collaborative skills.

So let's put all the principles together into one list of best teaching practices for faculty:

1. Interact with students as much as possible.
2. Give students opportunities to work in small groups.
3. Build in active learning.
4. Provide students with plenty of practice in the desired performances, spacing and interleaving that practice and varying the sense in which students get it. Of course, the teaching methods that afford the most effective practice will vary by the type of performance outcome.
5. Give students feedback that is prompt and targeted toward improving their competency in the desired performance.
6. Ensure students spend as much time as possible learning the material.

7. Set and communicate high expectations of students.

8. Find out students' course-related prior knowledge, remediate or activate it, have them self-assess their familiarity with it, and correct their errors and misconceptions.

9. Ensure that the organization of students' prior knowledge is valid. If it is valid, help students make more interconnections between important and meaningful features such as concepts and principles. If it is not valid, devise ways to make students' faulty mental model look inferior to your discipline's (see chapter 4).

10. Build desirable difficulties into student learning with challenging assignments and activities, spaced and interleaved practice sessions, and extended wait time after questions.

11. To motivate students, enhance the value of the material by displaying enthusiasm for it, rewarding students for achieving outcomes and demonstrating the relevance of the material to real-world applications and students' current and future lives.

12. Create a supportive environment for learning by aligning outcomes, learning activities, and assessments, incorporating early assessments that build student confidence, teaching students how to learn the material, clearly explaining expectations for performance, and building in choice and reflection on the learning process.

13. Help develop mastery by decomposing complex tasks into component skills, giving students practice in their weaker skills in different contexts, including the integration of skills in assessments, challenging students to link contextual learning experiences to general principles, and giving them practice in deciding where different skills and knowledge apply in various contexts.

14. Create a positive, inclusive, personalized course climate that allows different points of view, answers to questions, and approaches to a problem but requires evidence in student expression and honors ground rules for interaction.

15. Engage students in activities and assignments in which they practice self-regulated learning: planning, monitoring, and evaluating their learning and modifying their strategies to optimize it. These activities and assignments may involve goal setting, task analysis, rubric analysis, analysis of excellent and poor models, self-assessment, self-correction, assessment of peers' work, and assessment of study strategies.

16. Educate students about brain plasticity and their effort, self-awareness, and persistence that learning requires.

17. Inject emotions into presentations, activities, assignments, and reflections, and help students become more aware of their emotions by having them talk and write about them.

The online environment does not preclude an instructor from respecting any of these principles, even if scholars developed them with the traditional classroom in mind. In fact, most of practices and principles that appear in the instructional design literature can transfer to online courses. The specific ways that faculty can make this transfer, however, are not obvious.

In online courses, some kind of technology mediates the interactions with and among students, as well as the communications, practice opportunities, discussions, feedback, assessments, and motivational elements. But technology doesn't make the students' learning experiences and social relationships with others in the course any less real. Furthermore, in the candid words of several future-oriented instructional designers, adding "intellectual nutrition" to online courses will take us beyond "snake-oil salesmen and hucksters who favor style over substance" and generate principles for the next generation in online learning (Moller et al., 2012, p. 1). We will not have simply Internet-based courses, they write, but will create "technology-enabled learning environments" (p. 2).

At the moment, faculty are not getting the help they need to translate high-quality classroom pedagogy to the online environment. As a result, student success in online courses lags, and many instructors view online education with skepticism.

The work summarized in this section makes critical contributions to both the classroom and online teaching literature, but none provides a comprehensive compendium of all the universally applicable teaching and learning principles. We add more principles and apply them to online learning as we proceed through this book.

Each of chapters 2 through 7 addresses a best teaching practice—really a number of related best practices—and how faculty can build online courses around them. Some of these have received little mention in the lists of learning principles and best teaching practices we've examined here. Two of the lists do acknowledge the importance of content relevance, but this is only one aspect of significant learning outcomes, the focus of chapter 2. Similarly, Ambrose et al. (2010) recommend alignment among learning outcomes, activities, and assessment as one way (among many) to foster student motivation through supporting learning, but we regard coherent course design as a much more central best practice, one that the online learning literature skims over, so we devote all of chapter 3 to it. Accessibility isn't on any of the lists we have presented, and some would argue that it is only a design feature, but we consider it a best practice worthy of its own chapter (chapter 7). We just as strongly endorse informing your teaching with all the cognitive science research on learning possible on best practices, and we assemble the findings with an eye toward online application in chapter 4. We share with Ambrose et al. (2010) the conviction that student motivation underpins learning and so provide a more comprehensive list of motivators in chapter 5, along with ways to incorporate them into online courses.

Reflections

At the end of each chapter in this book, we list questions for faculty, instructional designers, and administrators to reflect on. This section also serves as a summary of the knowledge to be applied from this chapter. Our intent is to facilitate application.

For Instructors

- What is the target course you wish to design online?
- What learning principles do you already use in your classroom or online teaching?
- What is the content structure of your target course?
- What kinds of learning activities will fit well with your learning outcomes, content, and the principles of learning you want to apply in your course?
- How do you envision students' progression through learning activities from week to week (such as simple-to-complex, cause-effect, or some other progression)?

For Instructional Designers

- Where in the stages of instructional design would you begin to integrate the principles of learning with the events and conditions of learning?
- What preliminary course map could you develop from answers to the questions asked of instructors?

For Administrators

- How do you support collaboration of faculty with instructional designers or others to integrate principles of learning with technology training?
- What culture of faculty development would you like to create to support online course design and teaching?

■ REFERENCES

Allen, I. E., & Seamon, J. (2015, February). *Grade level: Tracking online education in the United States*. Babson Survey Research Group and Quahog Research Group. Retrieved from http://www.onlinelearningsurvey.com/reports /gradelevel.pdf

Ambrose, S. A., Bridges, M. W., DiPietro, M., Lovett, M. C., & Norman, M. K. (2010). *How learning works: Seven research-based principles for smart teaching*. San Francisco, CA: Jossey-Bass.

Atchley, W., Wingenbach, G., & Akers, C. (2013). Comparison of course completion and student performance through online and traditional courses. *International Review of Research in Open and Distance Learning, 14*(4), 104–116. Retrieved from ERIC database. (EJ1017510)

Barber, W., King, S., & Buchanan, S. (2015). Problem-based learning and authentic assessment in digital pedagogy: Embracing the role of collective communities. *Electronic Journal of E-Learning, 13*(2), 59–67.

Barshay, J. (2015, April 27). Five studies find online courses are not working well at community colleges. *Hechinger Report*. Retrieved from http://hechingerreport.org/five-studies-find-online-courses-are-not-working-at -community-colleges/

Best Value Schools. (2014, September). *25 colleges with high freshman retention rates*. Retrieved from http://www .bestvalueschools.com/high-freshman-retention-roi/

Boston, W., Diaz, S. R., Gibson, A., Ice, P., Richardson, J., & Swan, K. (2009). An exploration of the relationship between indicators of the community of inquiry framework and retention in online programs. *Journal of Asynchronous Learning Networks, 13*(3), 67–83. Retrieved from ERIC database. (EJ909838)

Bransford, J. D., Brown, A. L., & Cocking, R. R. (1999). *How people learn: Brain, mind, experience, and school*. Washington, DC: National Academy Press.

Brewer, P. E., & Brewer, E. C. (2015). Pedagogical perspectives for the online education skeptic. *Journal on Excellence in College Teaching, 26*(1), 29–52.

Broida, J. (n.d.). *Learner-centered model is cost-effective: Effective practice summary*. Retrieved from http://olc.onlinelearning consortium.org/effective_practices/learner-centered-model-cost-effective

Burnsed, B. (2010, October 22). Online universities: Retention rate data. *U.S. News & World Report: Education*. Retrieved from http://www.usnews.com/education/online-education/articles/2010/10/22/online-universities -retention-rate-data

Chickering, A. W., & Ehrmann, S. C. (1996). Implementing the seven principles: Technology as lever. *AAHE Bulletin, 49*(2), 3–6. Retrieved from https://www.aahea.org/articles/sevenprinciples.htm

Chickering, A. W., & Gamson, Z. F. (1987, March). Seven principles for good practice in undergraduate education. *AAHE Bulletin, 39*(7), 3–7. Retrieved from https://www.aahea.org/articles/sevenprinciples1987.htm

Chickering, A. W., & Gamson, Z. F. (1999). Development and adaptations of the seven principles for good practice in undergraduate education. *New Directions for Teaching and Learning, 80*, 75–81.

Clark, R. C., & Mayer, R. E. (2011). *E-learning and the science of instruction: Proven guidelines for consumers and designers of multimedia learning* (3rd ed.). San Francisco, CA: Jossey-Bass.

Conrad, R., & Donaldson, J. A. (2012). *Continuing to engage the online learner: More activities and resources for creative instruction*. San Francisco, CA: Jossey-Bass.

Davis, J. R., & Arend, B. D. (2013). *Facilitating seven ways of learning: A resource for more purposeful, effective, and enjoyable college teaching*. Sterling, VA: Stylus.

Dick, W., Carey, L., & Carey, J. O. (2015). *The systematic design of instruction* (8th ed.). Upper Saddle River, NJ: Pearson.

Dooley, K. E., Lindner, J. R., & Dooley, L. M. (2005). *Advanced methods in distance education: Applications and practices for educators, administrators, and learners.* Hershey, PA: IGI Global.

Elkilany, E. A. (2015). The impact of applying instructional design principles on students' attitudes towards the learning content. *Journal of Arab and Muslim Media Research, 8*(2), 147–169. doi:10.1386/jammr.8.2.147_1

Finley, F. N. (1983). Science processes. *Journal of Research in Science Teaching, 20*(1), 47–54.

Funk, J. T. (2007). *A descriptive study of retention of adult online learners: A model of interventions to prevent attrition.* (Order No. 3249896). Available from ProQuest Dissertations and Theses Global. (304723480)). Retrieved from http://search .proquest.com/openview/e6183a94ca54e333bab714da3b8d6870/1?pq-origsite=gscholar&cbl=18750&diss=y

Gagné, R. M., Wager, W. W., Golas, K. C., & Keller, J. M. (2005). *Principles of instructional design* (5th ed.). Belmont, CA: Wadsworth/Thomson Learning.

Guidera, S. G. (2003). Perceptions of the effectiveness of online instruction in terms of the seven principles of effective undergraduate education. *Journal of Educational Technology Systems, 32*(2/3), 139–178.

Harlen, W., & Doubler, S. (2004). Can teachers learn through enquiry online? Studying professional development in science delivered online and on-campus. *International Journal of Science Education, 26*(10), 1247–1267.

Hathaway, K. L. (2014). An application of the seven principles of good practice to online courses. *Research in Higher Education Journal, 22.* Retrieved from http://www.aabri.com/manuscripts/131676.pdf

Hattie, J. (2009). *Visible learning: A synthesis of over 800 meta-analyses relating to achievement.* New York, NY: Routledge.

Hiltz, S. R., & Goldman, R. (Eds.). (2005). *Learning together online: Research on asynchronous learning networks.* Mahwah, NJ: Erlbaum.

Hirumi, A. (2009). Learning online: Adapting the seven principles of good practice to a web-based instructional environment. In A. Orellana, T. L. Hudgins, & M. Simonson (Eds.), *The perfect online course: Best practices for designing and teaching.* Charlotte, NC: Information Age.

Iatradis, M. D. (1993). *Teaching science to children* (2nd ed.). New York, NY: Garland.

Jaffe, R., Moir, E., Swanson, E., & Wheeler, G. (2006). Online mentoring and professional development for new science teachers. In C. Dede (Ed.), *Online teacher professional development: Emerging models and methods* (pp. 89–116). Cambridge, MA: Harvard Education Publishing Group.

Jia, J. (2012). *Educational stages and interactive learning: From kindergarten to workplace training.* Hershey, PA: IGI Global.

Johnson, L., Adams Becker, S., Estrada, V., & Freeman, A. (2015). *NMC horizon report: 2015 higher education edition.* Austin, TX: New Media Consortium. Retrieved from https://net.educause.edu/ir/library/pdf/HR2015.pdf

Johnson, S. (2014). Applying the seven principles of good practice: Technology as a lever—in an online research course. *Journal of Interactive Online Learning, 13*(2), 41–50.

Jonassen, D. H. (2000). Toward a design theory of problem solving. *Educational Technology Research and Development, 48*(4), 63–85.

Jonassen, D. H. (2004). *Learning to solve problems: An instructional design guide.* San Francisco, CA: Jossey-Bass.

Jonassen, D. H. (2014). Assessing problem solving. In M. Spector, M. D. Merrill, J. Elen, & M. J. Bishop (Eds.), *Handbook of research on educational communications and technology* (pp. 269–287). New York, NY: Springer Science & Business Media.

Jonassen, D., & Land, S. M. (Eds.). (2012). *Theoretical foundations of learning environments* (2nd ed.). London, UK: Routledge.

Koeckeritz, J., Malkiewicz, J., & Henderson, A. (2002). The seven principles of good practice: Applications for online education in nursing. *Nurse Educator, 27*(6), 283–287.

Koslow, A., & Piña, A. A. (2015). Using transactional distance theory to inform online instructional design. *International Journal of Instructional Technology and Distance Learning*. Retrieved from http://www.itdl.org/Journal/Oct_15/Oct15.pdf

Lai, A., & Savage, P. (2013). Learning management systems and principles of good teaching: Instructor and student perspectives. *Canadian Journal of Learning and Technology, 39*(3).

Ley, K., & Gannon-Cook, R. (2014). Learner-valued interactions: Research into practice. *Quarterly Review of Distance Education, 15*(1), 23–32. Retrieved from http://www.aect.org/pdf/proceedings13/2013/13_16.pdf

Lineweaver, T. T. (2010). Online discussion assignments improve students' class preparation. *Teaching of Psychology, 37*, 204–209. Retrieved from http://dx.doi.org/10.1080/00986283.2010.488546

Lokken, F., & Mullins, C. (2015, April). *2014 Distance Education Survey results—Trends in e-learning: Tracking the impact of e-learning at community colleges.* Washington, DC: Instructional Technology Council. Retrieved from http://www.itcnetwork.org/attachments/article/1171/AnnualSurvey2014PublishedApril2015FinalWeb.pdf

Lu, M., Todd, A. M., & Miller, M. T. (2011). Creating a supportive culture for online teaching: A case study of a faculty learning community. *Online Journal of Distance Learning Administration, 14*(3). Retrieved from http://scholarworks.sjsu.edu/cgi/viewcontent.cgi?article=1009&context=comm_pub

Lumadue, R., & Waller, R. (2014). *Introduction to presentation design.* Retrieved from https://itunes.apple.com/us/book/intro.-to-presentation-design/id884768442?mt=13

Martin, B. L., & Briggs, L. J. (1986). *The affective and cognitive domains: Integration for instruction and research.* Englewood Cliffs, NJ: Educational Technology Publications.

Mayer, R. E. (2014). Commentary: Incorporating motivation into multimedia learning. *Learning and Instruction, 29*, 171–173. doi:10.1016/j.learninstruc.2013.04.003

McCabe, D. B., & Meuter, M. L. (2011). A student view of technology in the classroom: Does it enhance the seven principles of good practice in undergraduate education? *Journal of Marketing Education, 33*(2), 149–159.

Merrill, D. M. (2002). First principles of instruction. *Educational Technology Research and Development, 50*(3), 43–59.

Mewhinney, C. (2009). *Interaction of learning approach with concept integration and achievement in a large guided inquiry organic class* (Doctoral dissertation). Retrieved from http://digital.library.unt.edu/ark:/67531/metadc12163/

Meyer, K. A. (2014). An analysis of the research on faculty development for online teaching and identification of new directions. *Journal of Asynchronous Learning Networks, 17*(4), 93–112. Retrieved from http://sloanconsortium.org/sites/default/files/8-meyer.pdf

Meyer, K. A., & Murrell, V. S. (2014). A national study of training content and activities for faculty development for online teaching. *Journal of Asynchronous Learning Networks, 18*(1). Retrieved from http://files.eric.ed.gov/fulltext/EJ1030527.pdf

Moller, L., Robison, D., & Huett, J. B. (2012). Unconstrained learning: Principles for the next generation of distance education. In L. Moller & J. B. Huett (Eds.), *The next generation of distance education: Unconstrained learning* (pp. 1–19). New York, NY: Springer Science and Business Media.

Newlin, M. H., & Wang, A. Y. (2002). Integrating technology and pedagogy: Web instruction and seven principles of undergraduate education. *Teaching of Psychology, 29*(4), 325–330.

Nilson, L. B. (2013). *Creating self-regulated learners: Strategies to strengthen students' self-awareness and learning skills.* Sterling, VA: Stylus.

Orellana, A., Hudgins, T. L., & Simonson, M. (Eds.). (2009). *The perfect online course: Best practices for designing and teaching*. Charlotte, NC: Information Age Publishing.

Park, J. H., & Choi, H. J. (2009). Factors influencing adult learners' decision to drop out or persist in online learning. *Educational Technology and Society, 12*(4), 207–217.

Pelech, J., & Pieper, G. (2010). *The comprehensive handbook of constructivist teaching: From theory to practice*. Charlotte, NC: Information Age Publishing.

Persellin, D. C., & Daniels, M. B. (2014). *A concise guide to improving student learning: Six evidence-based principles and how to apply them*. Sterling, VA: Stylus.

Rabe-Hemp, C., Woolen, S., & Humiston, G. S. (2009). A comparative analysis of student engagement, learning, and satisfaction in lecture hall and online learning settings. *Quarterly Review of Distance Education, 10*(2), 207–218.

Richey, R. C., Klein, J. D., & Tracey, M. W. (2011). *The instructional design knowledge base: Theory, research, and practice*. London, UK: Routledge.

Riel, M., & Polin, L. (2004). Online learning communities: Common ground and critical differences in designing technical environments. In S. A. Barab, R. Kling, & J. H. Gray (Eds.), *Designing for virtual communities in the service of learning* (pp. 16–50). Cambridge, UK: Cambridge University Press.

Ritter, M. E., & Lemke, K. A. (2000). Addressing the "Seven Principles for Good Practice in Undergraduate Education" with Internet-enhanced education. *Journal of Geography in Higher Education, 24*(1), 100.

Schwen, T. M., & Hara, N. (2004). In S. A. Barab, R. Kling, & J. H. Gray (Eds.), *Designing for virtual communities in the service of learning* (pp. 16–50). Cambridge, UK: Cambridge University Press.

Shachar, M., & Neumann, Y. (2010). Twenty years of research on the academic performance differences between traditional and distance learning: Summative meta-analysis and trend examination. *MERLOT Journal of Online Learning and Teaching, 6*(2). Retrieved from http://jolt.merlot.org/vol6no2/shachar_0610.pdf

Shea, P., Vickers, J., & Hayes, S. (2010). Online instructional effort measured through the lens of teaching presence in the community of inquiry framework: A re-examination of measures and approach. *International Review of Research in Open and Distributed Learning, 11*(3). Retrieved from http://www.irrodl.org/index.php/irrodl/article/view/915/1648?

Sheridan, K., & Kelly, M. A. (2010). The indicators of instructor presence that are important to students in online courses. *MERLOT Journal of Online Learning and Teaching, 6*(4). Retrieved from http://jolt.merlot.org/vol6no4/sheridan_1210.htm

Simonson, M., & Schlosser, C. (2009). We need a plan. In A. Orellana, T. L. Hudgins, & M. Simonson (Eds.), *The perfect online course: Best practices for designing and teaching* (pp. 3–21). Charlotte, NC: Information Age Publishing.

Simonson, M., Smaldino, S., & Zvacek, S. (2015). *Teaching and learning at a distance: Foundations of distance education* (6th ed.). Charlotte, NC: Information Age Publishing.

Smith, P. L., & Ragan, T. L. (2005a). *Instructional design* (3rd ed.). Hoboken, NJ: Wiley.

Smith, P. L., & Ragan, T. L. (2005b). *Instructor companion site*. Retrieved from http://bcs.wiley.com/he-bcs/Books?action=index&itemId=0471393533&itemTypeId=BKS&bcsId=2112

Smith, R. M. (2014). *Conquering the content: A blueprint for online course design and development* (2nd ed.). San Francisco, CA: Jossey-Bass.

Spector, M., Merrill, M. D., Elen, J., & Bishop, M. J. (Eds.). (2014). *Handbook of research on educational communications and technology* (4th ed.). New York, NY: Springer Science & Business Media.

Stavredes, T., & Herder, T. (2014). *A guide to online course design: Strategies for student success*. San Francisco, CA: Jossey-Bass.

Stone, I. (2014, December). The 30 best online colleges 2014. *Best Value Schools*. Retrieved from http://www .bestvalueschools.com/best-online-colleges-2014/

Straumsheim, C. (2016, October 24). Doubts about data: 2016 Survey of Faculty Attitudes on Technology. *Inside Higher Ed*. Retrieved from https://www.insidehighered.com/news/survey/doubts-about-data-2016-survey-faculty -attitudes-technology

Tallent-Runnels, M. K., Thomas, J. A., Lan, W. Y., Cooper, S., Ahern, T. C., Shaw, S. M., & Liu, X. (2006). Teaching courses online: A review of the research. *Review of Educational Research, 76*(1) 93–135.

Tirrell, T., & Quick, D. (2012). Chickering's seven principles of good practice: Student attrition in community college online courses. *Community College Journal of Research and Practice, 36*(8), 580–590. Retrieved from ERIC database. (EJ971607).

US Department of Education. (2010). *Evaluation of evidence-based practices in online learning: A meta-analysis and review of online learning studies.* Washington, DC: Author. Retrieved from http://www2.ed.gov/rschstat/eval/tech/evidence -based-practices/finalreport.pdf

Vrasidas, C., & Glass, G. V. (Eds.). (2004). *Current perspectives in applied information technologies: Online professional development for teachers.* Greenwich, CT: Information Age Publishing.

Waterhouse, S. (2005). *The power of e-learning: The essential guide for teaching in the digital age.* Upper Saddle River, NJ: Pearson.

Xu, D., & Jaggars, S. S. (2013). *Adaptability to online learning: Differences across types of students and academic subject areas* (CCRC Working Paper No. 54). Community College Research Center, Columbia University. Retrieved from http://ccrc.tc.columbia.edu/media/k2/attachments/adaptability-to-online-learning.pdf

York, C. S., & Richardson, J. C. (2012). Interpersonal interaction in online learning: Experienced online instructors' perceptions of influencing factors. *Journal of Asynchronous Learning Networks, 16*(4), 83–98. Retrieved from http:// files.eric.ed.gov/fulltext/EJ982684.pdf

Zhang, J., & Walls, R. T. (2009). Instructors' self-perceived pedagogical principle implementation in the online environment. In A. Orellana, T. L. Hudgins, & M. Simonson (Eds.), *The perfect online course: Best practices for designing and teaching* (pp. 87–104). Charlotte, NC: Information Age Publishing.

CHAPTER 2

Setting Significant Outcomes

As foundations for online course design, criteria like sophisticated technology and comprehensive content fail to enhance student persistence. Rather, the first stage of course design should answer the "so what?" questions. The answers lend meaning and relevance to course content and should shape instructional goals, objectives, outcomes, and ultimately the whole design of a course. Connecting course content to real-world problems, for example, gives the knowledge and skills application and purpose. This chapter will show how focusing on significant learning provides the most effective strategy for course design, one that adds more value than any lock-step approach that only covers the content, teaches to the test, or basks in the glitter of technology.

The advent of online learning and the availability of information on the Internet have made our focus on deeper and richer experiences of teaching and learning ever more important.
—D. Barbezat, A. Zajonc, P. J. Palmer, and M. Bush (2014)

■ THE NEED FOR REFLECTING ON WHAT WE TEACH

Online learning faces the same challenge as classroom learning: reversing the trend of underachieving colleges (Bok, 2013) and academically adrift students (Arum & Roksa, 2011). Faculty can meet this challenge when they design and teach courses with a clear purpose and relevance for their students (Bhowmik, 2013; Fox, 2010). Unfortunately, the siren of technology often veers online course design off-track with bells and whistles, as if to make a tech-savvy impression rather than create "functional relevance" for students (Snelbecker, Miller, & Zheng, 2008, p. 6).

Several factors seduce faculty into this misplaced focus: genuine excitement about using new tools, well-meaning technical support that inadvertently ignores pedagogy, and little or no support from experienced peers or faculty development staff. Minimum standards for online course design offer little help because they tend to steer clear of identifying the teaching practices needed for effective learning (Hirumi, 2009). Moreover, the input and analysis stage in instructional design models omits any decision about what counts as significant learning in a course (Dick, Carey, & Carey, 2015; Gagné, Wager, Golas, & Keller, 2005; Smith & Ragan, 2005). Rather, these models move straight to analyzing course outcomes and objectives and proceeding with course design and development. This pervasive omission springs from the historically value-free nature of instructional systems design (Briggs, 1977): "The design model advocated here determines only the methodology of problem-solving, not the nature of the goals, objectives, or outcomes to be sought, nor the method of instruction. . . . The model presented is 'value free'" (p. 9).

Briggs appeared to shift this perspective slightly by challenging a group of prospective instructional designers to determine the relationship of "models of teaching" to "models of instructional design" (1978). Later, he added the importance of including values and attitudes types of objectives because of their "pervasive force in all our endeavors" (Martin & Briggs, 1986, p. 140). Yet these concerns only touch on what we mean by significant learning. Our reflection on what counts should highlight what will have enduring value for our students, not just list some course objectives that focus on values and attitudes.

Over time, we see a distinction made between *instructional design* and *instructional systems design*. The former embraces the "So what?" questions and learning theories and therefore comes closer to dealing with significant learning, whereas the latter contains procedural steps for developing a course (Andrews & Goodson, 2011; Branch & Kopcha, 2014; Briggs, 1977; Martin & Briggs, 1986; Reiser, 2007). Unfortunately, many practitioners use the terms interchangeably. But when you are designing an online course, you definitely want to start with instructional design.

Faculty generally assume responsibility for course design and development as well as for interpreting content, teaching, and assessing students (American Association of University Professors, n.d.; Nelson, 2010). In teaching and learning centers, instructional designers share this responsibility with the faculty, who are the subject matter experts with their own disciplinary ideas on how to teach the material (Dempsey, Albion, Litchfield, Havard, & McDonald, 2007). But faculty models of pedagogy may not align with those of instructional designers. Determining the pedagogy that drives the course design matters because the interaction of pedagogy and content influences what students will learn.

Simply satisfying students is not the same as significant learning. Unfortunately, the research on online course retention and attrition concentrates on satisfaction and overlooks the value that students perceive (Andreson, 2009; Hart, 2012; Moore, 2014; Kuo, Walker, Belland, & Schroder, 2013; Levy, 2006). To illustrate the difference, Levy recalls the time when AT&T received 90 percent or higher ratings on customer satisfaction yet was still losing customers. Some of the literature shows that content relevancy, course organization, and interaction matter (Grandzhol & Grandzhol, 2010; Hoskins, 2012; Lee, Dickerson, & Winslow, 2012; Park & Choi, 2009; Strachota, 2003). But for the many online students who hold jobs, carry family responsibilities, and have mature expectations for their courses, value can be an overriding factor (Lawlor, 2007; Rovai, 2003). It can make the difference in whether a student stays with and successfully completes a course or drops out.

HOW CONTENT BECOMES THE WRONG DRIVER

Students cite many reasons for dropping out of online courses, including the irrelevance and inapplicability of the content (Chyung & Vachon, 2013; Levy, 2006; Park & Choi, 2009). Dense content becomes a barrier to significant learning because it leaves too little time for an instructor to show its relevance and build in opportunities for students to apply it. Typically, content coverage balloons because of faculty's genuine passion for their field of expertise and their desire to share this with students. Content grows "like the mythical Hydra of Greek legend" with "two more heads growing in place of each head that is cut off, making it a very difficult monster to tame" (Monahan, 2015, ¶1). Where is there time for comprehension in the course? Where does the development of critical analysis and problem-solving skills fit in? Encyclopedic content coverage leaves little wiggle room for this higher-value, higher-order learning (Florida Department of Education, Bureau of Curriculum and Instruction, 2008). We teach a lot of content that will not matter much in students' lives, that is not life-worthy, that has no authentic purpose or meaning in the real world (Burkholder, 2014; Perkins, 2014). Consequently, students end up with only "acquaintance knowledge" (Perkins, 2014, p. 33). What is the point of teaching just content when so much of it is readily accessible without taking a college course? For example, anyone can quickly find even trivial information on the Internet, such as the name for the "dot over the letter *i*" (Perkins, 2014, p. 34). The Internet tells us it is a *tittle,* which also appears over the letter *j.* How relevant is this factoid to significant learning? As Gagné and Merrill (2000) plainly wrote:

> People may learn facts, but what for? They may learn new concepts, but how are these to function in the context of the larger task that they as human individuals do? Learners can acquire procedures, but in the context of what larger scale activity? Placing student learning outcomes in the context of real-world problems gives purpose and meaning to knowledge and skills. (p. 129)

We need to think differently about content and shift our focus from covering it to getting students to use it (Burkholder, 2014; Monahan, 2015; Sipress & Voelker, 2011; Weimer, 2014). Students are more likely to stick with a course when they must apply the content and see its relevance (Chyung & Vachon, 2013; Gentry, 2014; Hart, 2012; Holton, 2013; Müller, 2008; Park & Choi, 2009; CECS Student Success Center at Wright State University, n.d.; Yoder, 2005).

A MEANINGFUL DESTINATION FOR THE LEARNING ENTERPRISE

The power of design comes from leading students to a meaningful destination. This end shapes the instructional goals, objectives, outcomes, and ultimately the whole focus of a course and generates more relevant means. To exploit the power of design, we need to:

- Start with a "purposeful enterprise"—learning that will have lasting value for the students (Fink, 2013; Gagné & Merrill, 2000; Richey, 1996; Smith & Ragan, 2005).
- Select technology to support "functional relevance" (Snelbecker et al., 2008).
- Use content for a relevant purpose (Burkholder, 2014; Monahan, 2015; Weimer, 2014).
- Create learning activities that will lead to genuine accomplishment for the student (Wiggins & McTighe, 2011).

The "So what?" questions are broader than the goals, objectives, or outcomes you will list in a syllabus or course module. They come from thinking about what you expect your students to be able to do intellectually, emotionally, and physically after the course (Bain, 2004)—not how much content to include but what role to give it. A more life-worthy purpose may be to teach students to think critically or think like a disciplinary specialist—a mathematician, historian, or scientist—to read the literature, master threshold concepts, speak and write with authority, reason and research in the field, grasp the big issues, answer the big questions, and create complex new knowledge (Fink, 2013; Perkins, 2014). You can challenge students to tackle some big questions toward the end of a course, encouraging them to integrate their new knowledge and skills to formulate tentative answers and solutions (Fink, 2013).

A vision of significant learning reveals the wider aim of what students are learning (Gronlund cited in Marken & Morrison, 2013). Consider what you want them to remember and know how to do five years from now (Burkholder, 2014; Fink, 2013; Monahan, 2015; Weimer, 2014). Might they look back and realize that the value of your course lay not so much in the content itself but their ability to apply it (Monahan, 2015)? Might they care enough to take informed actions in the real world (Fink, 2013; Perkins, 2014)? This vision guides your decisions about course outcomes, approaches to teaching and learning, and student activities. It prompts examples of student performance that would realize this vision, such as solving problems using the content, making predictions, or explaining a concept or phenomenon.

Once you develop a clear vision, students will experience better teaching because the vision clarifies the purpose and goals, teaching strategies, and learning activities. You then are in a better position to help students understand how and why they are moving forward in the course. Not surprisingly, teacher clarity correlates with student learning (BrckaLorenz, Cole, Kinzie, & Ribera, 2011; Ribera, BrckaLorenz, Cole, & Lair, 2012). In fact, faculty who value clarity rank high student engagement and deep learning among their major goals (Ribera et al., 2012). Student data also reveal "significant, positive relationships between teaching clarity and all subscales of deep learning and student-reported gains" (BrckaLorenz et al., 2011, ¶17). In sum, significant learning, once defined, leads to active and meaningful learning experiences.

■ EXAMPLES OF SIGNIFICANT LEARNING FROM INSTRUCTIONAL DESIGN

While models of instructional systems design bypass the vision of significant learning, several scholars of instructional design embrace it fully. For assessing students, they recommend assigning an appropriate, authentic challenge (e.g., Reigeluth, 2016; Reigeluth & Carr-Chellman, 2009; Gagné & Merrill, 2000), as do educators and evaluators (Fink, 2013; McTighe & Wiggins, 2014; Monahan, 2015; Perkins, 2014; Weimer, 2014; Wiggins & McTighe, 2011). Instructional designers also offer examples of learning goals that illustrate several types of significant learning: values, ways of thinking, complex knowledge, and problem solving (Reigeluth, 1999; see figure 2.1).

Figure 2.1   Significant Learning Domains

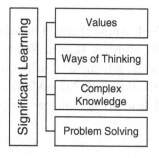

Values

- Preparing students for "valued adult roles" (Gardner, 1999, p. 70)
- Preparing students to become responsible citizens in a democratic society, convincing them that "they can make a difference" through political, social, and community action (Kovalik & McGeehan, 1999, p. 372)
- Experiencing learning "in the context of a goal that is relevant, meaningful, and interesting to the student" and "closely related to how students will use it outside the learning environment" (Schank, Berman, & Macpherson, 1999, p. 163)

Ways of Thinking

- Using multiple perspectives and divergent thinking to address "fuzzy, ill-defined, and ill-structured problems" that are realistic and relevant to students' lives (Hannafin, Land, & Oliver, 1999, p. 117)
- Learning "general methods of thinking (for success in education, industry, and today's information society)" and "general logical structures of various subject matters" (Landa, 1999, p. 342)

Complex Knowledge

- Learning "how to learn, as well as what to learn" and how to construct knowledge (Mayer, 1999, p. 142)
- Learning "content knowledge in complex domains, problem-solving and critical thinking skills, and collaboration skills" with authenticity and relevance within a "situated, learner-centered, integrative, and collaborative" learning environment (Nelson, 1999, p. 234)
- Using a "diversity of expertise" from others to "deal with complex issues" and learning how to "work with people" as well as "how to learn" (Bielaczyc & Collins, 1999, p. 270)

Problem Solving

- Meaningful and authentic "problem solving, collaboration and communication" in a "problem-based" context, and then in a "project-based" context involving several models for how to think, tolerate ambiguity, explore independently, and articulate one's thinking (Schwartz, Lin, Brophy, & Bransford, 1999, p. 185)
- "Problem solving and conceptual development" that is "driven by an ill-defined or ill-structured problem (or question, case, project) and 'owned' by the learner," and during which the learning is an authentic and active process where students can construct knowledge based on their experiences (Jonassen, 1999, p. 216)

■ EXAMPLES OF SIGNIFICANT LEARNING FROM COLLEGE COURSES

Examples from college courses illustrate the power that setting significant learning goals can have for students in artistic activities like creative thinking and design, in health and social services, in quantitative reasoning and technology, and in scientific fields like chemistry and environmental science.

Creativity and Design

Creative Thinking

What counts for significant learning in creativity and creative thinking? According to a review of the sources of innovation and creativity conducted for the National Center on Education and the Economy (Adams, 2005), it is not just technical expertise but an intersection of creative thinking skills, motivation, procedural and technical knowledge, metacognitive awareness, and a commitment to the creative process. In this framework, students begin with an end product or artifact as a personal goal, and the instructor coaches them to think about how they are thinking as they complete their projects and solve creative problems. Proof of success resides in the students' gains in creativity (Seng cited in Adams, 2005, p. 18).

Fashion Design

At first, In-Sook Ahn planned to develop her online course with content and objectives handed to her by someone else, along with the designated textbook. The book portrayed only one culture's body type and focused on personal wardrobe analysis. After Ahn met with an instructional designer, she broadened her focus to a multicultural context that would help "students develop a vision and disposition toward the aesthetics of fashion design in a way that would serve them as they engaged in the highly competitive workplace" (Goodson & Ahn, 2014, p. 204). Students looked beyond their closets and limited fashion choices in their small town to the international world of fashion inspiration and design. Assessments, participation in discussions, and formative evaluation showed that students not only learned but also expected what they learned to be useful in their future fashion careers.

English

To prepare for a major English assignment, students first identified the communities to which they felt a sense of belonging. The assignment then challenged them to apply the principles of communication on behalf of the communities they claimed. One of the students, Regina Gordon, chose to create a support group for people with sarcoidosis and an awareness campaign, including a blog, flyers, and a day for observing this rare, debilitating disease. The sarcoidosis awareness project gave Regina, who lives with this disease, an active voice in public space to creatively actualize her personal passion for awareness and advocacy (R. Gordon, personal communication, February 22, 2016).

The Sciences

Chemistry

In rethinking his teaching methods for classroom and online applications in his chemistry courses, Paul Edwards decided to teach computer applications that would make the computer a tool of the profession. With this in mind, he replaced traditional drill-and-practice applications with scientific word processing and spreadsheets for laboratory calculations. One "expert" had recommended giving students templates to follow. However, Edwards decided to have his students create the templates themselves instead of "plugging and chugging" numbers in someone else's vision. For at least one student, the impact was considerable. After graduation, she entered a master's program in industrial chemistry and a two-year internship at an industrial chemistry lab. The project she was given involved calculations on a spreadsheet with an estimated time line of a full two years to complete the task. However, because of her experience in applied spreadsheet calculations, she was able to complete the project in six months (P. Edwards, personal communication. August 14, 2015).

Environmental Science

In their online environmental science course, Deksissa, Behera, and Harkness (2014) wanted their students to acknowledge and change their beliefs about water. Specifically, they wanted students to replace their misconceptions about water being abundant and free with a more realistic view, develop a deep interest in environmental science, and see its relevance to their personal lives. Toward these ends, the course provided opportunities for students to practice critical thinking, problem solving, data analysis and interpretation, laboratory analysis, the scientific method, technical writing skills, and oral presentation skills. They used Fink's (2003) areas of foundational knowledge, application, integration, human dimension, caring, and learning how to learn as their assessment framework. Test results and confidence surveys showed significant student gains in all areas.

Quantitative Reasoning and Information Technology

Quantitative Reasoning

Alicia Graziosi Strandberg of the Villanova School of Business and Kathleen Campbell of Saint Joseph's University went beyond teaching just the quantitative content (Strandberg & Campbell, 2014). Their online students had to use data and quantitative thinking to solve multifaceted realistic problems that had no definite answers. To align the course with industry standards and expectations, Strandberg and Campbell required that students create organized visual displays of data (graphs, figures, tables) that helped inform decisions. They worked in teams to develop solutions for these problems. Like most other real-world problems, getting to a solution required melding the perspectives of different team members. Teams had to provide data, visual representations of the data, and related explanations for their decisions. For Strandberg and Campbell, dealing only with the quantitative content for technical competence would have fallen short of functional relevance and significant learning in their classes.

Computer Information Technology

Jeff Straw incorporated significant learning and functional relevance into his online computer programming course by deemphasizing programming languages, which change over time, and focusing instead on "the thought processes and problem-solving approach" of the field (Straw, 2011, p. 1). He reported that students better understood the meaning and purpose of computer programming, were more engaged in learning, and expressed metacognitive gains. In addition, they were in a better position to decide if computer programming was the right career choice for them.

Health and Social Sciences

Community Health

Kathleen Lux admitted, "I had never thought about the human dimension, caring, and learning how to learn 'taxonomies' related to course design, which is ironic as nursing is all about caring for humans" (Lux, 2011, p. 6). She redesigned her hybrid course, Community Health Promotion, with this human dimension in mind and its "big purpose" to get students excited about health promotion. Her collection of student comments suggested the course achieved this purpose—for example, "I perceive community health nursing in a much more positive way" (Lux, 2011, p. 20).

Social Sciences

In a course in the Department of Geography and another in the Department of Educational Studies, Dan Trudeau and Tina Kruse added civic engagement experiences—Trudeau in his course on urban social inequality and Kruse in her course on youth development—to increase the significance of the learning (Trudeau & Kruse, 2014). They believed that community experiences would be of value in students' lives long after each course. They located and secured community partners, set protocols for student-partner interactions, gave students opportunities to select experiences matching their own interests, created frameworks for thinking and reflection, and added methods for sharing mutual student and partner findings. Trudeau and Kruse reported (pp. 25–26):

> As a way of fostering significant learning experiences, students who participate in civic engagement are highly motivated and engaged in their learning. . . . Another important reason is that the learning which the students experience through civic engagement is personally—and socially—relevant, long-lasting, and sometimes transformative, and is thus more substantive than a lecture-discussion approach to learning.

• • •

More examples from college courses are available in:

- *Designing Courses for Significant Learning: Voices of Experience* (Fink & Fink, 2009)
- *Creating Significant Learning Experiences* (Fink, 2013)
- Fink's Designing Significant Learning Experiences website: http://www.designlearning.org/

■ EXAMPLES OF SIGNIFICANT LEARNING FROM ADAPTIVE LEARNING

Here we look at two examples of adaptive learning courses that incorporate significant learning outcomes. Both use the Smart Sparrow platform (Smart Sparrow, n.d.). The company promotes itself as offering personalization and the use of learning analytics as the key to better learning. But the case studies of courses using this platform reveal that significant learning is the springboard for design.

In the first example, a learning designer at St. Leo University redesigned the online Marketing 101 course to incorporate real-world scenarios requiring students to think through and make choices about an entrepreneur's best decision in different marketing contexts (Instructional Designer, n.d.). In the second example, Ariel Anbar and learning designer Lev Horodyskj created the Habitable Worlds course at Arizona State University. It had the big purpose of creating "an introductory science course designed for students—particularly non-science majors—to apply their knowledge in a project-based manner, using logic and reasoning to solve problems" and engage students in understanding "the science behind the compelling question of whether we are alone in the universe" (Anbar, n.d., ¶2). This emphasis represented a sharp departure from teaching the introductory course as encyclopedic content to be memorized. It also drove the learning activities away from traditional lecture and toward online exercises and video tutorials designed for "question-motivated problem solving" (Anbar, n.d., ¶3).

Dror Ben Naim, the CEO of Smart Sparrow, contends that "course design is key to improving student engagement." Engagement sags, he says, "when the learning experience is distilled to simply posting course materials online and asking students to 'discuss' on a web forum" (Naim, 2015, ¶16, 24). He adds, "Each lesson should have one action-oriented objective to ensure your lesson design process is focused" (¶28).

■ THE PROCESS OF REFLECTION

Various scholars propose ways for instructors to begin reflecting on the significant learning potential of their courses. For instance, Wilcoxson (2013, p. 3) suggests focusing on learning rather than a particular task, noting that "'build a model of a dam' differs from 'simulate the principle of how dams work.'" You might start with the following reflective questions (McTighe & Wiggins, 2014, p. 2): "What should students know, understand, and be able to do?" and "What enduring understandings are desired?"

Or you might begin by looking around for real problems in local news outlets and asking how practitioners in the field view these situations and solve these problems (Jonassen, 1999). Then ask students to research cases that illustrate approaches or solutions. Are there problems of strategic performance, policy issues, design problems, dilemmas—any authentic problem that will allow students to use the content, evaluate multiple perspectives, develop rationales, and assess plausible solutions? Can you pose rule-using, policy, troubleshooting, or design problems (Jonassen, 2011)? Decisions about choices, judgments, and the process of constructing knowledge lead students to find solutions for problems that matter to them. Or you might ask what actions could benefit your community with service-learning or advance social justice with civic engagement experiences (Guthrie & McCracken, 2010; Waldner, Widener, & McGorry, 2012).

Goodson and Ahn (2014) integrate front-end analysis from instructional design (Dick et al., 2004; Gagné et al., 2004) with Fink's approach to designing significant learning (Fink, 2003, 2013; Fink & Fink, 2009), and with cultural analysis (Saxena, 2011). They pose the following questions (p. 202):

- What is worth caring about in the course?
- What are the most important concepts and why do they matter?
- Who are the students? One culture or diverse? Both male and female?
- What is important and relevant to these students?
- How and why would these students apply what they learn from the course?
- How will the course address the broader goal of helping students to learn how to learn and to learn how to think?

Keller (2010) considers what will hold students' attention, relate to their personal goals and lives, build their confidence in achieving the learning outcomes, and convince them that their investment in learning has been worth the time and effort.

Fink (2013, p. 10) defines significant learning in several ways, beginning with this probe: "In your deepest, fondest dreams, what kind of impact would you most like to have on your students?" In a course design template, he adds questions about the "big purpose" of a course, its value for students, the life situations in which they will find the course valuable, and the needs that the course will address (Fink, n.d.). He poses these additional questions for the initial phase of course building (2013, pp. 293–294):

- Where are you? What are your situational factors: the context, the nature of the subject, the student and instructor characteristics, and the special pedagogical challenges?
- Where do you want to wind up? That is, what do you want students to gain from the course in terms of foundational knowledge, application, integration, human dimension, caring, and learning how to learn?
- How will you and your students know if you get there? What kinds of feedback and assessments will you use to measure your students' progress?

Whatever questions foster your reflection about what counts as a meaningful learning enterprise or significant learning, students need to anchor their knowledge to the situations where the real-life purpose of that knowledge is clear (Ouyang & Stanley, 2014). In one instance, a faculty member designing an online course began with a simple question:

> The first question you have to ask yourself is, "What do I want the students to learn?" And I had never asked myself that question in all the years [I'd been teaching, and] I've been teaching for a long time. . . . You make the lecture the night before you go in, you draw all over the board, you come out, and you say, "It wasn't so bad" or "It was great" or "It was horrible" or whatever it was, it was. You say, "Well, next time maybe I'll do something differently." I never actually asked myself, "What do I want the students to learn?" It was online, when you're sitting there saying, "Oh dear, what do I want them actually to learn and how am I going to get there?" (Russell, 2012, p. 54)

The Reflections section poses some related questions, starting with eight to help faculty make decisions about significant learning. Instructional designers in turn need to know an instructor's responses to those questions, so we add two questions for designers. Finally, because administrators oversee the online course design process and may even review and certify online courses, they affect how significant learning plays out, so they too have two questions for reflection.

Reflections

For Instructors

- What is worth caring about in the online course you are designing?
- What are the most important concepts, and why do they matter?
- What are the most important tasks students should do, and why do they matter?
- Who are the students? Do they represent one culture or diverse cultures? What is their gender distribution?
- What is important and relevant to these students?
- How and why would these students apply what they learn from the course?
- How will the course address the broader goal of helping students learn how to learn and learn how to think?
- How will the course address the broader goal of helping students in their future life situations?

For Instructional Designers

- What do you know about the answers to the faculty reflection questions listed?
- How will the answers influence the strategies you recommend for designing the course?

For Administrators

- In what ways do the campus mission and goals for graduation suggest the kind of significant learning that should be happening in your institution's online courses?
- How do you support faculty reflections about what counts as significant learning in their online courses?

■ REFERENCES

Adams, K. (2005, July). *Sources of innovation and creativity: A summary of the research.* Washington, DC: National Center on Education and the Economy. Retrieved from http://www.ncee.org/wp-content/uploads/2010/04/Sources-of -Innovation-Creativity.pdf

American Association of University Professors. (n.d.). *Academic freedom of students and professors, and political discrimination.* Retrieved from http://www.aaup.org/academic-freedom-students-and-professors-and-political-discrimination

Anbar, A. (n.d.). *Habitable worlds.* Retrieved from https://www.smartsparrow.com/case-studies/habworlds/

Andresen, M. A. (2009). Asynchronous discussion forums: Success factors, outcomes, assessments, and limitations. *Journal of Educational Technology and Society, 12*(1), 249–257.

Andrews, D. L., & Goodson, L. A. (2011). A comparative analysis of models of instructional design. In G. J. Anglin (Ed.), *Instructional technology: Past, present, and future* (3rd ed., pp. 205–225). Santa Barbara, CA: Libraries Unlimited.

Arum, R., & Roksa, J. (2011). *Academically adrift: Limited learning on college campuses.* Chicago, IL: University of Chicago Press.

Bain, K. (2004). *What the best college teachers do.* Cambridge, MA: Harvard University Press.

Barbezat, D., Zajonc, A., Palmer, P. J., & Bush, M. (2014). *Contemplative practices in higher education: Powerful methods to transform teaching and learning.* San Francisco, CA: Jossey-Bass.

Bhowmik, J. (2013). Enhancing student learning through local and global examples in a statistics unit. *American Journal of Educational Research, 1*(8), 290–293.

Bielaczyc, K., & Collins, A. (1999). Learning communities in classrooms: A reconceptualization of educational practice. In C. M. Reigeluth (Ed.), *Instructional-design theories and models* (pp. 269–292). Mahwah, NJ: Erlbaum.

Bok, D. (2013). *Higher education in America.* Princeton, NJ: Princeton University Press.

Branch, R. M., & Kopcha, T. J. (2014). Instructional design models. In M. M. Spector, M. D. Merrill, J. Elen, & M. J. Bishop (Eds.), *Handbook of research on educational communications and technology* (pp. 77–88). New York, NY: Springer Science and Business Media.

BrckaLorenz, A., Cole, E., Kinzie, J., & Ribera, A. (2011). *Examining effective faculty practice: Teaching clarity and student engagement.* Paper presented at the annual meeting of the American Educational Research Association, New Orleans, LA. Retrieved from http://cpr.indiana.edu/uploads/AERA%202011%20Teaching%20Clarity%20Paper.pdf

Briggs, L. M. (1977). Introduction. In L. M. Briggs (Ed.), *Instructional design: Principles and applications* (pp. 5–20). Englewood Cliffs, NJ: Educational Technology Publications.

Briggs, L. M. (1978). *Models of teaching course.* Tallahassee: Florida State University.

Burkholder, P. (2014). A content means to a critical thinking end: Group quizzing in history surveys. *History Teacher, 47*(4), 551–578.

CECS Student Success Center at Wright State University. (n.d.). *A national model for increasing the number, caliber and diversity of engineering and computer science graduates.* Retrieved from http://engineering-computer-science.wright .edu/sites/default/files/page/attachments/WhitePapers_dean_v4.pdf

Chyung, S. Y., & Vachon, M. (2013). An investigation of the satisfying and dissatisfying factors in e-learning. *Performance Improvement Quarterly, 18*, 97–114.

Deksissa, T., Liang, L., Behera, P., & Harkness, S. J. (2014). Fostering significant learning in the sciences. *International Journal for the Scholarship of Teaching and Learning, 8*(2). Retrieved from http://digitalcommons.georgiasouthern.edu /ij-sotl/vol18/iss2/12

Dempsey, J. V., Albion, P., Litchfield, B. C., Havard, B., & McDonald, J. (2007). What do instructional designers do in higher education? A written symposium. In R. A. Reiser & J. V. Dempsey (Eds.), *Trends and issues in instructional design and technology* (2nd ed., pp. 221–233). Upper Saddle River, NJ: Prentice Hall.

Designing significant learning experiences. (n.d.). [website]. Retrieved from http://www.designlearning.org/

Dick, W., Carey, L., & Carey, J. O. (2015). *The systematic design of instruction* (8th ed.). Upper Saddle River, NJ: Pearson.

Fink, D. (n.d.). *Template for examples of good course design.* Retrieved from http://www.designlearning.org/wp-content/uploads/2015/09/DBLE-Short-Template-for-Examples2.doc

Fink, L. D. (2003). *Integrated course design* (Idea Paper 42). Manhattan, KS: IDEA Center. Retrieved from http://ideaedu.org/wp-content/uploads/2014/11/Idea_Paper_42.pdf

Fink, L. D. (2013). *Creating significant learning experiences: An integrated approach to designing college courses.* San Francisco, CA: Jossey-Bass.

Fink, L. D., & Fink, A. K. (Eds.). (2009). *Designing courses for significant learning: Voices of experience* (New Directions for Teaching and Learning, 119). Retrieved from http://onlinelibrary.wiley.com/doi/10.1002/tl.370/abstract

Florida Department of Education, Bureau of Curriculum and Instruction. (2008). *Priorities for evaluating instructional materials: Research update.* Retrieved from http://www.cimes.fsu.edu/files/researchReport.pdf

Fox, J. (2010, May). Establishing relevance. *Teaching Professor, 24*(5).

Gagné, R. M., & Merrill, M. D. (2000). Integrative goals for instructional design. In R. C. Richey (Ed.), *The legacy of Robert M. Gagné* (pp. 127–140). Syracuse, NY: Clearinghouse on Information Technology.

Gagné, R. M., Wager, W. W., Golas, K. C., & Keller, J. M. (2005). *Principles of instructional design* (5th ed.). Belmont, CA: Wadsworth/Thomson Learning.

Gardner, H. E. (1999). Multiple approaches to understanding. In C. M. Reigeluth (Ed.), *Instructional-design theories and models: Vol. 2. A new paradigm of instructional theory* (pp. 69–89). Mahwah, NJ: Erlbaum.

Gentry, R. (2014, August). Sustaining college students' persistence and achievement through exemplary instructional strategies. *Research in Higher Education Journal, 24,* 1–12.

Goodson, L. A., & Ahn, I. S. (2014). Consulting and designing in the fast lane. In A. P. Mizell & A. A. Piña (Eds.), *Real-life distance learning: Case studies in research and practice.* Bloomington, IN: Division of Distance Learning, Association for Educational Communications and Technology.

Grandzol, J. R., & Grandzol, C. J. (2010). Interaction in online courses: More is NOT always better. *Online Journal of Distance Education Administration, 13*(2). Retrieved from http://www.westga.edu/~distance/ojdla/summer132/Grandzol_Grandzol132.html

Guthrie, K. L., & McCracken, H. (2010). Teaching and learning social justice through online service-learning courses. *International Review of Research in Open and Distributed Learning, 11*(3). Retrieved from http://www.irrodl.org/index.php/irrodl/article/view/894/1628

Hannafin, M., Land, S., & Oliver, K. (1999). Open learning environments. In C. M. Reigeluth (Ed.), *Instructional-design theories and models: Vol. 2. A new paradigm of instructional theory* (pp. 115–140). Mahwah, NJ: Erlbaum.

Hart, C. (2012). Factors associated with student persistence in an online program of study: A review of the literature. *Journal of Interactive Online Learning, 11*(1). Retrieved from http://www.ncolr.org/jiol/issues/pdf/11.1.2.pdf

Hirumi, A. (2009). In search of quality: An analysis of e-learning guidelines and specifications. In A. Orellana, T. L. Hudgins, & M. Simonson (Eds.), *The perfect online course: Best practices for designing and teaching* (pp. 39–67). Charlotte, NC: Information Age Publishing.

Holton, D. (2013, July 17). *Two courses that made a difference in student retention.* Retrieved from https://edtechdev.wordpress.com/2013/07/17/two-courses-that-made-a-difference-in-student-retention/

Hoskins, B. J. (2012). Connections, engagement, and presence. *Journal of Continuing Higher Education, 60*, 51–53.

Instructional Designer. (n.d.). *Marketing 101.* Retrieved from https://www.smartsparrow.com/case-studies/marketing-101/

Jonassen, D. (1999). Designing constructivist learning environments. In C. M. Reigeluth (Ed.), *Instructional-design theories and models: Vol. 2. A new paradigm of instructional theory* (pp. 215–239). Mahwah, NJ: Erlbaum.

Jonassen, D. (2011). Supporting problem solving in PBL. *Interdisciplinary Journal of Problem-Based Learning, 5*(2). Retrieved from http://docs.lib.purdue.edu/ikpbl/vol15/iss2/8/

Keller, J. M. (2010). *Motivational design for learning and performance: The ARCS model approach.* New York, NY: Springer.

Kovalik, S. J., with McGeehan, J. R. (1999). Integrated thematic instruction: From brain research to application. In C. M. Reigeluth (Ed.), *Instructional-design theories and models: Vol. 2. A new paradigm of instructional theory* (pp. 371–396). Mahwah, NJ: Erlbaum.

Kuo, Y., Walker, A. E., Belland, B. R., & Schroder, K.E.E. (2013, March). A predictive study of student satisfaction in online education programs. *International Review of Research in Open and Distance Learning, 14*(1). Retrieved from http://www.irrodl.org/index.php/irrodl/article/view/1338

Landa, L. N. (1999). Landamatics instructional-design theory for teaching general methods of thinking. In C. M. Reigeluth (Ed.), *Instructional-design theories and models: Vol. 2. A new paradigm of instructional theory* (pp. 341–369). Mahwah, NJ: Erlbaum.

Lawlor, D. S. (2007, September). *Student retention in online courses: A mixed methods study.* Master's thesis, University of Regina. Retrieved from https://www.editlib.org/p/124451/

Lee, C., Dickerson, J., & Winslow, J. (2012). An analysis of organizational approaches to online course structures. *Online Journal of Distance Learning Administration, 15*(1). Retrieved from http://www.westga.edu/~distance/ojdla/spring151/lee_dickerson_winslow.html

Levy, Y. (2006). *Assessing the value of e-learning systems.* Hershey, PA: Information Science.

Lux, K. (2011, September). *Example of a well-designed course in: Nursing.* Retrieved from http://www.designlearning.org/wp-content/uploads/2011/09/K.-Lux-Comm.-Hlth-Nursing-2nd-v.pdf

Marken, J., & Morrison, G. (2013). Objectives over time: A look at four decades of objectives in the educational research literature. *Contemporary Educational Technology, 4*(1), 1–14.

Martin, B. L., & Briggs, L. J. (1986). *The cognitive and affective domains: Integration for instruction and research.* Englewood Cliffs, NJ: Educational Technology Publications.

Mayer, R. H. (1999). Designing instruction for constructivist learning. In C. M. Reigeluth (Ed.), *Instructional-design theories and models: Vol. 2. A new paradigm of instructional theory* (pp. 141–159). Mahwah, NJ: Erlbaum.

McTighe, J., & Wiggins, G. (2014). *Improve curriculum, assessment, and instruction by using the Understanding by Design framework.* Alexandria, VA: ASCD. Retrieved from http://jaymctighe.com/wordpress/wp-content/uploads/2011/04/UbD-White-Paper-June-2014.pdf

Monahan, N. (2015, October). More content doesn't equal more learning. *Faculty Focus.* Retrieved from http://www.facultyfocus.com/articles/curriculum-development/more-content-doesnt-equal-more-learning/

Moore, J. (2014). Effects of online interaction and instructor presence on students' satisfaction and success with online undergraduate public relations courses. *Journalism and Mass Communication Educator, 69*(3), 271–288.

Müller, T. (2008). Persistence of women in online degree-completion programs. *International Review of Research in Open and Distance Learning, 9*(2), 1–18.

Naim, D. B. (2015, November). Online learning can work if universities just rethink the design of their courses. *Conversation: US Pilot.* Retrieved from http://theconversation.com/online-learning-can-work-if-universities-just-rethink-the-design-of-their-courses-50848

Nelson, C. (2010, December 21). Defining academic freedom. *Inside Higher Ed.* Retrieved from https://www
.insidehighered.com/views/2010/12/21/nelson_on_academic_freedom

Nelson, L. M. (1999). Collaborative problem solving. In C. M. Reigeluth (Ed.), *Instructional-design theories and models:
Vol. 2. A new paradigm of instructional theory* (pp. 241–267). Mahwah, NJ: Erlbaum.

Ouyang, J. R., & Stanley, N. (2014). Theories and research in educational technology and distance learning instruction through Blackboard. *Universal Journal of Educational Research, 2*(2), 161–172.

Park, J. H., & Choi, H. J. (2009). Factors influencing adult learners' decision to drop out or persist in online learning.
Educational Technology and Society, 12(4), 207–217.

Perkins, D. N. (2014). *Future wise: Educating our children for a changing world.* San Francisco, CA: Jossey-Bass.

Reigeluth, C. M. (Ed.). (1999). *Instructional-design theories and models: Vol. 2. A new paradigm of instructional theory.* Mahwah, NJ: Erlbaum.

Reigeluth, C. M. (2016). Instructional theory and technology for the new paradigm of education. *Revista de Education
a Distance, 50*(1). Retrieved from http://www.um.es/ead/red/50/reigeluth_eng.pdf

Reigeluth, C., & Carr-Chellman, A. C. (Eds.). (2009). *Instructional-design theories and models: Vol. 3.* New York, NY:
Routledge.

Reiser, R. A. (2007). Learning and instructional systems design. In R. A. Reiser & J. V. Dempsey (Eds.), *Trends and
issues in instructional design and technology* (2nd ed.). Upper Saddle River, NJ: Pearson Education.

Ribera, T., BrckaLorenz, A., Cole, E. R., & Lair, T.F.N. (2012, April). *Examining the importance of teaching clarity: Findings from the faculty survey of student engagement.* Paper presented at the Annual Meeting of the American Educational
Research Association, Vancouver, BC, Canada. Retrieved from http://fsse.indiana.edu/pdf/2011/Examining%20
the%20importance%20of%20Teaching%20Clarity.pdf

Richey, R. C. (1996). R. M. Gagné's impact on instructional design theory and practice of the future. In *Proceedings
of Selected Research and Development Presentations at the 1996 National Convention of the Association for Educational Communications and Technology.* Retrieved from http://files.eric.ed.gov/fulltext/ED397828.pdf

Rovai, A. P. (2003). In search of higher persistence rates in distance education online programs. *Internet and Higher
Education, 6*, 1–16.

Russell, A. K. (2012). *Catalysts for re-examining pedagogical assumptions: A phenomenological inquiry into higher education
faculty designing and teaching online courses* (Order No. 3494490). Available from ProQuest Dissertations & Theses
Global. (921908429). Retrieved from http://search.proquest.com.ezproxy.library.ipfw.edu/docview/921908429?ac
countid=11649

Schank, R. C., Berman, T. R., & Macpherson, K. A. (1999). Learning by doing. In C. M. Reigeluth (Ed.), *Instructional-
design theories and models: Vol. 2. A new paradigm of instructional theory* (pp. 161–181). Mahwah, NJ: Erlbaum.

Schwartz, D., Lin, X., Brophy, S., & Bransford, J. (1999). Flexibly adaptive instructional design). In C. M. Reigeluth
(Ed.), *Instructional-design theories and models: Vol. 2. A new paradigm of instructional theory* (pp. 183–213). Mahwah, NJ:
Erlbaum.

Sipress, J. M., & Voelker, D. J. (2011). The end of the history survey course: The rise and fall of the coverage model.
Journal of American History, 97(4), 1050–1066.

Smart Sparrow. (n.d.). Retrieved from https://www.smartsparrow.com/

Smith, P. L., & Ragan, T. L. (2005). *Instructional design* (3rd ed.). New York, NY: Wiley.

Snelbecker, G. E., Miller, S. M., & Zheng, R. Z. (2008). *Functional relevance and online instructional design. In* R. Zheng
& S. P. Ferris (Eds.), *Understanding online instructional modeling: Theories and practices* (pp. 1–17). Hershey, PA: IGI Global.

Strachota, E. M. (2003). *Student satisfaction in online courses: An analysis of the impact of learner-content, learner-instructor, learner-learner and learner-technology interaction*. (3100902). Available from ProQuest Dissertations and Theses Global. (305284514). Retrieved from http://search.proquest.com/docview/305284514

Strandberg, A., & Campbell, K. (2014, October). Online teaching best practices to better engage students with quantitative material. *Journal of Instructional Pedagogies, 15*. Retrieved from http://www.aabri.com/manuscripts/152142.pdf

Straw, J. (2011, March). *Example of a well designed course*. Retrieved from http://www.designlearning.org/wp-content/uploads/2011/03/DBL_Example-Jeff_Straw.pdf

Trudeau, D., & Kruse, T. P. (2014). Creating significant learning experiences through civic engagement: Practical strategies for community-engaged pedagogy. *Journal of Public Scholarship in Higher Education, 4*. Retrieved from https://jpshe.missouristate.edu/assets/missouricompact/2014–2_Trudeau.pdf

Waldner, L. S., Widener, M. C., & McGorry, S. Y. (2012). E-service learning: The evolution of service-learning to engage a growing online student population. *Journal of Higher Education Outreach and Engagement, 16*(2). Retrieved from http://openjournals.libs.uga.edu/index.php/jheoe/article/view/792

Weimer, M. (2014, September 24). Diversifying the role course content plays. *Faculty Focus*. Retrieved from http://www.facultyfocus.com/articles/teaching-professor-blog/course-content-can-fulfill-multiple-roles/

Wiggins, G., & McTighe, J. (2011). *The understanding by design guide to creating high-quality units*. Alexandria, VA: ASCD.

Wilcoxson, C. (2013). The top 10 things new teachers should know: Professional reference for teachers. Retrieved from http://www.teachers2be.org/images/main/general/Top_Ten_Things_Teachers_Should_Know_2013.pdf

Yoder, M. B. (2005). *Supporting online students: Strategies for 100% retention*. Paper presented at the 19th Annual Conference on Distance Learning, Madison, WI. Retrieved from http://www.uwex.edu/disted/conference/Resource_library/proceedings/03_87.pdf

CHAPTER 3

Designing a Coherent Course

After summarizing online course design standards from educational institutions and accreditation agencies, the chapter reviews the evidence that the course coherence and alignment required by these standards result in better learning. To support coherence and alignment, the chapter draws on the literature from both teaching and learning and instructional systems to offer the graphic syllabus, outcomes map, online course templates, and course maps. Because learning outcomes provide the foundation for a course, this chapter addresses how to write assessable ones, with attention to occupational and professional standards. It then moves on to the assessments, which should simply mirror the outcomes and ways to help ensure online academic integrity. Since learning activities help students achieve these outcomes, we advise how to identify those that will give students practice in performing the outcomes. Finally, the chapter deals with practical online course development issues: choosing online course content, constructing a syllabus, complying with online copyright guidelines, and organizing files for yourself and your students.

An online course can meet minimum technical standards for course design, yet fail to measure up in a "cognitive walk-through."

—R. E. Youger and T. C. Ahern

■ ONLINE COURSE DESIGN STANDARDS

Probably the best way to prepare to teach an online course is to take a couple of online courses yourself and experience them from the student's perspective. But whether or not you have, the most important guideline to follow is to ensure tight coherence, or alignment, among all your course components. For example, you should be able to take any assessment item, whether an assignment or a test item, and match it up to a course outcome. If you can do this, you can improve learning as much as fourfold (Cohen, 1987; Squires, 2009). We also have some not-so-surprising evidence that online students choose what content to study based on what they think will make a difference in their performance on assignments and assessments, and they will simply ignore the rest (Murray, Pérez, Geist, & Hedrick, 2012).

Aligning all parts of your course will help your students achieve your intended learning outcomes and make a positive impression (Delaney, Johnson, Johnson, & Treslan, 2010; Fink, 2013; Lee, 2014; Moore, Downing, & York, 2009; Peterson & Cruz, 2004; Reisetter & Boris, 2009; Sun & Chen, 2016; Wiggins & McTighe, 2011). These research findings anchor the online course standards we review here. You can make more of your courses than what the standards mandated by educational institutions and accrediting agencies require, but these standards furnish a set of quality checkpoints. Some are the same as for face-to-face classes, and others apply to your use of technology and your digital rather than physical presence in your online classes. Some campuses have their own sets of standards, some outsource quality review to a separate organization, and some have no published standards at all.

Following are lists of the standards from a sampling of colleges and universities and accreditation agencies. We then lay out the common checkpoints for quality.

Examples of Colleges and Universities That Set Quality Standards

- Quality Matters rubric, copyrighted by MarylandOnline, to which many colleges and universities subscribe by paying a fee (Quality Matters Higher Education Program, n.d.; Roehrs, Wang, & Kendrick, 2013)
- California State University campuses (Quality Online Learning and Teaching, n.d.; QOLT program background, n.d.)
- Illinois Online Network (Quality Online Course Initiative, n.d.)
- Grand Rapids Community College (*GRCC Distance Learning Standards*, 2015)
- Purdue University Fort Wayne (formerly Indiana University–Purdue University Fort Wayne) (IPFW Online Course Design Standards, 2016)
- Pennsylvania State University, which ranks as a top online bachelor's degree program (US News & World Report, 2016; *Web Learning @ Penn State*, n.d.)

Examples of Accreditation Agencies That Set Quality Standards

- Accrediting Council for Independent Colleges and Schools (2016)
- Council of Regional Accrediting Commissions (2011)
- Commission on Colleges–Southern Association of Colleges and Schools (2000, 2011, 2014)
- Distance Education Accrediting Commission (2016)
- Southern Regional Education Board (2006)
- Keil & Brown, (2014)—review of six US regional accrediting commissions and two national accrediting organizations

We also present an integrated summary of the basic expectations for online course quality in exhibit 3.1.

Exhibit 3.1: Expectations for Online Course Quality

Orientation: Make the overall course design and structure clear to students with a course orientation, a syllabus, introductions, overviews, and summaries.

Outcomes: Provide measurable student-centered learning outcomes in the syllabus and other places—at the course level, for each unit or module, and at the lesson level—and connect the outcomes to program competencies, degree goals, general education outcomes, and any professional accreditation standards.

Assessments: Derive assessments directly from the learning outcomes. Administer short assessments of different types periodically so that students can monitor their progress during the course rather than waiting until the midterm or end-of-course exam. Explain to students how completing their assignments will help them achieve the learning outcomes. Also collect comments from students during the term to improve the course.

Course materials: Use materials that directly support the students' achievement of the learning outcomes. Make sure materials are relevant, accurate, comprehensive, free of extraneous content, and organized in a logical sequence of meaningful chunks.

Instructional strategies: Use instructional strategies that incorporate the best practices in the discipline and online instructional design. Align learning activities with the outcomes, and provide students with support in how to study. Include estimates of time required to complete assignments. Integrate Chickering and Gamson's (1987) seven principles of good practice in undergraduate education into the instructional strategies. Include opportunities for student engagement and interactions with the instructor, the content, and other students.

Technology and multimedia: Use learning outcomes, assessments, teaching methods, and technical considerations, such as the learning management system (LMS) capabilities, to guide choices about the technology and multimedia. Know how to use all tools that the students will use. In the course materials, explain how to use the tools and identify the sources of support and troubleshooting for students.

Navigation and accessibility: Make navigation easy and accessible for students. Make sure that the course organization and the location of all materials and assignment submission sites are easy to find and access.

◼ PHASES OF COURSE DESIGN

Procedural templates for instructional design typically display a linear process: you start at one step, complete it, then start the next, complete it, and move on, one step at a time (Dick, Carey, & Carey, 2015). This is a proven methodology (Salifu, 2015). But in practice, some phases occur cyclically or simultaneously (Smith & Ragan, 2005). You may return to a certain phase as you discover what course components work well or need improvement. Nonetheless, this simple model, as shown in figure 3.1, provides a well-established grounding in essential phases of course design.

Figure 3.1 Phases of Course Design

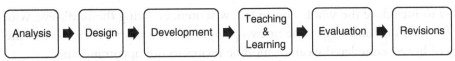

Analysis ➡ Design ➡ Development ➡ Teaching & Learning ➡ Evaluation ➡ Revisions

Analysis begins after determining significant learning (see chapter 2). It proceeds with ensuring that outcomes, activities, and assessments lead to the vision of significant learning. Start with a wide-angle view of the vision and then zoom in to other parts of instruction with a general-to-detailed and simple-to-complex organization of all course lessons (Reigeluth, 1999, 2007). Should the sequence of the lessons be chronological, hierarchical, processual, procedural, spiral, or something else? At each stage of analysis, decide how one part of a course fits with the wide-angle view, and design every part so that students' final grades reflect their achievement of one or another learning outcome. The order of topics also affects how students learn (Ritter, Nerb, Lehtinen, & O'Shea, 2007), a topic we address in chapter 4.

■ STRUCTURING YOUR COURSE

Students see and value your effort in course design, choice of content, and relevance of assignments (Morrison & Anglin, 2009). Explicit organization and clearly labeled segments reduce student anxiety, help students better understand the learning process, and facilitate their time management (Briggs, 1977; Fink, 2007; Lee, Dickerson, & Winslow, 2012; Martin, 2011; Reisetter & Boris, 2009; Savenye, Olina, & Niemczyk, 2001). Indeed, clarity of structure is a hallmark of outstanding online course design (Dooley, Lindner, & Dooley, 2005; Dyckman & Davis, 2008; Helms et al., 2011; Lee et al., 2012; Reisetter & Boris, 2009; Simonson & Schlosser, 2009; Simonson, Smaldino, & Zvacek, 2015; Smith, 2014; Welch, Orso, Doolittle, & Areepattamannil, 2015).

Course Design Structure

Students benefit from a clear content focus and well-crafted titles for each week, module, or lesson (Reisetter & Boris, 2009). For example, *Week 1: Chapter 1* conveys nothing about content. In contrast, *Week 1: The Medical vs. Psychosocial Model* indicates that students will compare two models in a given week and time frame. Some instructors prefer *module* or *lesson* rather than *week* to make it easier to adapt to changes in schedules, such as a fifteen-week semester format and a six-week summer session format for the same course. Use of a calendar tool or listing of weekly dates along with topic titles helps students plan their time, such as *Module 1: The Medical vs. Psychosocial Model [August 6–12]*. Beyond titles and time frames, displaying relationships among weeks also helps, even when labeling course sections as modules. Methods for figuring out the best way to structure a course include these:

- Making outlines
- Developing a concept map
- Making notes on colored sticky papers or index cards that you can easily rearrange
- Making a graphic of the course structure (see figure 3.2 for an example)

A simple flowchart also supports the structure of course design, as displayed in figure 3.3. This flowchart starts with a course overview followed by weekly previews and summaries to build bridges between chunks of content (Smith, 2014). These connections not only show the course structure but also allow students to see the progression of the topic they are studying. Include the following sections:

- An overview to introduce the whole course (a few sentences giving the bird's-eye, wide-angle view)
- A preview for each unit and week (one or two paragraphs or a short bulleted list of the week's focus)
- A summary of how a completed week or module relates to the upcoming one
- A summary for the end of a unit and its connections to the upcoming unit

Figure 3.2 Example of Unit Structure for Course Weeks

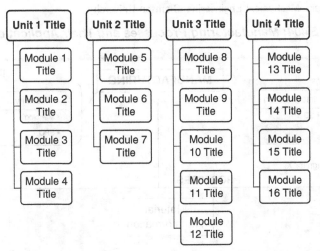

Figure 3.3 Connections across Weeks of Study

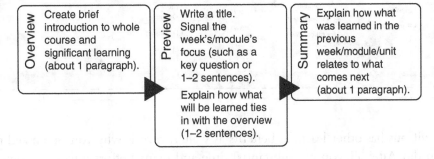

The Graphic Syllabus

The most elaborate and informative graphic for showing relationships among topics is the *graphic syllabus*. Not to be confused with the standard text syllabus, it is a content-focused flowchart, graphic organizer, or diagram of the sequencing and organization of the major course topics through the term. Figure 3.4 shows an example.

Along with clarifying the complex connections among topics, a graphic syllabus provides the big picture of your course content—the structure of the knowledge as an integrated whole and a cohesive system of interpreting phenomena—giving students a deeper understanding of the course material than they would otherwise have (Medina, 2008; Vekiri, 2002). Because it is a relational graphic, it influences how students organize learning content (Clark & Mayer, 2011). The knowledge structure enables them to better process, comprehend, and retain the material (Marzano, 2003). That structure is what prior knowledge is all about. New material is integrated not into an aggregate of facts and terms but into a preexisting organization of learned knowledge (Ausubel, 1968; Baume & Baume, 2008; Bransford, Brown, & Cocking, 1999; Carlile & Jordan, 2005; Hanson, 2006; Svinicki, 2004; Wieman, 2007; Zull, 2002, 2011). Acquiring the discipline's mental structure of knowledge advances a learner from novice toward expert (Alexander, 1996; Bransford et al., 1999; Chi, Glaser, & Rees, 1982; Royer, Cisero, & Carlo, 1993).

Figure 3.4   Graphic Syllabus of a Manufacturing Course
Source: Courtesy of Laine Mears, Mechanical Engineering, Clemson University.

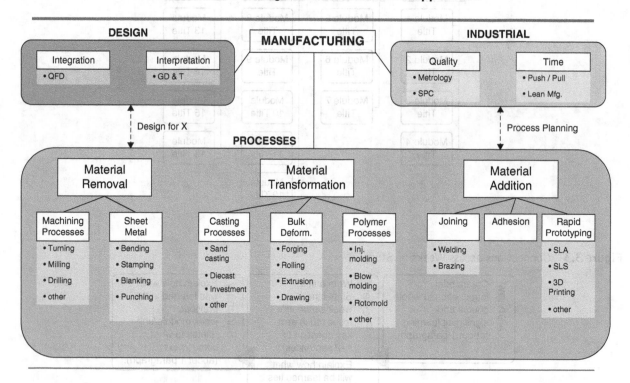

A graphic syllabus has other learning benefits as well. It reveals why you organized the course content the way you did. After all, you put substantial time and mental effort into your topical organization, but students, who have no background in the field and no command of the vocabulary, cannot possibly follow your sophisticated logic. Figure 3.4 shows the conceptual relationships using spatial arrangements and arrows. It also cues the associated textual information, which means that simply recalling the shape of the visual can help a student remember the words within it. A final learning boost of the graphic syllabus and graphics in general is their ability to communicate better than text across cultural, language, and ability barriers (Tversky, 1995, 2001). They can increase the accessibility of the materials and help us meet the learning needs of a diverse student population.

A graphic syllabus may notate the calendar schedule of the topics, the major activities and assignments, and the tests. But however much information it contains, it cannot include everything that a regular text syllabus should, so it is meant to be a supplement, not a replacement for it. Nilson (2002, 2007) provides many more examples and much more information about the use of the graphic syllabus.

In designing any graphic or part of your course, avoid cognitive overload (see chapter 4). The exact size of a chunk or segment of learning depends on the kinds of practice, the degree of difficulty, and the amount of content delivered at one time (Hung, Randolph-Seng, Monsicha, & Crooks, 2008; Reisetter & Boris, 2009). Course chunks that are too large inhibit learning. Segmented chunks reduce complexity, prevent students from feeling overwhelmed, and make the content easier to grasp, even if the amount of information remains the same (Clark & Mayer, 2011). Then organize the chunks into a logical sequence of meaningful interrelated sections.

■ COURSE TEMPLATES AND MAPS: AIDS TO COURSE DESIGN

Although the LMS comes with default course menus, they may not make good instructional sense. Several campuses use online course templates to create a more logical organization and set of names or labels for course areas and course menus. In addition to these kinds of templates, course maps help you plan all the essential course components before building them directly into the LMS.

Course Templates

You or your institution may be able to customize your course site within the LMS. For example, at Purdue University Fort Wayne, the Center for the Enhancement of Learning and Teaching provides several customizable templates for online courses that Goodson (2014) designed in consultation with faculty and technology specialists. Course menu items are grouped into three categories for students and one with tips and resources for instructors hidden from the student view. The sample template in exhibit 3.2 shows the menu items for each category.

- Content
- Communication Tools
- Support Resources
- Instructor Areas

Exhibit 3.2: Sample Course Template Menu

Content

Course Home Page
Syllabus and Schedule
Weekly Folders
MY GRADES

Communication Tools

Online Office
Announcements
E-mail
MY GROUP

Support Resources

Student Support Services
Blackboard Help

Instructor Areas

Instructor Guide
Online Course Design Standards
Course Notifications
Discussion Forums
Tools

The course home page provides placeholders with directions for adding these items to the home page:

- A course banner (a decorative enclosure with the name and number of a course)
- Welcome
- Start Here (including an online readiness self-assessment survey)
- Online Office
- What You Will Study in This Course

The home page also has a link to the weekly folders, which contain all the materials students need to study and the activities and assignments to complete each week. This type of organization makes sense to students (Smith, 2014). Each placeholder contains suggestions for what to include and how an instructor can make edits. Images of students and icons signal the location of folders, items, assignments, quizzes, and discussions. Weekly folders contain placeholders for:

- An introduction
- Learning outcomes
- A study guide
- Activities for the week in a checklist format

The first weekly folder also holds common start-up activities to give students practice with the technology, like a low-stakes practice quiz about the university's mascot, color brand, and meaning of the university acronym (1 point for each correct answer). Notes within this folder encourage faculty to give the quiz before the graded syllabus quiz or start-here quiz. The quiz settings allow students multiple attempts to earn all 3 points, and directions encourage them to give at least one wrong answer on one of the attempts so that they can see how the automated feedback works for both correct and incorrect answers. Such practice items familiarize students easily and quickly with the course technology with scarcely any risk.

Common customizations to the template include the addition of a "student café" or "lounge area" for students to use for social discussions and the elimination of the My Group category when the course does not use small groups. Some instructors add a link to the department website or specialized content such as tutorials. In some cases, assignments appear not only in the weekly folders but also in an assignments area linked on the course menu.

Other universities, like Fresno State, furnish course templates and menus from which to choose (e.g., Fresno State University, n.d.). If you lack access to such templates, you can create your own unless your institution prohibits it. Even within fixed menu labels, the course can be consistently and clearly organized to include the same types of course items.

Course Maps

A course map makes it easier to fit your course design into whatever electronic spaces are available to you at your institution. It helps you sequence your course topics, learning activities, and materials. Just select a map template and customize it to make sense for your course (Distance@FSU; Purdue University Course Development Plan; Simonson et al., 2015; UCONN eCampus, n.d.). Topics considered later in this chapter and in chapter 6 will help you develop your map further. The Pennsylvania State University College of Earth and Mineral Sciences (2016) uses a questionnaire to help faculty design new online courses:

- *What are the learning outcomes of your course?* See the next section on learning outcomes.
- *What is the general description of your course?* The flow of the course, your approach to teaching, segments of lessons and topics, content to draw on in building the course, and plan for assessment
- *How do you envision the course being delivered?* Kinds of student experiences, activities previously used in face-to-face classes to carry over to the online course, any real or simulated lab requirements, concepts that require demonstration, kinds of student interactions, technologies, time required for each lesson
- *What general resources will your students need for the course?* Required and supplementary materials such as textbooks, articles, workbooks, media, online materials or websites, and preferred citation-style format (e.g., APA, MLA, Chicago)

Answers round out the information in a worksheet for:

- Lesson and title
- Learning outcomes
- Level of outcomes
- Accompanying assessments (such as quiz, exam, blog post, lab report)
- Grade category (participation, quizzes, exams)
- Lesson topics
- Multimedia needs
- Textbook chapter and/or external reading/links

Other institutions offer similar course maps, some with additional categories or areas for content, module concept labels, deliverables, or technology strategies.

Let's examine a course map worksheet in some depth. The actual layout appears on a horizontal long sheet with multiple columns. Denise Jordan at Purdue University Fort Wayne includes a section for student deliverables in her online community health nursing course (D. Jordan, sample course map, 2016). She prepared the course map in Microsoft Word so that she could easily review and make edits before placing the content into her online course site:

Part 1: At the top of each weekly map: title and summary of learning focus: "In this module, settings for community health nursing are addressed; key functions of public health nursing, funding, and governmental structure are included in the discussion. Specialty areas such as schools, correctional facilities, home health, and hospice are examined."

Part 2: List of deliverables to expect from students and point values
- Writing Assignment: Home Health Settings, 10 points
- Discussion Board: Nutritional Assessment in Schools, 3 points
- Writing Assignment: Dealing with Clients in Correctional Settings, 4 points
- Web Assignment: Explore DHHS Website and Select Priority Health Issue, 3 points

Part 3: Six columns:

1. *Competencies:* Course-level learning outcomes, accreditation standards, and university expectations for graduation at the baccalaureate level
2. *Learning Outcomes:* For each weekly module (such as "Explain the focus of the nursing process and how community health nurses use it to provide care in their communities")
3. *Resources:* Introductory videos, websites, and topic videos organized to match different learning outcomes (such as the Quality and Safety Education for Nurses website, Video: Just the Job, at http://www.youtube.com /watch?v=VwfkIoEPfHk; Video: Working in Corrections at http://www.youtube.com/watch?v=p1f0SVEH_k)
4. *Activities:* Reading, analysis, critical thinking, discussion, and writing activities (such as Discussion Board: Nutritional Assessment of School Age Children)
5. *Assessments:* Chapter quizzes, assessment of writing activities, and unit exams
6. *Rubrics:* Column to check if a rubric is required to guide grading

Part 4: Detailed deliverables—for example:

Writing Activity:

Settings—Correctional Facility and Hospice

Write no less than 150 and no more than 500 words for this assignment:

As a correctional nurse, you will deal with people from a variety of backgrounds, social classes, and past crimes. Answer these questions:

1. How can your values and attitudes toward criminal activity impact your treatment of the inmates?
2. Does social class, race, age, or gender make any difference in how you feel about them?
3. Consider the Levels of Prevention, Pyramid Health Issue: Sexually Transmitted Diseases in Correctional Facilities on page 1010 in the textbook. What are your thoughts as you consider how to apply these interventions in the local juvenile detention center?
4. Reflect on the video, *Dying in Prison* (http://www.youtube.com/watch?v=W8rd18hKaiY). How does the prison experience depict the essential characteristics of hospice nursing practice? (Jordan, 2016)

Listing the video URLs in her map allowed Jordan to easily embed them into their titles later when she began building the actual course site. This system worked very well in planning a complex course with multiple higher-level outcomes in which some students worked entirely online and others in a hybrid environment where students attended some class sessions on campus and completed learning activities online for other days.

■ WRITING AND SEQUENCING LEARNING OUTCOMES

Aligning your learning outcomes with a vision of significant learning deserves your utmost attention (see chapter 2). The outcomes state what students should be able to do or perform to demonstrate learning, such as, "The student will be able to classify given rocks as igneous or metamorphic," or, "The student will be able to identify the parts of a computer system." As identified in the basic standards for online course design, outcomes should be:

- Measurable
- Student-centered

- Listed in the syllabus and other places at the course level, for each unit or module, and at the lesson level
- Connected to program competencies, degree goals, general education outcomes, and professional accreditation standards

Measurable outcomes center on action verbs (e.g., *define, classify, construct, compute, design, assess*) rather than nebulous verbs reflecting internal states that cannot be observed (e.g., *know, learn, understand, realize,* and *appreciate*). They should also specify conditions under which the student's performance will be assessed. For example, will the student differentiate among and classify igneous, metamorphic, and sedimentary rocks in writing or orally, and will the rocks be actual samples, or drawn, or photographed? Will the student identify parts of a computer system on a diagram or in an actual computer? Two sets of examples contrast vague versus explicit learning outcomes.

- *Example Set 1* (Clair & Baker, 2000, cited in Heywood, 2005, p. 21):
  Vague: "At the end of this course in Engineering Graphics, the student will know how to use a computer-aided-design (CAD) software package."

  Explicit: "At the end of this course in Engineering Graphics, the student will be able to draw a multi-view representation of a solid object using a computer aided-design software package."

- *Example Set 2* (Dick et al., 2015, p. 130):
  Vague: "The student will be able to lead group discussions aimed at solving problems."

  Explicit: "During simulated problem-solving meetings attended by master's students in the leadership department and held in the department's conference rooms, the student will successfully lead group discussions aimed at solving given problems."

We tend to display our learning outcomes to students in a list, but this fails to represent the relationships they have to each other. In fact, outcomes later in a course build on earlier outcomes, making a course a true learning process. A flowchart of the learning process through which you plan to lead students is called an *outcomes map*. Instructional designers start with this same type of map in developing the instructional task analysis for any course. It is the most important part of the design process (Dick et al., 2015; Jonassen, Tessmer, & Hannum, 1999; Smith & Ragan, 2005).

The outcomes map illustrates your course design to students, making their learning process evident in visual form. It starts with your early foundational outcomes (those critical during the first part of the course), progresses through your mediating outcomes, and finally arrives at your ultimate (end-of-course) outcomes. It visually represents the sequence, flow, and cumulative progression of the skills and abilities that students should be able to demonstrate at various times during the course. It shows students how achieving one or more outcomes should enable them to achieve subsequent ones, and it orients them to your course more effectively than a linear list does (Nilson, 2007). You can provide your students with your outcomes map as part of the orientation to your course, whether it is fully online or in a classroom course with technology support. Figure 3.5 shows an example.

Learning outcomes represent our top-priority content and abilities for our students to master (Anderson, 2002; Fink, 2013; Youger & Ahern, 2015). Don Slater in the College of Science at Technology at Georgia Southern University started with the major topics for his Site Construction course. Then for each topic, he created a list of tasks students should be able to accomplish by the end of the course, such as, "Use a

Figure 3.5   Outcomes Map of an E-Commerce and Tourism Marketing Course
Source: Courtesy of Irem Arsal, Parks, Recreation and Tourism Management, Clemson University.

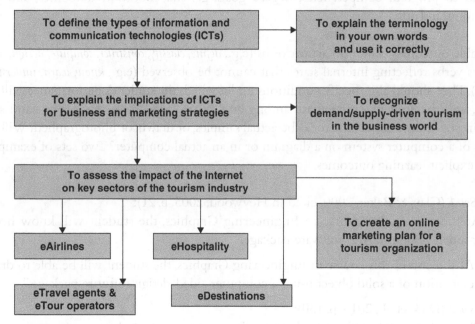

hand level, Jacob staff, and folding rule to conduct a vertical survey" (Goodson, Slater, & Zubovic, 2015). Making his topic and task lists visible revealed some gaps and overlaps in what he was teaching and testing. This is precisely the kind of revelation that other faculty who do an instructional analysis experience. You can also start with an inventory of all previous assessment items used for a course, sequence them before mapping them to levels of learning, and then make adjustments to fill in the gaps.

For certain subject areas, professional standards mandate the outcomes that also should go into an outcomes map, as in the following examples:

Engineering: Students should be able to design and conduct engineering experiments as well as analyze and interpret data (Criteria for Accrediting Engineering Programs, 2017–2018).

Nursing: Students should be able to pass a licensure exam and achieve successful employment (Accreditation Commission for Education in Nursing, 2013).

Psychology: Students at the doctorate level should be able to follow communication protocols for challenging interactions, challenges to professional values, and ways to resolve them (American Psychological Association, 2011, n.d.; Fouad et al., 2009).

In fact, professional standards and requirements can shape the whole design of an online course, as in the next examples:

Psychopathology: In professional practice, Veronika Ospina-Kammerer's students must be able to use the *Diagnostic and Statistical Manual of Mental Disorders* (DSM) and make decisions in spite of some controversies about its content. She designed her course to require students to use the DSM, analyze controversies between the medical and the psychosocial model, and write research-based analyses of its strengths, weaknesses, and usefulness in professional practice (L. Goodson, personal communication including course design review, 2003–2004, 2016).

Fashion design: InSook Ahn took stock of the professional competencies needed in the worldwide fashion design industry rather than limiting the course to personal style for one's stereotyped body type. Her course outcomes included the ability to find and implement inspirations for design, explain the cultural diversity of design, and create elements of design (Goodson & Ahn, 2014).

Organizational leadership: Anna Gibson considered the responsibilities and actions of different types of team leaders and followers in actual organizations. She then designed her course to enable her students to practice expected leadership styles, spearhead organizational change, work within group dynamics, and make sound decisions about the ethical, personal, and organizational issues that students are likely to encounter in leadership and follower roles (L. Goodson, personal communication including course design review, 2016–2017).

■ DEVELOPING VALID ASSESSMENTS

Instructional designers and teaching and learning scholars alike agree on this added leading-edge strategy: design your assessments at the start, before developing the instructional materials, to bring into sharp focus your analysis for your course design (Briggs, 1977; Dick et al., 2015; Fink, 2013; Gagné, Wager, Golas, & Keller, 2005; Simonson et al., 2015; Smith & Ragan, 2005; Wiggins & McTighe, 2011). In the basic online course design standards, the following requirements apply:

- Derive assessments directly from the learning outcomes.
- Administer short assessments of different types periodically throughout the course to enable students to assess their progress.
- Explain to students how completing assignments and assessments will help them achieve the learning outcomes.

All course design standards call for multiple forms of assessment, and students prefer their learning to be assessed a variety of ways (Battalio, 2009). As the following example shows, adding frequent short assessments also improves student learning (Sharpe & Oliver, 2007, p. 43):

> There was a problem in the course [introductory chemistry] with a 73 percent overall pass. . . . The students had complained about the time lag for feedback on the eight practical reports and the inconsistency in quality of feedback and grading. . . .
> The course was redesigned to include both high and low stakes [assessments]. . . . The low stakes assessments were made available for a week, students were allowed unlimited attempts and their best mark was recorded. High stakes assessments were unseen and conducted under examination invigilation conditions in computer labs.
> The pass rate improved to 93 per cent and student feedback and analysis of logs identified the low stakes assessments as being critical. Students completed each of the five low stakes assessments on average three or four times and received instant feedback that provided clues to the answer, but not the actual answer.
> Student feedback was extremely positive and students identified the multiple attempts with feedback as highly motivating and helpful.

Assessments should measure the student performance they claim to measure. If you want to determine how well your students can do X, Y, and Z, then assess them doing X, Y, and Z. Hirumi (2009, p. 48) had this to say: "If an objective states that students will be able to list key concepts, assessments should ask students to list key concepts. If an objective states that learners will be able to analyze a case, the assessment should ask learners to analyze a case."

Many different forms of assessment appear in resources like these:

- Bloom's taxonomy (Bloom, 1956) for the cognitive domain, which contains excellent examples for different types of learning
- Classroom assessment techniques (Angelo & Cross, 1993)
- MIT's Teaching and Learning Lab (MIT Teaching and Learning Laboratory, n.d.)
- *Teaching at Its Best* (Nilson, 2016)
- Teach the Earth (Science Education Resource Center, Carleton College, n.d.)
- Handbooks of strategies and examples for developing and validating test items (e.g., Haladyna & Rodriguez, 2013; Lane et al., 2016)

Beyond well-designed assessments, what about the possibility that students will plagiarize or cheat? Actually, despite such fears, online students self-report no more academic dishonesty than do classroom students (Beck, 2014; Weimer, 2015), and students themselves perceive opportunities for cheating in online courses as no greater than those in most classroom courses (Chiesl, 2009). But in an online course, strategic assessment design matters no less than in a campus classroom. To begin, cheating is less likely under the following conditions (All, 2011; Chiesl, 2009; Simonson et al., 2015):

- Assessments align with learning outcomes.
- The class and campus create a climate of academic integrity.
- Students receive frequent short assessments.
- Grades are based on achievement rather than a curve.

We suggest additional ways to minimize academic dishonesty in the following sections. But first, we consider the different kinds of assessment you might want to use and offer recommendations for designing them.

Objective Tests and Quizzes

Test banks that accompany textbooks specialize in objective items—true/false, matching, multiple-choice, and multiple-answer/true-false—that assess students' recall of facts, terms, definitions, processes, causes, effects, results, and similar pieces of information available in the course materials. Short-answer items are also classified as objective, but you must read and grade each one, which undermines the efficiency advantage of objective items. A cleanly written objective item avoids two tricky pitfalls: diverting a knowledgeable student away from the correct response and cluing a poorly prepared student toward the correct response (Suskie, 2009). Faulty phraseology or construction can do either.

Multiple-Answer/True-False Items

Multiple-answer/true-false items have a stem and a list of responses, as do multiple-choice items. However, students do not select just one right response; they decide whether each option is true or false in relation to the stem. This type of item has the following format (Bellchambers, Davies, Ford, & Walton, 2015).

With regards to thermoregulation, which of the following are correct?

A. Rectal temperature is an accurate way to assess core temperature.
B. Heat stroke can be life-threatening.
C. Genetic factors predispose to heat stroke.
D. Heat stroke is rare in elderly patients, as they are more susceptible to hypothermia.
E. The hypothalamus is not involved in temperature regulation in patients with heat stroke.

This type of item is flexible enough to accommodate any number of correct answers and represents the statistically strongest and most efficient type of objective question. Each option—and there may as many as eight or ten—presents a decision point and, in essence, a separate item. So with just ten stems, you can easily generate forty to eighty items, and the more items a test has, the more reliable it is (Ebel, 1978; Frisby & Sweeney, 1982.) Furthermore, multiple true-false choices remove the process-of-elimination strategy.

Short-Answer/Recall Items

Recall items in frequent quizzes make excellent compliance checks of reading, viewing, and listening, and recall has its place in learning, but not as the end of college-level or professional education. You should set, teach, and assess learning outcomes to include higher-level thinking, such as interpretation, nonroutine problem solving, application, analysis, inference, generalization, synthesis, conclusion drawing, and evaluation. Contrary to popular myth, you can assess these cognitive skills with most objective items. You can, for example, have students rewrite a false statement to make it true or have them explain why they chose a certain multiple-choice option. But like short-answer items, only you, not the computer, can grade them.

Clicker Databases

In the sciences, mathematics, and a few other disciplines, you can find many concept-oriented multiple-choice items in clicker question databases on the web, such as these:

- Carl Wieman Science Education Initiative at the University of British Columbia: http://www.cwsei.ubc.ca/resources/clickers.htm#questions
- Agile Learning: Derek Bruff's Blog on Teaching and Technology: http://derekbruff.org/?page_id=2
- Vanderbilt University Center for Teaching: Classroom Response System ("Clickers") Bibliography: https://cft.vanderbilt.edu/docs/classroom-response-system-clickers-bibliography/#education
- Clickers in Statistics Courses at Oklahoma University: http://www.ou.edu/statsclickers/clickerQuestions.htm

You might also search the web using "clicker questions" + "teaching" and look for your discipline.

Even if you do not plan to use clickers, you can use these types of items in creating self-assessments, practice quizzes, and, in some cases, prompts for online discussions.

Stimulus-Based Items

You can also compose your own higher-level-thinking multiple-choice and multiple-answer/true-false items around a realistic stimulus—a table, graph, diagram, flowchart, drawing, photo, map, schematic, equation, data set, description of an experiment, report, statement, quotation, passage, poem, situation, or short case—that students must interpret or analyze accurately and intelligently to answer the items correctly. These have been called "interpretive exercises" (Suskie, 2009), but "stimulus-based items" is the more descriptive term we use here. Usually you can create a series of items around one stimulus. Multiple-choice items built around a stimulus frequently appear in professionally written standardized tests, such as the Scholastic Assessment Test, the Graduate Record Examination, and the California Critical Thinking Skills Test (CCTST), as well as licensing exams, such as the National Council of Licensure Examinations for registered and practical nurses.

Be creative in choosing stimuli, and use different kinds. Just make sure to give your students prior practice in interpreting and analyzing the types of stimuli you put on the test and in performing the thinking skills each item requires. Try to minimize interlocking items—that is, items that responding to correctly require having responded correctly to previous items in the series. While you have to find the stimuli yourself, you will see them all around you when you start looking for them.

Distracters

To develop plausible distracters (wrong answers), you can juggle the elements (or variables) in the correct responses. For example, if you have students interpret a table from which they should conclude that more industrialized nations have lower birthrates and infant mortality rates than less industrialized nations, the elements are a nation's degree of industrialization, birthrate, and infant mortality rate. You can mix these variables together in an assortment of ways. You can also introduce other variables that students often confuse with the elements—for instance, population density and population growth, which some students mistakenly equate with birthrate. In addition, make all responses grammatically parallel and about the same length, and order them alphabetically, numerically, or chronologically to reduce the possibility of cluing students or falling into a pattern (Suskie, 2009).

Reducing Cheating

Whether you select your objective items from a test bank or compose your own, you can give more robust tests and minimize the cheating opportunities if you develop a pool of different but equivalent items for each learning outcome (Helms et al., 2011). Your LMS should have a tool to create a test by sampling items or question sets randomly from the item pools so that each student will have comparable but different assessments. An instructional designer may be able to create sets of equivalent items using LMS tools so students see different variations of each item but in the same order.

On your own, you can use LMS settings to make a test available for a limited period of time, such as forty-eight hours, and set a time limit just long enough for knowledgeable students to complete the test. You might also select "show one question at a time" and "no backtracking," as well as "allow multiple attempts," and students would get a new test for each attempt (Chiesl, 2009). Let students know the scope, types of assessments, and limits in advance.

Perhaps you can convince students that cheating is not in their best interests. This was the strategy that chemistry professor Paul Edwards followed in writing the cover page for his online diagnostic test (P. Edwards, personal communication, August 14, 2015):

> In order to offer this Diagnostic Test online, we are relying on your maturity and personal integrity to complete the test yourself without help from other people or resources. More specifically, the Chemistry Department expects you to comply with XXX University's Code of Conduct, particularly Section II titled Statement of Academic Integrity.

It is also important for you to understand that if you do get outside help, you could find yourself enrolled in a course for which you are NOT prepared. A low grade in a four-credit course such as *General Chemistry* or *Principles of Chemistry 1* can jeopardize not only your academic standing but also your financial aid early in your academic career!

Edwards also added an item at the end of his test stating that by submitting the test, the student was verifying that the work was his or her own and agreed to be bound by the university's code of conduct.

Just about every LMS has a tool for monitoring student activity. In this case, Edwards chose to monitor coincident log-ins and students' responses for patterns suggesting cheating. On the rare occasions when he or his colleagues detected cheating, they followed the institutional procedures in place for proctored testing. But in his view and experience, students are no more likely to cheat on online tests than classroom tests. The key lies in the character of the student. If the student is already inclined to cheat, the student will do so in any context, and the converse also holds true for honesty.

Papers, Graphics, and Projects

While these take longer to grade than an objective test, student-constructed work like essays, papers, graphics, and projects may be the only way to assess student performance on certain outcomes, such as the ability to conduct research, organize a project, set up a business, make ethical decisions, and communicate in writing. Avoid stock paper topics and analyses of textbook cases because students may be able to purchase them on the web. Many capable entrepreneurs operate online paper mills available equally to classroom and online students (Ko & Rossen, 2010; Simonson et al., 2015).

To avoid stock assignments, customize your assessments to what your outcomes specify and what you teach, and devise topics and deliverables that require originality, creativity, personalization, and relevance. For instance, you can have students create a product relevant to their current or future job: a website, a piece of equipment, an oral or video presentation, a treatment plan, a business plan or strategy, or marketing materials. Or ask them to select a problem they are facing in their workplace or personal life and conduct research to identify possible solutions. Or have them analyze a challenging new case that describes a situation they are likely to face someday. Alternatively, you can ask for a graphic of important course material, such as a flowchart, a schematic diagram, a decision map, a concept map, or a mind map. You may even be able to give students a choice of presentation media. No technology solves the problems caused by poor assignments (Council of Writing Program Administrators, 2003; McCord, 2008).

Students need resources and guidance in the process of developing their papers and projects. Make your plagiarism and citation policies clear, and give students resources and exemplars of citation practices— either your own or those available elsewhere. For example, the Purdue Online Writing Lab (OWL, 2017) supplies students with guides and exemplars on writing, research, and citation practices. You can further discourage cheating by breaking down and chunking major assignments into manageable pieces that have spaced due dates and providing feedback for improvements. This strategy discourages students from procrastinating as well as cheating. A good first chunk might require annotations of research articles before asking for any other writing.

Grading with a rubric can save you and teaching assistants some time, as well as improve your students' work (Howell, 2011; Jönsson & Svingby, 2007). Students have a right to see your rubric in advance so they will know the criteria on which they should focus. Make sure to explain how your rubric aligns with the outcomes. Your LMS may have a built-in rubric tool that allows you to give comments as well as score student assignments. Suskie (2009) identifies and gives examples of these types of rubrics: checklists, rating scales, holistic rating scales, and descriptive rubrics. You can find many examples at these websites:

- Association of American Colleges and Universities VALUE Rubrics: https://www.aacu.org/value /rubrics
- Carnegie Mellon University, Whys & Hows of Assessment: http://www.cmu.edu/teaching/assessment /howto/assesslearning/rubrics.html
- Carnegie Mellon University Eberly Center, Examples by College: http://www.cmu.edu/teaching /assessment/examples/programlevel-bycollege/index.html

In addition to designing meaningful assignments that align with course outcomes, make sure you know the limits of plagiarism detection tools. After all, manufacturers explicitly caution that the instructor, not the tool itself, is responsible for plagiarism detection. Such tools have limited databases, and you need to know whether they include the ones your students are able to use. Turnitin and SafeAssign, for example, do not check work against all subscription databases, online encyclopedias, textbooks not posted online, or purchased papers (Kaner & Fiedler, 2008). Some faculty use such detection tools just for teaching students about what counts as originality. You simply need to make informed choices about how to use them (Goodson, 2007). If in doubt about a tool's value or use, check with your librarian or instructional designer or others who have knowledge and experience with it. You may find that a web search of selected phrases serves just as well for suspiciously constructed student prose (Ko & Rossen, 2011; McKeever, 2004; MIT Comparative Media Studies: Writing, n.d.).

Self-Assessments and Reflections

Assignments and activities that require self-assessment and reflection enhance the performance of online students (US Department of Education, 2010), usually without generating a heavy grading workload. Students can assess their learning using online readiness surveys, knowledge surveys, flash cards, and practice quizzes. You can place reflection prompts in discussion forums, blogs, chats, or short paper assignments—for example:

- "What did you find to be the 'muddiest point' in the week's lesson?" (Angelo & Cross, 1993).
- "What are you doing to learn the material?" (Fink, 2013).
- "What are your personal goals for this course?" followed at the end of the term by, "What have you learned in this course?" (Weimer, 2012).

In a portfolio, students can reflect on their improvements, strengths, and weaknesses. In an "exam wrapper" (questions to prompt error analysis about study and test-taking strategies), they can assess how effectively they prepared for the exam, what else they could have done, what kinds of mistakes they made, and how they will better prepare for the next exam (Ambrose et al., 2010; Barkley, 2009; Lovett, 2013). If your prompts ask students to analyze or react to their peers' work (they should not ask students to evaluate the way we do), peer feedback also encourages self-assessment (Nilson, 2003). The student author cannot help but assess her communication skills, especially if her peer reviewers misunderstood her intended message.

Figure 3.6   Example of an Activity with an Attached File

Qualitative versus Quantitative Data

Attached Files: 📄 Adding Confidence to Knowledge PDF 🔽 (131.301 KB)

The attached manuscript by Goodson, Slater, and Zubovic describes the type of data collected and analyzed in "knowledge surveys," which they call "confidence surveys." They use both quantitative and qualitative data. Your task is to review the article and answer the following questions.

- What data in the manuscript is quantitative?
- What data in the manuscript is qualitative?

With online course sites, whether teaching fully online or hybrid, you have many resources and ways for delivering course content:

- *Traditional textbooks.* Generally an author or publisher holds the copyright, students purchase the textbook, and instructors build learning activities around the textbook. (Instructors and instructional designers can contact the publisher for a free preview copy.)
- *Content-rich supplemental online publisher resources to accompany textbooks,* such as Pearson's *Mastering Astronomy* site (Pearson, 2016), for which students pay an access fee. You must password-protect access to any digital content sold with a textbook.
- *E-textbooks,* such as Wiley-Blackwell's *Environment and Society,* which comes with companion websites of instructor and student resources (Robbins, Hintz, & Moore, 2014). Some faculty build their own e-textbooks to customize and align the content to their outcomes (Coussement, Johnson, & Goodson, 2016).
- *Web-based multimedia and open-educational resources.* You can find an untold number of online resources—scholarly articles, images, podcasts, videos (TED Talks, YouTube), animations, simulations, and more—for both content presentation and learning activities (see chapter 6).
- *Personally recorded podcasts or videos.* Be sure to divide up your video and audio lectures into five- to seven-minute segments. Recordings are not difficult to produce yourself and may be well worth it for your students' learning (see chapter 4 for guidelines).
- *Original content files added directly to the LMS.* Figure 3.6 shows how an item with attached files might look at a course site.

◼ ONLINE COPYRIGHT GUIDELINES

Because you have many resources from which to draw when building an online course, you need to pay attention to copyright. How much attention depends on what material you use and how you use it. You probably already know that copyright law protects all creative work: literary (fiction and nonfiction), musical (including lyrics), dramatic (including accompanying music), choreographic, sculptural, pictorial, graphic, architectural, audio, and audiovisual (including motion pictures). Copyright law does *not* protect facts, ideas, discoveries, inventions, words, phrases, symbols, designs that identify a source of goods, and some US government publications (you must check on each one). However, we still have to cite the sources of our facts, other people's ideas, and certain key phrases.

You can use some material more freely than others and need to take care to avoid copyright infringement. Let's start with some basic legal definitions of free use, fair use, and public domain before looking at the restrictions on certain kinds of materials.

Free use means no license or written permission from the copyright holder is required to copy, distribute, or electronically disseminate the work. Whether a given case qualifies depends on three rather gray criteria: (1) your use is *fair use*, (2) the material you wish to use is factual or an idea, and (3) the work you wish to use is in the *public domain*.

In general, *fair use* allows limited use of materials for purposes of teaching, scholarship, research, criticism, comment, parody, and news reporting. Legal determinations of fair use are made on a case-by-case basis. The amount and significance of material used from the protected work also figure into the determination. A tiny amount should not raise concerns unless it is of substantial importance—such as the heart of the copied work, a trademarked logo, or content that would harm an author's or copyright holder's sales market.

Public domain is a clearer legal concept but is sometimes redefined. A work published in the United States is now in the public domain if (1) it was published on or before 1923, (2) ninety-five years have elapsed since its publication date if it was published between 1923 and 1977, or (3) seventy years have elapsed since the author's death if it was published after 1977. However, if a work was published between 1923 and 1963 and the copyright owner did not renew the copyright after the twenty-eight-year term that once applied, the work has come into public domain. Corporate works published after 1977 enter the public domain ninety-five years after publication.

Restrictions on Online Course Materials

Here is what you can freely use in an online course:

- Your own original work if it is not published or otherwise owned by another agency
- Materials that explicitly give you permission for their use, such as those made available under Creative Commons Licenses
- Materials for which your institution has purchased a license to allow use in courses (which may include media)
- Materials in the public domain
- Links to websites with appropriate citation

With respect to websites, you can link to but may not copy the content at a website without permission. These linked sites may include media resources, such as iTunesU, YouTube Education, TED Talks, and many more listed in chapter 6.

9. Students learn new material better and can remember it longer when they receive it multiple times and in different ways—that is, through multiple senses and in multiple modes that use different parts of their brain—than when they receive it just once or multiple times in the same way (Doyle & Zakrajsek, 2013; Hattie, 2009; Kress, Jewitt, Ogborn, & Charalampos, 2006; Shams & Seitz, 2008; Tulving, 1967, 1985; Vekiri, 2002; Winne & Nesbit, 2010; Zull, 2002, 2011). Learning styles seem not to exist. Numerous studies have found that teaching to a person's style fails to improve his or her learning over teaching to other styles (Howard-Jones, 2014; Pashler, McDaniel, Rohrer, & Bjork, 2008).

10. Students learn new material better and can remember it longer when they receive it in an organized structure or when they organize and structure it themselves (if they are ready to do so). In fact, the only way people remember anything long term is in a coherent, logically organized structure based on patterns and relationships among interconnected parts. Without a coherent big picture of prior knowledge in their minds, students cannot comprehend and retain new material (Ambrose et al., 2010; Bransford et al., 1999; Hanson, 2006; Svinicki, 2004; Wieman, 2007). Structures are shown most clearly in graphics, which also serve as retrieval cues.

11. Students learn new material better and can remember it longer when they receive it in connection with easy-to-understand stories and example cases (Bower & Clark, 1969; Graesser, Olde, & Klettke, 2002; Haberlandt & Graesser, 1985).

12. Students learn new material better and can remember it longer when they receive it in connection with a number of examples that vary by content, conditions, discipline, and level of abstraction (Hakel & Halpern, 2005).

13. Students learn new material better and can remember it longer when the material evokes emotional and not just intellectual or physical involvement. This principle mirrors the biological base of learning, which is the close communication between the frontal lobes of the brain and the limbic system. From a biological point of view, learning entails changes in the brain in which new or fragile synapses are formed or strengthened (Leamnson, 1999, 2000; Zull, 2002, 2011).

14. Students learn new material better and can remember it longer when they review or practice new material at multiple, intervallic times than when they review it all at one time (Brown, Roediger, & McDaniel, 2014; Butler, Marsh, Slavinsky, & Baraniuk, 2014; Cepeda, Pashler, Vul, Wixted, & Rohrer, 2006; Dunlosky, Rawson, Marsh, Nathan, & Willingham, 2013; Hattie, 2009; Rohrer & Pashler, 2010; Winne & Nesbit, 2010). This schedule of practice is called "spaced" or "distributive," and it can take the form of being tested or self-testing (see item 17 in this list).

15. Students learn new material better and can remember it longer when that review or practice is "interleaved" than when it is "blocked." In other words, students benefit when they occasionally review earlier material as they are learning new material (Butler et al., 2014; Dunlosky et al., 2013; Rohrer & Pashler, 2010).

16. Students learn new material better and can remember it longer when they actively and effectively plan, monitor, and evaluate their learning (self-regulated learning). This means observing their cognitive learning strategies (metacognition), emotional reactions to the material, and physical reactions to their learning environment (Ambrose et al., 2010; Bransford et al., 1999; Hattie, 2009; Nilson, 2013; Winne & Nesbit, 2010; Zimmerman, Moylan, Hudesman, White, & Flugman, 2011).

17. Students learn new material better and can remember it longer when they are tested or test themselves on it than they do when they just reread it (even multiple times), as the former involves retrieval practice and more effortful cognitive processing (see item 14) (Brown et al., 2014; Dempster, 1996, 1997; Dunlosky et al., 2013; Karpicke & Blunt, 2011; McDaniel, Howard, & Einstein, 2009; Roediger &

Karpicke, 2006; Rohrer & Pashler, 2010; Rohrer, Taylor, & Sholar, 2010; Winne & Nesbit, 2010). This is called the *testing effect*.

18. Students can remember material longer after repeated testing when they expect a final comprehensive exam. They will keep material more accessible in memory when they expect to have to recall it in the future than when they do not (Szupnar, McDermott, & Roediger, 2007).

19. Students learn new material better and can remember it longer when they have to produce answers and not just recognize correct ones—that is, when they expect to have to free-recall material for short answer or essay questions (Butler & Roediger, 2007; McDaniel, Anderson, Derbish, & Morrisette, 2007; Tulving, 1967). This is called the generation effect.

20. Students learn new material better and can remember it longer when they have to work harder to learn it—that is, when they have to overcome what are called *desirable difficulties* (Bjork, 1994, 2013; Bjork & Bjork, 2011; Brown et al., 2014; McDaniel & Butler, 2010). These difficulties can help students generate multiple retrieval paths and stretch their abilities.

21. Students learn new material better when it creates impasses in their current mental models—that is, contradictions, conflicts, anomalies, uncertainties, and ambiguities, which stimulate curiosity, inquiry, questioning, problem solving, and deep reasoning to restore "cognitive equilibrium" (Chinn & Brewer, 1993; Graesser & McMahen, 1993; Graesser, Lu, Olde, Cooper-Pye, & Whitten, 2005; Graesser & Olde, 2003).

22. Students understand new material better when instructors train them to ask deep thinking and explanation questions such as *why, how,* and *what if* as opposed to simple recall questions (Craig, Sullins, Witherspoon, & Gholson, 2006; Graesser & Person, 1994; Rosenshine, Meister, & Chapman, 1996).

23. Students learn new material better and can remember it longer when they can correct and learn from errors. Research on mice has revealed a biological base: when an organism gets an error signal, its brain releases calcium, which enhances the brain's ability to learn and change, that is, its *neuroplasticity* (Najarfi, Giovannucci, Wang, & Medina, 2014).

24. Students learn from their mistakes more effectively when they receive immediate feedback on an assignment, quiz, or test (Anderson, Corbett, Koedinger, & Pelletier, 1995; McTighe & O'Connor, 2005; Roediger & Marsh, 2005; Shute, 2006).

25. Students learn new material better and can remember it longer when they read it from printed text than from e-textbooks and websites (Baron, 2015; Daniel & Willingham, 2012; Daniel & Woody, 2013; Kolowich, 2014; Mangen, Walgermo, & Brønnick, 2012; Sanchez & Wiley, 2009; Tanner, 2014; Wästlund, Reinikka, Norlander, & Archer, 2005; Zhang, Yan, Kendrick, & Li, 2012).

■ HOW THESE PRINCIPLES CAN INFORM ONLINE COURSE DESIGN AND TEACHING

Some of these principles have ramifications for teaching that are quite straightforward, but the practical meaning of others is not quite so clear.

Principle 1: The Sequence of Procedural and Processual Steps

The teaching implications of this principle are obvious for all platforms: when designing and teaching a course, make sure to sequence the steps of a procedure and process in the same order that students will perform them. The Khan Academy provides many examples of this strategy for teaching problem-solving procedures in its online videos (Murphy, Gallagher, Krumm, Mislevy, & Hafter, 2014).

Principle 2: Active Learning

Just about any student-active teaching method that works well in a traditional classroom environment supports active engagement in an online course. Whatever the platform, students learn more when given opportunities for reflective writing (Means et al., 2014; US Department of Education, 2010), student-to-student interaction (Carr, Gardner, Odell, Munsch, & Wilson), and group work such as jigsaw (Huang, Huang, & Yu, 2011; Shaaban, 2006). Other activities that engage students include these (Eberlein et al., 2008; Nilson, 2016):

- Quizzes
- Interviews
- Surveys
- Debates and constructive controversy, which can foster critical analysis and evaluation
- Interactive videos, especially those that integrate questions and reflection prompts
- Interactive learning objects
- Blogs
- Group projects
- Wikis
- Well-moderated discussions, especially those that incorporate elements of self-reflection and self-evaluation
- Process-oriented guided inquiry learning in science courses (POGIL)
- Peer-led team learning in math and sciences (PLTL)
- The case method and problem-based learning (PBL)
- Role plays, which can encourage understanding of different perspectives
- Simulations followed by debriefing
- Expert panels to which students ask questions

These methods allow students to construct knowledge collaboratively and adapt well to discussion boards, wikis, and GoogleDocs, both whole class and small group. Chapter 6 offers more on these and other active learning techniques.

Principle 3: Targeted Feedback

To provide targeted feedback, the assessment criteria must first clearly delineate what a student product should accomplish, what elements it should contain, and what questions it should answer. In addition, students must understand the criteria, so it is best to furnish models and set up a discussion thread on just the criteria. Targeted feedback means focusing on helping students improve their performance in the next similar assessment and telling them what they are doing well. This type of feedback is constructive, improvement directed, and process centered (Means et al., 2014), and research confirms that it enhances student performance and pass rates in online courses (Bonnel & Boehm, 2011; Gosmire, Morrison, & Van Osdel, 2009; Ley & Gannon-Cook, 2014; Online Learning Consortium, 2016; Shaw, 2013). It is not surprising that online students greatly value timely and informative feedback (Northrup, 2011; Yuan & Kim, 2015).

Targeted feedback zeros in on how students can close the gap between their current and the desired performance, whether an art project, computer program, statistical analysis, physics demonstration, chemistry experiment, mathematical problem solution, writing assignment, or other project. It emphasizes what students have to learn now and may set a specific target for their next assignment (Coffield with Costa, Müller, & Webber, 2014; Duncan, 2007). Give praise where deserved because students may not know what they are doing right. But focus on praising the effort and the process students went through to produce the work to help ensure they keep putting forth the necessary effort (Coffield et al., 2014; Dweck, 2007; Halvorson, 2014). No one excels by sitting on their laurels.

On objective quizzes and tests, most learning management systems (LMSs) allow you to preload feedback for correct and incorrect answers—for example, for an incorrect response: "Social Anxiety Disorder is not the best choice. Please refer to . . ." and for a correct response: "Yes! Body Dysmorphic Disorder is the correct label for . . ." Such feedback is simple to prepare yet often neglected. You can also set the timing of the feedback to be immediate or delayed until all students have submitted the same quiz or test.

For essays and papers, your comments should concentrate on major writing issues such as content, reasoning, and organization, and less on style and grammar. If your feedback fails to improve a student's performance, consider giving the student additional clarification and models to help him or her understand and implement your feedback (Falkenberg, 1996; Means et al., 2014; Wiggins, 2012). If possible, provide feedback in multiple forms using freely available technology tools, such as highlighting and adding comments on a student's file and supplementing your written feedback with Skype, FaceTime, VoiceThread, or a telephone call (Yuan & Kim, 2015). Avoid social media to keep the feedback private.

Consider making a follow-up assignment in which students paraphrase or summarize your feedback back to you. This way, they have to review all of your feedback carefully and make sense of it (Nilson, 2013). We in turn can find out how our students interpret our comments and corrections and will be able to clarify what they misunderstand. Perhaps the words, symbols, and abbreviations we use are alien or ambiguous to them. Only when students attend to and accurately understand our feedback can we expect them to improve their work. When students will revise a piece of work, have them write out their goals and plans for revision and explain the changes they plan in response to the feedback they have received (Nilson, 2013).

Feedback can come from several sources and use several media:

- *You:* Individual e-mails or Skype or FaceTime sessions for private communication such as comments on assignments; affirmation to students on track; tips to those off track on how to improve or catch up; e-mail announcements or feedback to groups or the whole class; reflective summaries or "my thoughts" after students have discussed an issue; discussion board postings to a group or the whole class; recorded audio or video; embedded feedback in study and quiz tools; feedback templates and rubrics accompanying submitted work; additional comments on a rubric; error analyses; additional practice; or more modeling of correct strategies for incorrect problem solutions (Means et al., 2014)
- *Fellow students:* Through replies from classmates in discussion forums; in response to nonevaluative prompts that ask for identification of required elements in the work or reactions (Nilson, 2003); on a team evaluation form in which students assess their own contributions as well as those of their teammates (Goodson, 2004a; Leader, 2002)
- *External experts:* Invited into a discussion or chat space for a specific purpose and time frame (Bonk, 2013; Goodson, 2004b)
- *Programmed software:* Student self-assessments such as flash cards or readiness-reflection quizzes; preloaded, automated feedback for correct and incorrect responses to quizzes and tests; preloaded publisher feedback in quizzes and tutorials; web-based interactive learning objects that include quizzes

Principle 4: The Validity and Organization of Prior Knowledge

The mind filters all new incoming information according to its compatibility with what it also knows or thinks it knows. This means that you have to start teaching from your students' current mental models of your content. If you are not sure what those models are, you should find them out by asking your students how they think some phenomenon works or comes into being or giving them a multiple-choice test with distracters that reflect possible or likely misconceptions.

Once you know your students' mental models, you must convince them that your discipline's models provide better explanations—more robust, comprehensive, plausible, evidence based, whatever—than their faulty models (Baume & Baume, 2008; Taylor & Kowalski, 2014). If what you teach fails to fit into their models, your lessons will not stick. You can address and correct student misconceptions in a variety of ways: demonstrations, animations, videos, simulations, and even readings. Or give students opportunities to test the validity of their misconceptions (CIRTL, n.d.). (See principles 10 and 21.)

Once you know that your students have a valid mental model, relate new knowledge to their prior knowledge as much as possible. This will help them elaborate the models and more easily store the new knowledge.

Principle 5: A Safe, Welcoming Environment

At the beginning of your course, set the tone for the style of communication you expect. Get to know your students, and let them get to know you. Share some information about your professional background, your interest in the course content, and your positive feelings about teaching it. If you have posted an inviting introduction for yourself, you can assume that students who wish to respond will do so. You might also incorporate one or two social icebreakers that allow students to get acquainted with each other and begin to build a classroom community. Consider whether students might already know each other from previous courses. In any case, you can set up a discussion forum where students share information about themselves. You can ask about their geographical locations, majors or occupations, reasons for taking the course, and perhaps something they are proud of having done or become. Otherwise you can let the introductions run their course so that students can get to know each other in their own ways. Watch for occasions when it makes more sense to send a private e-mail in reply to a student's introduction.

Strive to relate to your students on a quasi-personal level. Send them positive, motivating messages every so often (see chapters 5 and 6). Show and tell them that you care about their welfare and their success in your course. In addition, show that you care about their opinions by soliciting their feedback about how the course is going on a fairly regular basis. (Chapter 6 addresses the kinds of instructor-student interaction that have the most favorable effects.)

When you set up content-focused discussion areas, keep in mind that your postings can sometimes decrease student participation (Fortner & Murphy, 2014). Your words can carry such power that they shut out student exchanges. You may want to save your additional postings for times when you need to redirect students to the right path for progress in your course. Keep your messages short with a specific purpose (Liu & Kaye, 2016; Van Voorhis & Falkner, 2004). In other words, "be actively engaged, but avoid prominence" (Helms et al., 2011, p. 65). We are responsible for creating and maintaining inclusive opportunities. When possible, integrate course content that includes the scholarly and artistic contributions and perspectives of all genders and cultural, ethnic, and racial groups. Avoid asking diverse students to represent their group. Whatever their group, it is too internally diverse to be represented by one or a few members.

Use gender-neutral language. Call a group by the name that its members prefer. Do not stay away from course-appropriate topics related to diversity because they are sensitive, controversial, or applicable to only a minority of people. Some students may see your avoidance as prejudicial.

We must also be poised to prevent and respond to disruptive, offensive discussion posts. Rather than waiting until an ill-considered post appears, have clear communication policies from the beginning of the course and advise students on how to optimize the value of their online discussions. The web offers some excellent choices—for example:

- Code of Conduct, Geek Feminism: http://geekfeminism.org/about/code-of-conduct/
- Netiquette, Virginia Shea: http://www.albion.com/netiquette/index.html
- Online Forums—Responding Thoughtfully, Jennifer Janechek, Writing Commons: http://writingcommons.org/open-text/new-media/online-forums/651-online-forums-responding-thoughtfully

Of course, you must enforce your communication policies. Early on, monitor one or two fairly low-risk discussions for insulting comments and unfounded attacks on assigned work or ideas, and privately counsel any offenders. Explain why you are concerned, what kinds of comments are more appropriate, and why. Students new to online discussions can make careless missteps such as flaming without actually realizing their negative impact, and some gentle informative guidance can put them on track. After that, enforce consequences as stated in your syllabus and institution policies against harassment. For the protection of other classmates, you may need to remove a student's offending posts or confine his or her comments to a private discussion forum or journal area (Salter, 2015).

Principle 6: Attention Attractors and Holders

Because chapters 2 and 5 treat the personal relevance of material in depth, we focus here on the implications of other attention attractors and holders.

Students cannot learn if their attention is somewhere other than the lesson. With mobile devices practically ubiquitous in the student population, this distraction problem plagues the classroom environment (McCoy, 2013; Tindell & Bohlander, 2012). Computers and mobile devices interfere with work done outside a classroom as well (Parry, 2013; Patterson, 2017), where faculty cannot monitor and restrict their use. This means that almost all online learning and assessment activities are subject to distractions.

All that you can do is to try to make content presentation as compelling as possible. Where possible, show your face. Find ways to display enthusiasm and drama. Add relevant, interesting images. Use visuals strategically, avoid dense text, and keep the cognitive load low (Daniel, 2014). In your recordings, vary your facial expressions, vocal intonations, speaking pace, and movements, even if the technology allows only hand gestures. Produce videos of your lectures in short installments, and select similarly brief videos from other sources. Students attentively watch only about six minutes of a video (Guo, Kim, & Rubin, 2014), and videos under eight minutes are the ones most viewed on YouTube (*Wired,* 2011). On occasion, however, you may want to show a really superb speech in its entirety (MiniMatters, n.d.) or show one of the professionally produced, well-coached, and well-rehearsed TED talks (www.ted.com), all of which are limited to eighteen to twenty minutes (Gallo, 2014).

Text-dense slide presentations rarely attract and hold student attention. Reserve slides for what the students need to *see*—for pictures, photographs, diagrams, and other visuals (Elder, 2009)—and supplement them with your narration (Daniel, 2014). Put dense text in Word documents with visual images added, and save them in PDF format, which makes them faster and easier for students to open, view, and print. When you must place text on a slide or in a video, use intense colors and tasteful color contrasts, such as dark blue text on a white or yellow background or white or yellow text on a dark blue background.

In general, varying your media among videos, audio, graphics, and text helps keep your students' attention. For a broad array of possibilities, go to Cathy Moore's blog, where you will find graphics, videos, animations, simulations, cases, multimedia scenarios, and infographics, many of them interactive:

- Elearning Samples, Cathy Moore—Let's Save the World from Boring Training: http://blog.cathy -moore.com/resources/elearning-samples/

Principle 7: Elaborative Rehearsal for Long-Term Memory

To be able to recall new material long term, students must think about it while holding it in working memory. Specifically, they need to reflect on its importance, its deeper meaning, and its connection to what they already know or believe to be true. But they need inducement and time to do this. While such pauses for reflection often seem awkward in the traditional classroom, online courses offer superior opportunities for elaborative rehearsal. You can simply insert questions and prompts before, during, and after videos, podcasts, or other content presentations and collect student responses (Williams, 2013). The questions may be as simple as, "This video is about _____. What do you already know about this topic?" or, "What have you learned about why this topic is important?" Students should submit their responses, which you can grade pass or fail with a few points for pass and zero for fail (see principle 16).

Principle 8: Cognitive Load Minimized

How can you minimize the cognitive load of learning for students? This principle has several corollaries from cognitive psychology and instructional design that lay out concrete guidelines.

a. Students learn new material better and can remember it longer when they receive it in chunks that reduce the number of pieces of new information by collapsing them into categories or logical groups (Gobet et al., 2001; Hanson, 2006; Mayer & Moreno, 2003; Miller, 1956; Wieman, 2007). Therefore, try to help your students categorize and classify material whenever possible. Teach them that a concept is a category that groups similar observations and facts and thereby makes learning more efficient. Give them exercises in classifying subconcepts under more general ones, as a concept map might show—for example, "Which of these concepts is most general and is a category under which the others fall: liquid rain, freezing rain, precipitation, hail, and snow?" (Precipitation.)

b. Students learn new material better and can remember it longer when they receive a complex lesson in shorter segments rather than as one long continuous lesson (Clark & Mayer, 2011; Mayer, 2005; Mayer & Moreno, 2003). Called the *segmentation principle*, it has special importance in the online context. Any continuous exposition of content, whether videos, podcasts, or animations, needs to be divided into short segments of three to ten minutes. Even text should be segmented by headings and subheadings, and you should avoid assigning too much text at one time.

c. Students learn new material better and can remember it longer when the learning is scaffolded to build new information and skills on those previously acquired or approximated. In other words, you should design learning to be incremental, adding complexity in stages or layers. When students begin learning something new, you need to provide the most help and hints—training wheels, if you will—which you should progressively withdraw as students practice more and progress. The following techniques illustrate the kind of scaffolding you might provide (Hmelo-Silver, Duncan, & Chin, 2007; Kirschner, Sweller, & Clark, 2006; Mayer & Moreno, 2003):

- Modeling a procedure or method of reasoning, as you might in a video or podcast
- Making models available of the work you want students to produce on the course LMS or website
- Explaining abstract content with practical examples
- Guiding students' early practice with step-by-step hints and feedback, given in either one-on-one or group communication
- Showing students worked examples (problem solutions) to start and only partially worked examples as they progress
- Launching new topics with a graphic organizer of their sequenced components

   d. Students learn new material better and can remember it longer when its presentation uses both words and graphics rather than just words. This is termed the *multimedia principle* (Clark & Mayer, 2011; Mayer & Moreno, 2003), and it means that online learning should not rely on text-based presentations and readings alone. Rather, you should display graphics (e.g., pictures, photographs, diagrams, flowcharts, animations, videos, concept maps, mind maps) as much as possible to illustrate phenomena, principles, examples, processes, procedures, and causal and conceptual relationships. Of course, labels, descriptions, and explanations should accompany the graphics. In fact, students are more likely to remember graphics than words, and the graphics then cue the words. The human mind processes, stores, and retrieves visuals more easily and with less effort than it does text. Graphics facilitate thinking about the material—drawing inferences, analyzing relationships, and making new connections between elements—and do not require the elaborate cognitive transformations that written words do (Tulving, 1967, 1985; Vekiri, 2002; Zull, 2011).

   e. Students learn new material better and can remember it longer when its presentation aligns words to their corresponding graphics in close proximity (Clark & Mayer, 2011). Complementing the multimedia principle (principle 8d), this contiguity principle recommends that the labeling, descriptive, or explanatory text be physically close to its accompanying graphic element.

   f. Students learn new material better and can remember it longer when its presentation relies on words in an audio narration than in written text (Clark & Mayer, 2011; Moreno, 2006). This principle states that you should find or make an audio recording of online content whenever possible rather than use text alone. However, accessibility guidelines require you to make verbal material available in both audio and text formats as well as visual whenever possible (see chapter 7).

   g. Students learn new material better and can remember it longer when its presentation explains the graphics with audio narration or written text but not both (Clark & Mayer, 2011). The *redundancy principle*, as it is called, advises you to have your students either listen to the audio recording or read the text that accompanies a graphic. That is, you should tell students to obtain the descriptions and explanations in one form or the other, but not both at the same time. However, for accessibility, both forms should available.

   h. Students learn new material better and can remember it longer when its presentation highlights the main points and avoids extraneous audio, graphics, and text (Clark & Mayer, 2011; Kalyuga, Chandler,

& Sweller, 1999; Kozma, 2000; Mayer, 2001; Mayer & Moreno, 2003). Called the *coherence principle*, it counsels you to present online content cleanly and simply in whatever medium you use. Get right to the point and do not elaborate more than is necessary.

i. Students learn new material better and can remember it longer when its presentation features a visible speaker using an informal, conversational style (Clark & Mayer, 2011). This personalization principle reiterates this recommendation in principle 6 about attention attractors and holders that you should use technology that shows your face. In addition to personalizing the presentation, this allows you to display enthusiasm and drama in your vocal variety, facial expressions, and gestures.

Principle 9: Multimodal Repetition

Whenever possible, give students the opportunities to process your online content in at least two or three modalities involving multiple senses. Allow them to read, hear, talk, write, see, draw, think, act, and feel new material into their system, involving as many parts of the brain in their learning as you can. If your students first read or listen to the material, follow up with having them do two of the following: discuss it, make a graphic of it, watch a video or animation of it, role-play or simulate it, or free-write about it.

Principle 10: Structured Knowledge

Structure is key to how people learn. It is what distinguishes knowledge from disparate, isolated pieces of information. Knowledge is a structured set of patterns that we have identified through careful observation, a grid that we have superimposed on a messy world to allow us to make predictions and applications (Kuhn, 1970). It encompasses useful concepts; widely accepted generalizations; well-grounded inferences; credible hypotheses; and evidence-backed theories, principles, and probabilities. Without knowledge, science and advanced technology wouldn't exist.

The human mind gravitates to structure. It is designed to seek patterns in its observations of reality and then build these patterns into explanatory structures. This means that it may make up connections to fill in the blanks in its understanding of phenomena. Some of these made-up connections stand up to scrutiny and scientific testing. For example, Charles Darwin did not observe mutations happening in nature; rather, he hypothesized their occurrence to explain species diversity. Although no one was around to watch the big bang, the theory fills in quite a few missing links in cosmology. Astronomers have never directly observed dark matter, but the theory of this undetectable phenomenon accounts for unexpected gravitational effects on galaxies and stars. Of course, not all made-up connections stand the test of time or science. Superstitions and prejudice exemplify false patterns. The belief of many people, including many students, that one's intelligence is fixed and immutable also fails under careful study.

Students lack the background knowledge to perceive the structure of our disciplines. They do not see the big picture of the patterns, generalizations, and abstractions that experts recognize so clearly, so they struggle to identify the central, core concepts and principles (Kozma, Russell, Jones, Marx, & Davis, 1996). Without having a knowledge structure in their head, they also fail to comprehend and retain new material (Bransford et al., 1999; Svinicki, 2004). The mind processes and stores information only within a big-picture structure of prior knowledge, only as a coherent, logically organized framework into which new material can fit (Ausubel, 1968; Baume & Baume, 2008; Bransford et al., 1999; Carlile & Jordan, 2005; Hanson, 2006; Svinicki, 2004; Wieman, 2007; Zull, 2002, 2011).

How long might it take for students to organize a disciplinary structure on their own? How long did it take us? Most of us needed years of specialized study and apprenticeship to discover the structure of our discipline and acquire expertise. We do not have that kind of time with our students, so we need to help them acquire the structure quickly. We must make the organization of our discipline's knowledge explicit by providing them an accurate, ready-made structure.

The best tool for displaying a big-picture structure is a graphic. Recall from principle 8 that graphics minimize cognitive load while clarifying the organization of concepts, processes, principles, and the like. They also facilitate storage and retrieval of knowledge. This is why a graphic syllabus of your course (see chapter 3) provides such a powerful learning framework. You should also furnish students with graphic representations of theories, conceptual interrelationships, and knowledge schemata and then have them develop their own graphics to clarify their understanding of the material.

Principle 11: Stories and Cases

Long before any society invented the written word, people handed down their culture and belief structure from generation to generation in the form of stories and parables. As teaching tools, stories still work well because they are easier to identify with and remember than abstract ideas. But now stories can take many forms: illustrative anecdotes, case studies, and problem-based learning problems conveyed in text, audio recordings, animations, or videos. Online courses can draw on all these story forms and media.

Principle 12: Varied Examples

Examples that represent different contexts, conditions, disciplines, and levels of abstraction enable students to induce the most robust and useful generalizations and conclusions. You can use illustrative anecdotes and assign case studies and problem-based learning problems as situational examples—the more varied they are, the better for student learning.

Principle 13: Emotions

Emotional involvement enhances students' learning and long-term retention of new material. Not only do emotions bring additional neurotransmitters into creating and reinforcing synaptic connections, but they also enhance motivation, which is so important in determining how much effort and persistence students put into their learning (Ambrose et al., 2010). Some of the attention-attracting elements listed in principle 6 double as motivators, such as instructor enthusiasm and the personal relevance of the material. In addition, motivation can involve emotions like curiosity, intrigue, fascination, wonder, surprise, compassion, humor, self-esteem, affiliation, and a sense of autonomy and control. In fact, motivation so deeply affects learning that we devote the next chapter to this topic.

Any medium can evoke emotions. Animations can be whimsical and amusing as well as instructive. Video and audio recordings can tell moving or intriguing stories as well as illustrate situations and principles. Demonstrations can yield surprising results. Readings can generate compassion or curiosity. Free writing can reinforce students' sense of autonomy and control. When choosing animations, videos, writing topics, and the like for your courses, look for those that can engage students emotionally as well as cognitively.

Principle 14: Spaced Practice

Build in activities and assignments that have students review and practice retrieving the same content at spaced intervals. Also tell students that they will perform better on tests if they space their pre-exam study sessions over several days and get a good night's sleep the night before a test instead of cramming.

Principle 15: Interleaved Practice

Interleave this spaced review and retrieval practice by having students work with prior content as they are learning new content. In other words, intersperse among the problems and exercises on new material a few problems and exercises from previously learned material. This way, students will also get practice in deciding the kind of problem they have to solve and what skills they will need.

Principle 16: Self-Regulated Learning

The process of goal-setting and planning strategies before a learning process, monitoring one's learning during it, and evaluating one's learning after it is called *self-regulated learning*. This process takes place on several dimensions: one's cognitive learning strategies (metacognition), one's emotional reactions to the material, and one's reactions to the physical environment one has chosen for learning. It requires a learner's focused self-awareness, honest introspection and self-assessment, willingness to change strategies, and acceptance of responsibility for one's learning (Pintrich, 2000; Zimmerman, 2001, 2002; Zimmerman & Schunk, 2001). You can teach your students to practice self-regulated learning by giving them assignments that engage them in doing it (Nilson, 2013). Online courses can accommodate the following activities.

As bookends for your course, you can have your students at the beginning write an informal, goal-setting essay, "How I Earned an A in This Course" (Zander & Zander, 2000), and at the end an informal, self-assessment essay, "How I Earned an A in This Course—or Not." Or you can ask them to reflect in writing on the nature of the course material at the beginning (Kraft, 2008; Suskie, 2009) and then again at the end. Or have them write take-a-stance-and-justify essays on course material at the beginning and correct and rewrite those essays, possibly as the final exam, at the end. Or administer a knowledge survey—really a survey of students' confidence in their ability to answer questions and perform tasks (Goodson, Slater, & Zubovic, 2015; Nuhfer & Knipp, 2003)—on the course learning outcomes and skills at the beginning and repeat the survey at the end. If you let students compare their before-and-after products, the last three options will make students aware of all they have learned during the course.

After content presentations in any medium, ask students to write short answers to two or three of the following questions (Chew, quoted in Lang, 2012; Kalman, 2007; Mezeske, 2009; Schell, 2012; Wirth, n.d.):

- What is the most useful or valuable thing you learned?
- What are the most important concepts or principles?
- What do you not understand clearly?
- What helped or hindered your understanding?
- What idea or fact surprised you?
- What comparisons and connections can you draw between this new material and your earlier learning in this course and other courses?

- What stands out in your mind?
- How did what you learned confirm or conflict with your prior beliefs, knowledge, or values?
- How did you react emotionally to what you read, heard, or watched?

Along with homework assignments, have students write reflections like these, appropriate to the assignment (Brown & Rose, 2008; Jensen, 2011; MacDonald, 2013; Mezeske, 2009; Rhode Island Diploma System, 2006; Suskie, 2009):

- Describe the process that you followed in doing this assignment, such as the steps you took, the strategies you chose, the problems you had, and the solutions you developed.
- What was the value of this assignment in developing your skills and expanding your knowledge for your future use?
- If you were to do this assignment again, how would you do it differently?
- What learning outcomes did this assignment help you achieve?
- What key concepts and principles did this assignment help you understand better?
- How well did you achieve your goals for this assignment?
- What advice would you give to future students in this course about this assignment? What approach should they take? How can they avoid likely problems? What skills should they work on improving?
- For every problem you did not complete correctly, describe where you went wrong (or describe the correct strategy for solving it) and resolve the problem (or a similar problem) (Zimmerman et al., 2011).

After a simulation or academic game, ask students to describe and evaluate their goals, decisions, strategies, and responses to the actions of other students.

After you return graded exams, have students reflect on and analyze their results by answering questions like these (Barkley, 2009):

- How did your actual performance compare with what you expected? How do you feel about your actual performance?
- How many hours did you study for this exam, and what study strategies did you use? Did you study long enough? How well did your study strategies work?
- Look at where you lost points. What patterns do you see in why you lost points?
- How will you prepare differently for the next exam?

While students should submit these assignments, you need grade them only pass or fail and attach some nominal number of points to passing. To pass, students have to complete the assignments (e.g., answer all the questions) and meet a minimum word requirement that you set. If you want students to delve into considerable depth, you should develop a rubric and use it to grade the assignments (Nilson, 2013).

Principle 17: The Testing Effect

Build into your course plenty of assessment opportunities, including low-stakes quizzes and exams, practice tests, and homework assignments that can tell students how much they are really learning and give them retrieval practice (Roediger & Butler, 2010). Also teach students how to most effectively read text, listen to audio recordings, and watch videos and animations. First, they should read, listen to, or watch the assignment; then free-recall as much as they can by writing it down or reciting it aloud; and finally review the assignment to find what they forgot, missed, or recalled incorrectly. This technique, which incorporates self-testing, is much more efficient than just rereading the material, even many times (McDaniel et al., 2009; Roediger & Karpicke, 2006).

Principle 18: Comprehensive Exams

When students expect to have to recall content and perform skills again in the future, they will keep the content and skills more accessible in memory. The teaching implication is obvious: plan on giving a comprehensive final, and tell your students from the beginning that you will.

Principle 19: The Generation Effect

When students know that they will have to produce (e.g., write, design, or problem-solve) answers by free-recalling material, they will learn it more thoroughly than when they know they will only have to recognize correct answers on an objective test. Therefore, test students on the most important material using short-answer items, essay questions, and problems to solve. Ask for explanations, analyses, and evaluations. Tell students in advance what material merits short answers, essays, complete problem solutions, and the like so they will study accordingly.

Even before you test, accustom your students to generating answers to questions before, during, and after readings, podcasts, videos, animations, and exercises (Williams, 2013). Ask them the questions that foster elaborative rehearsal (see principle 7 above) about how the material relates to what they already know, what it means on a deeper level, or why it is important. Or you can ask them to free-recall descriptions, explanations, and analyses contained in the presentations or exercises. To ensure students answer these questions, have them submit their responses and grade these pass or fail.

Principle 20: Desirable Difficulties

These difficulties can help students generate multiple retrieval paths and stretch their abilities. However, avoid challenges that increase cognitive load. The following are ways to integrate desirable difficulties into student learning (Persellin & Daniels, 2014), not all of which may be under your control and oversight:

- Have students recast text material into a graphic format such as a concept map or flowchart.
- Vary the conditions and location of their practice opportunities.
- Have them transfer new knowledge to new situations.
- Have them handwrite notes on the assigned readings, podcasts, videos, and animations.
- Hold students to high standards—for example, refuse to accept or grade work that shows little effort.
- Assign especially creative, inventive, or challenging tasks to small groups.

Principle 21: Challenges to Current Mental Models

This principle connects with principle 4 about the learning effects of prior knowledge and mental models that students bring into your course. However, principle 4 focuses on the importance of overturning students' faulty mental models, while this one points out that students who seriously question their misconceptions reap the extra learning benefits of greater curiosity, more motivated inquiry, and deeper reasoning, which are needed to restore their cognitive equilibrium. This is another example of a desirable difficulty. In other words, identifying your students' faulty mental models provides you with powerful teachable moments as you reveal the superior explanatory strength of your discipline's model with telling demonstrations, animations, videos, simulations, videos, or readings.

Principle 22: Deep Thinking and Explanation Questions

To facilitate your students' learning, model asking challenging, thought-provoking questions that require high-level critical or creative thinking; avoid simple recall and descriptive questions. Prompts that begin with *why, how,* and *what if* are promising candidates. Discussion threads, reflective assignments, and untimed quizzes present excellent opportunities because students have the time to think deeply before responding.

You also want students to ask such questions themselves, so consider assignments where students develop thought-provoking questions on a reading, video, or other content presentation. You can use some of these questions as prompts for discussion threads or short writing assignments or as quiz and exam questions. When students know you will use them in some way, they will be motivated to suggest good ones.

Principle 23: Error Correction

This principle is somewhat related to principle 21 because both highlight the benefit of error. However, this one emphasizes that any kind of error provides a rich and memorable learning experience when students have the chance to correct it (Najafi, Giovannucci, Wang, & Medina, 2014). The idea of learning by one's mistakes may not appeal to students at first because mistakes cost them points, but you can explain to them the long-term payoffs.

Principle 24: Prompt Feedback on Errors

The teaching implication of this learning principle is obvious: return graded assignments and tests as soon as you can, while students can still remember what they were thinking when they were completing the assignment or test.

Principle 25: Print Text for Reading

While the mind normally does not shift gears when faced with the same material in a different medium, it may so do if it has been trained or has trained itself to operate differently. Research has uncovered some weaknesses in e-textbooks and web-based readings as learning tools, despite their money-saving virtues. Unfortunately, people tend to read any material on a screen quickly and superficially, the same casual way they read novels on an e-reader or social media or the news on the web. But reading course material demands focused mental processing. As a result, students learn and retain less when they read an e-textbook than a print textbook (Baron, 2015; Daniel & Willingham, 2012; Daniel & Woody, 2013; Kolowich, 2014; Wästlund et al., 2005). Similarly, reading from websites leads to lower comprehension than reading from a book, especially on complex topics and for students with less working memory capacity (Mangen et al., 2012; Sanchez & Wiley, 2009). One survey-based study that reported comparable course performance between students who selected the print textbook and those who chose the electronic version also found that the latter tended to print out their text to mark up and take notes on it (Rockinson-Szapkiw, Courduff, Carker, & Bennett, 2013).

The design of electronic materials can also inhibit storage and retrieval (Rosenfield, Jahan, Nuñez, & Chan, 2015). These materials offer fewer, if any, of the valuable, effortless retrieval cues that print textbooks do. Visual and tactile information such as page layouts, page location of content, paper texture, colors, and font features flow automatically into long-term memory when students are reading a book, especially one with varied page layouts. This information helps students retrieve text material more easily (Mangen et al., 2012; R. Pak, personal communication with L. Nilson, May 13, December 12, 2013).

In most research, students report that they cannot learn material as quickly and efficiently from an e-textbook as they can from a print version. They admit to wandering off into digital distractions that are just a few clicks away, while their peers reading a book are less tempted and more focused (Daniel & Willingham, 2012; Daniel & Woody, 2013). These distractions include text-embedded hyperlinks, which can be enrichening, but it turns out that reading is a linear mental process (Tanner, 2014; Zhang et al., 2012). Therefore, when you create your own online materials, avoid complex interfaces.

Publishers, however, can produce e-textbooks and web-based materials more quickly than print materials, so the information may be more up-to-date. In addition, well-designed materials provide opportunities for multimodal learning. In astronomy, some e-textbooks offer helpful and engaging visuals and animations. In music, e-materials may include audio samples of different types of music. Embedded videos and instructor annotations can also aid learning (Gu, Wu, & Xu, 2015). In one study conducted in Thailand, third-year professional students in medicine, a visually intensive discipline, learned just as much from the electronic version of their textbook as they did from the print version (Samrejrongroj, Boonsiri, Thunyaharn, & Sangarun, 2014). Therefore, even if online materials are not as good for reading as print, they can be valuable study aids when their content and exercises are high quality and the visual and audio enhancements complement the subject matter.

You might give students a choice between the print textbook and e-textbook when both are available with the same content. Show the e-book users how to highlight text and make annotations to augment their study strategies (Denoyelles, Raible, & Seilhamer, 2015).

When you choose online instructional materials, consider these all-important features:

- Overall organization
- Logical sequencing of topics
- Readability in language and layout
- Consistency of headings and subheadings
- Chunking and blocking of material
- Existence of introductions and summaries
- Utility of visuals and animations
- Attractiveness of the color treatments
- Compatibility with a screen reader so that students can listen to rather than read the text

In addition, look for call-out boxes or font styles that draw attention to the concepts you deem important for your learning outcomes rather than trivial bits of information (Florida Department of Education, 2008). If you are willing to customize online materials with your own annotations, choose an e-textbook that allows this option.

When creating your own materials, maximize online readability by selecting these two text features (Geraci, 2006):

- A sans serif font (like Arial or Verdana) because it lessens eyestrain and increases retention (a serif font, like Times Roman, is better for paper-based reading)
- Nonjustified paragraphs because they make words easier to read and increase retention

• • •

Cognitive psychology provides valuable insights into how people learn and how we can best teach students in online as well as classroom-based courses. The implications of this discipline's findings span course design, content organization and presentation, teaching strategies, assessment methods, social interaction, and feedback on assignments and exams. If we want to make learning as trouble free and gratifying as possible for our students and facilitate their success, we ignore this research at our own and their peril.

This chapter does not address one final principle: students learn new material better and can remember it longer when they get adequate sleep and exercise (Doyle & Zakrajsek, 2013). Unfortunately, these important factors are beyond your control. All that you can do is educate students about the considerable effects of sleep and exercise.

Reflections

For Instructors

- What principles of learning can you apply in the course you are designing?
- How do you want to use online technology to implement these principles?
- What procedures and processes are critical to learn in your course? How will you present them to students?
- What active learning strategies can you use in your course?
- How can you provide targeted feedback for the practice activities and assignments in your course?
- How can you reassure students that they will be learning in a supportive and welcoming environment?
- What faulty mental models do your students bring into your course, and how can you convince your students of the validity of your discipline's models?
- How can you personalize your course to share your passion for what you are teaching and ensure the personal relevance of the content to your students?
- What forms of elaborative rehearsal of new content can you incorporate to help students make connections to valid prior knowledge and consider the importance of the content?
- What material in your course may increase your students' cognitive load? How can you reduce that load?
- How can you ensure that your students review new material at least two or three times in different modalities?
- What can you do to help students see the big picture of your course content?
- What examples, stories, and cases can you draw on to advance students' learning? How can you ensure they are varied? Where can you best place them in your course?

- How can you add emotions to your content presentations and student activities? Do any of your examples, stories, and cases evoke emotions? How will you know what your students find challenging?
- What opportunities for review and practice can you provide? How can you space them to maximize learning?
- How will you incorporate self-regulated learning assignments and activities into your course?
- How can you add more chances to test your students or for them to test themselves?
- How can you teach your students to ask challenging, thought-provoking questions—those that begin with *why, how,* and *what if* and evoke high-level critical or creative thinking?
- What essay-type and short-answer questions can you inject into your discussion forums, chats, and tests?
- How can you add desirable difficulties into your course materials and learning activities without increasing cognitive load?
- How will you build in opportunities for students to correct and learn from their errors?
- How will you select and develop online materials for your students to read and study?
- If considering an e-textbook, make sure you find answers to the following questions:
  - Do students have the choice to buy a print-based edition with the same content?
  - Can students effortlessly download and print sections of the e-textbook?
  - What is the functionality for "turning" the pages—that is, moving from one to the next without getting lost or stuck? (Look for page-like rather than scrolling presentation.)
  - How easy is it to make annotations and access embedded multimedia within the e-textbook?
  - How well does the e-textbook work with a screen reader so that a student can choose to listen rather than read the text information?

For Instructional Designers

- How can you apply the principles of learning in helping the instructor design and develop the course?
- How can you use the tools in the LMS to apply those principles?

For Administrators

- How can you support your online faculty and instructional designers in applying these principles of learning in online courses?
- What kind of peer-sharing or peer-review process can encourage dialogue or review and feedback on ways to improve the integration of these principles?

■ REFERENCES

Ambrose, S. A., Bridges, M. W., DiPietro, M., Lovett, M. C., & Norman, M. K. (2010). *How learning works: Seven research-based principles for smart teaching.* San Francisco, CA: Jossey-Bass.

Anderson, J. R., Corbett, A. T., Koedinger, K. R., & Pelletier, R. (1995). Cognitive tutors: Lessons learned. *Journal of Learning Sciences, 4*(2), 167–207.

Ausubel, D. (1968). *Educational psychology: A cognitive view.* New York, NY: Holt.

Barkley, E. F. (2009). *Student engagement techniques: A handbook for college faculty.* San Francisco, CA: Jossey-Bass.

Baron, N. S. (2015). *Words onscreen: The fate of reading in a digital world.* New York, NY: Oxford University Press.

Baume, D., & Baume, C. (2008). *Powerful ideas in teaching and learning.* Wheatley, UK: Oxford Brookes University.

Bjork, E. L., & Bjork, R. A. (2011). Making things hard on yourself, but in a good way: Creating desirable difficulties to enhance learning. In M. A. Gernsbacher & J. Pomerantz (Eds.), *Psychology and the real world: Essays illustrating fundamental contributions to society* (2nd ed., pp. 56–64). New York, NY: Worth.

Bjork, R. A. (1994). Memory and metamemory considerations in the training of human beings. In J. Metcalfe & A. Shimamura (Eds.), *Metacognition: Knowing about knowing* (pp. 185–205). Cambridge, MA: MIT Press.

Bjork, R. A. (2013). Desirable difficulties perspective on learning. In H. Pashler (Ed.), *Encyclopedia of the mind.* Thousand Oaks, CA: Sage.

Bligh, D. A. (2000). *What's the use of lectures?* San Francisco, CA: Jossey-Bass.

Bonk, C. (2013, March). *Bring experts from around the world into your class.* Indiana University Bloomington. [website]. Retrieved from http://citl.indiana.edu/innovations/spotlights/bonk.php

Bonnel, W., & Boehm, H. (2011). Improving feedback to students online: Teaching tips from experienced faculty. *Journal of Continuing Education in Nursing, 42*(11), 503–509. doi.org/10.3928/00220124–20110715–02

Bonwell, C. C., & Eison, J. A. (1991). *Active learning: Creating excitement in the classroom* (ASHE-ERIC Higher Education Report No. 1). Washington, DC: George Washington University, School of Education and Human Development.

Bower, G. H., & Clark, M. C. (1969). Narrative stories as mediators for serial learning. *Psychonomic Science, 14,* 181–182.

Bransford, J. D., Brown, A. L., & Cocking, R. R. (1999). *How people learn: Brain, mind, experience, and school.* Washington, DC: National Academy Press.

Brown, P. C., Roediger III, H. L., & McDaniel, M. A. (2014). *Making it stick: The science of successful learning.* Cambridge, MA: Belknap Press of Harvard University Press.

Brown, T., & Rose, B. (2008, November). *Use of metacognitive wrappers for field experiences.* Session presented at the National Association of Geoscience Teachers Workshops: The Role of Metacognition in Teaching Geoscience, Carleton College, Northfield, MN. Retrieved from http://serc.carleton.edu/NAGTWorkshops/metacognition/tactics/28926.html

Butler, A. C., Marsh, E. J., Slavinsky, J. P., & Baraniuk, R. G. (2014). Integrating cognitive science and technology improves learning in a STEM classroom. *Educational Psychology Review.* doi:10.1007/s10648–014–9256–4

Butler, A. C., & Roediger, H. L. III. (2007). Testing improves long-term retention in a simulated classroom setting. *European Journal of Cognitive Psychology, 19*(4/5), 514–527.

Carlile, O., & Jordan, A. (2005). It works in practice but will it work in theory? The theoretical underpinnings of pedagogy. In G. O'Neill, S. Moore, & R. McMullan (Eds.), *Emerging issues in the practice of university teaching* (pp. 11–25). Dublin: All Ireland Society for Higher Education.

Carr, K., Gardner, F., Odell, M., Munsch, T., & Wilson, B. (2003, Fall). The role of online, asynchronous interaction in development of light and color concepts. *Journal of Interactive Online Learning, 2*(2). Retrieved from http://www.ncolr.org/jiol/issues/pdf/2.2.5.pdf

Cepeda, N. J., Pashler, H., Vul, E., Wixted, J. T., & Rohrer, D. (2006). Distributive practice in verbal recall tasks: A review and quantitative synthesis. *Psychological Bulletin, 132,* 354–380.

Chinn, C., & Brewer, W. (1993). The role of anomalous data in knowledge acquisition: A theoretical framework and implications for science instruction. *Review of Educational Research, 63,* 1–49.

CIRTL Network. (n.d.). *Overcoming misconceptions: Misconceptions as barriers to understanding science* [web log]. Retrieved from http://www.cirtl.net/node/2628

Clark, R. C., & Mayer, R. E. (2011). *E-learning and the science of instruction: Proven guidelines for consumers and designers of multimedia learning* (3rd ed.). San Francisco, CA: Pfeiffer/Wiley.

Coffield, F., with Costa, C., Müller, W., & Webber, J. (2014). *Beyond bulimic learning: Improving teaching in further education.* London, UK: Institute of Education Press.

Cornelius-White, J. (2007). Learner-centered teacher-student relationships are effective: A meta-analysis. *Review of Educational Research, 77*(1), 113–143. doi: 10.3102/003465430298563

Craig, S. D., Sullins, J., Witherspoon, A., & Gholson, B. (2006). The deep-level reasoning effect: The role of dialogue and deep-level-reasoning questions during vicarious learning. *Cognition and Instruction, 24*, 565–591.

Daniel, D. B. (2014). Practical PowerPoint: Promising principles for developing individual practice. In J. H. Wilson, D. S. Dunn, J. R. Stowell, & J. Freeman (Eds.), *Best practices for technology-enhanced teaching and learning* (pp. 87–104). New York, NY: Oxford University Press.

Daniel, D. B., & Willingham, D. T. (2012). Electronic textbooks: Why the rush? *Science, 333*, 1569–1571.

Daniel, D. B., & Woody, W. D. (2013). E-textbooks at what cost? Performance and use of electronic v. print texts. *Computers and Education, 62*, 18–23. Retrieved from http://www.sciencedirect.com/science/article/pii/S0360131512002448

Denoyelles, A., Raible, J., & Seilhamer, R. (2015, July 6). Exploring students' e-textbook practices in higher education. *Educause Review.* Retrieved from http://er.educause.edu/articles/2015/7/exploring-students-etextbook-practices-in-higher-education

Dempster, F. N. (1996). Distributing and managing the conditions of encoding and practice. In E. L. Bork & R. A. Bork (Eds.), *Human memory* (pp. 197–236). Orlando, FL: Academic Press.

Dempster, F. N. (1997). Using tests to promote classroom learning. In R. F. Dillon (Ed.), *Handbook on testing* (pp. 332–346). Westport, CT: Greenwood Press.

Deslauriers, L., Schelew, E., & Wieman, C. E. (2011). Improved learning in a large-enrollment physics class. *Science, 332*(6031), 862–864.

Doyle, T., & Zakrajsek, T. (2013). *The new science of learning: How to live in harmony with your brain.* Sterling, VA: Stylus.

Duncan, N. (2007). Feed-forward: Improving students' use of tutors' comments. *Assessment and Evaluation in Higher Education, 32*(2), 271–283.

Dunlosky, J., Rawson, K., Marsh, E., Nathan, M., & Willingham, D. (2013). Improving students' learning with effective learning techniques: Promising directions from cognitive and educational psychology. *Psychological Science in the Public Interest, 14*(1), 4–58.

Dweck, C. S. (2007). *Mindset: The new psychology of success.* New York, NY: Random House.

Eberlein, T., Kampmeier, J., Minderhout, V., Moog, R. S., Platt, T., Varma-Nelson, P., & White, H. B. (2008). Pedagogies of engagement in science. *Biochemistry and Molecular Biology Education, 36*, 262–273. doi:10.1002/bmb.20204

Elder, L. B. (2009). *Why you shouldn't use PowerPoints in (most) online courses* [web log]. Retrieved from https://nauelearning.wordpress.com/2009/10/21/nopptonline/

Falkenberg, S. (1996). *The feedback fallacy.* Retrieved from http://people.eku.edu/falkenbergs/feedback.htm

Feldon, D. F. (2010). Why magic bullets don't work. *Change, 42*(2), 15–21.

Florida Department of Education. (2008). *Priorities for evaluating instructional materials: Research update: Content, presentation, learning.* Retrieved from http://www.cimes.fsu.edu/files/researchReport.pdf

Fortner, R. A., & Murphy, C. A. (2014). Impact of instructor intervention on the quality and frequency of student discussion posts in a blended classroom. *MERLOT Journal of Online Learning and Teaching, 10*(3). Retrieved from http://jolt.merlot.org/vol10no3/Murphy_0914.pdf

Gallo, C. (2014, February 25). TED talks are wildly addictive for three powerful scientific reasons. *Forbes*. Retrieved from http://www.forbes.com/sites/carminegallo/2014/02/25/ted-talks-are-wildly-addictive-for-three-powerful -scientific-reasons/#22ca1b0251e9

Geraci, M. (2006). Web typography: Let your words speak. *Interface: The Journal of Education, Community, and Values, 6*. Retrieved from http://commons.pacificu.edu/cgi/viewcontent.cgi?article=1020&context=inter06

Gobet, F., Lane, P.C.R., Croker, S., Cheng, P.C.H., Jones, G., Oliver, I., & Pine, J. M. (2001). Chunking mechanisms in human learning. *Trends in Cognitive Sciences, 5*, 236–243. doi:10.1016/S1364–6613(00)01662–4

Goodson, L. A. (2004a, June). Constructive controversy in asynchronous time. *Proceedings of the Association for Educational Communications and Technology Conference* (pp. 94–108). Denton, TX. Retrieved from http://www.aect.org/pdf /AECT_UNT_Proceedings_2004.pdf

Goodson, L. A. (2004b, June). Face-to-face with an online expert panel. In *Proceedings of the Association for Educational Communications and Technology Conference* (pp. 124–137). Denton, TX. Retrieved from http://www.aect.org/pdf /AECT_UNT_Proceedings_2004.pdf

Goodson, L. A., Slater, D., & Zubovic, Y. (2015). Adding confidence to knowledge. *Journal of the Scholarship of Teaching and Learning, 15*(1), 20–37. Retrieved from http://josotl.indiana.edu/article/view/12761

Gosmire, D., Morrison, M., & Van Osdel, J. (2009). Perceptions of interactions in online courses. *Journal of Online Learning and Teaching, 5*(4), 609.

Graesser, A. C., Lu, S., Olde, B. A., Cooper-Pye, E., & Whitten, S. (2005). Question asking and eye tracking during cognitive disequilibrium: Comprehending illustrated texts on devices when the devices break down. *Memory and Cognition, 33*, 1235–1247.

Graesser, A. C., & McMahen, C. L. (1993). Anomalous information triggers questions when adults solve problems and comprehend stories. *Journal of Educational Psychology, 85*, 136–151.

Graesser, A. C., & Olde, B. A. (2003). How does one know whether a person understands a device? The quality of the questions the person asks when the device breaks down. *Journal of Educational Psychology, 95*, 524–53.

Graesser, A. C., Olde, B., & Klettke, B. (2002). How does the mind construct and represent stories? In M. C. Green, J. J. Strange, & T. C. Brock (Eds.), *Narrative impact: Social and cognitive foundations* (pp. 231–263). Mahwah, NJ: Erlbaum.

Graesser, A. C., & Person, N. K. (1994). Question asking during tutoring. *American Educational Research Journal, 31*, 104–137.

Granitz, N. A., Koernig, S. K., & Harich, K. R. (2009). Now it's personal: Antecedents and outcomes of rapport between business faculty and their students. *Journal of Marketing Education, 31*(1), 52–65.

Gu, X., Wu, B., & Xu, X. (2015). Design, development, and learning in e-textbooks: What we learned and where we are going. *Journal of Computers in Education, 2*(1), 25–41.

Guo, P. (2013, October 29). *Optimal video length for student engagement*. [web log]. Retrieved from http://blog.edx.org /optimal-video-length-student-engagement

Guo, P. J., Kim, J., & Rubin, R. (2014, March 3). *How video production affects student engagement: An empirical study of MOOC videos*. Retrieved from https://groups.csail.mit.edu/uid/other-pubs/las2014-pguo-engagement.pdf

Haberlandt, K., & Graesser, A. C. (1985). Component processes in text comprehension and some of their interactions. *Journal of Experimental Psychology: General, 114*, 357–374.

Hake, R. R. (1998). Interactive-engagement vs. traditional methods: A six thousand-student survey of mechanics test data for introductory physics courses. *American Journal of Physics, 66*, 64–74.

Hakel, M., & Halpern, D. F. (2005). How far can transfer go? Making transfer happen across physical, temporal, and conceptual space. In J. Mestre (Ed.), *Transfer of learning from a modern multidisciplinary perspective* (pp. 357–370). Greenwich, CT: Information Age Publishing.

Halvorson, H. G. (2014). *The key to great feedback? Praise the process, not the person.* Retrieved from http://99u.com/articles/19442/the-key-to-great-feedback-praise-the-process-not-the-person

Hanson, D. (2006). *Instructor's guide to process-oriented guided-inquiry learning.* Stony Brook, NY: Stony Brook University.

Hattie, J. (2009). *Visible learning: A synthesis of over 800 meta-analyses relating to achievement.* New York, NY: Routledge.

Helms, J. L., Marek, P., Randall, C. K., Rogers, D. T., Taglialatela, L. A., & Williamson, A. A. (2011). Developing an online curriculum in psychology: Practical advice from a departmental initiative. In D. S. Dunn, J. H. Wilson, J. Freeman, & J. R. Stowell (Eds.), *Best practices for technology enhanced teaching and learning: Connecting to psychology and the social sciences* (pp. 53–71). New York, NY: Oxford University Press.

Hmelo-Silver, C. E., Duncan, R. G., & China, C. A. (2007). Scaffolding and achievement in problem-based and inquiry learning: A response to Kirschner, Sweller, and Clark (2006). *Educational Psychologist, 42*(2), 99–107.

Hobson, E. H. (2002). Assessing students' motivation to learn in large classes. *American Journal of Pharmaceutical Education, 56,* 82S.

Howard-Jones, P. A. (2014, October). Neuroscience and education: Myths and messages. *Nature Reviews Neuroscience, 15,* 817–824.

Huang, T., Huang, Y., & Yu, F. (2011). Cooperative weblog learning in higher education: Its facilitating effects on social interaction, time lag, and cognitive load. *Educational Technology and Society, 14*(1), 95–106.

Jensen, J. D. (2011). Promoting self-regulation and critical reflection through writing students' use of electronic portfolio. *International Journal of ePortfolio, 1*(1), 49–60.

Jones-Wilson, T. M. (2005). Teaching problem-solving skills without sacrificing course content: Marrying traditional lecture and active learning in an organic chemistry class. *Journal of College Science Teaching, 35*(1), 42–46.

Kalman, C. S. (2007). *Successful science and engineering teaching in colleges and universities.* Bolton, MA: Anker.

Kalyuga, S., Chandler, P., & Sweller, J. (1999). Managing split-attention and redundancy in multimedia instruction. *Applied Cognitive Psychology, 13,* 351–371.

Karpicke, J., & Blunt, J. (2011). Retrieval practice produces more learning than elaborative studying with concept mapping. *Science, 331*(6018), 772–775. doi:10.1126/science.1199327

Kirschner, P. A., Sweller, J., & Clark, R. E. (2006). Why minimal guidance during instruction does not work: An analysis of the failure of constructivist, discovery, problem-based, experiential, and inquiry-based teaching. *Educational Psychologist, 41*(2), 75–86.

Kolowich, S. (2014, December 17). Five things we know about college students in 2014. *Chronicle of Higher Education.* Retrieved from http://chronicle.com/blogs/wiredcampus/5-things-we-know-about-college-students-in-2014/55313

Kozma, R. (2000). Reflections on the state of educational technology research and development. *Educational Technology Research and Development, 48*(1), 5–15.

Kozma, R. B., Russell, J., Jones, T., Marx, N., & Davis, J. (1996). The use of multiple linked representations to facilitate science understanding. In S. Vosniadou, E. DeCorte, R. Glaser, & H. Mandl (Eds.), *International perspectives on the design of technology-supported learning environments* (pp. 41–60). Mahwah, NJ: Erlbaum.

Kraft, K. (2008, November). *Using situated metacognition to enhance student understanding of the nature of science.* Session presented at the National Association of Geoscience Teachers Workshops: The Role of Metacognition in Teaching Geoscience, Carleton College, Northfield, MN. Retrieved from http://serc.carleton.edu/NAGTWorkshops/metacognition/kraft.html

Kress, G., Jewitt, C., Ogborn, J., & Charalampos, T. (2006). *Multimodal teaching and learning: The rhetorics of the science classroom.* London, UK: Continuum.

Kuhn, T. S. (1970). *The structure of scientific revolutions* (2nd ed.). Chicago, IL: University of Chicago Press.

Lang, J. M. (2012, January 17). Metacognition and student learning. *Chronicle of Higher Education.* Retrieved from http://chronicle.com/article/MetacognitionStudent/130327/

Leader, L. (2002). Peer and self-evaluation for improving student collaboration in online courses. In M. Driscoll & T. Reeves (Eds.), *Proceedings of E-Learn: World Conference on E-Learning in Corporate, Government, Healthcare, and Higher Education 2002* (pp. 1770–1773). Chesapeake, VA: Association for the Advancement of Computing in Education.

Leamnson, R. (1999). *Thinking about teaching and learning: Developing habits of learning with first year college and university students.* Sterling, VA: Stylus.

Leamnson, R. (2000). Learning as biological brain change. *Change, 32*(6), 34–40.

Ley, K., & Gannon-Cook, R. (2014). Learner-valued interactions: Research into practice. *Quarterly Review of Distance Education, 15*(1), 23–32, 45.

Liu, J. C., & Kaye, E. R. (2016). Preparing online learning readiness with learner-content interaction: Design for scaffolding self-regulated learning. In L. Kyei-Blankson, J. Blankson, E. Ntuli, & C. Agyeman (Eds.), *Handbook of research on strategic management of interaction, presence, and participation in online courses* (pp. 216–243). Hershey, PA: IGI Global.

Lundberg, C. A., & Sheridan, D. (2015). Benefits of engagement with peers, faculty, and diversity for online learners. *College Teaching, 68*(1), 8–15.

MacDonald, L. T. (2013). *Letter to next semester's students.* On Course Workshops. Retrieved from http://oncourseworkshop.com/staying-course/letter-next-semesters-students/

Mangen, A., Walgermo, B. R., & Brønnick, K. (2012). Reading linear texts on paper versus computer screen: Effects on reading comprehension. *International Journal of Education Research 58,* 61–68. doi:10.1016/ijer2012.12.002

Mayer, R. E. (2001). *Multimedia learning.* Cambridge, UK: Cambridge University Press.

Mayer, R. E. (2005). Principles for managing essential processing multimedia learning: Segmenting, pretraining, and modality principles. In R. E. Mayer (Ed.), *Cambridge handbook of multimedia learning* (pp. 169–182). Cambridge, UK: Cambridge University Press.

Mayer, R. E. (2009). *Multimedia learning* (2nd ed.). Cambridge, UK: Cambridge University Press.

Mayer, R. E., & Moreno, R. (2003). Nine ways to reduce cognitive load in multimedia learning. *Educational Psychologist, 38*(1), 43–52.

McCoy, B. (2013). Digital distractions in the classroom: Student classroom use of digital devices for non-class related purposes. *Journal of Media Education, 4*(4), 5–14.

McDaniel, M. A., Anderson, J. L., Derbish, M. H., & Morrisette, N. (2007). Testing the testing effect in the classroom. *European Journal of Cognitive Psychology, 19*(4/5), 494–513.

McDaniel, M. A., & Butler, A. C. (2010). A contextual framework for understanding when difficulties are desirable. In A. S. Benjamin (Ed.), *Successful remembering and successful forgetting: Essays in honor of Robert A. Bjork* (pp. 175–199). New York, NY: Psychology Press.

McDaniel, M. A., Howard, D. C., & Einstein, G. O. (2009). The read-recite-review study strategy: Effective and portable. *Psychological Science, 20*(4), 516–522.

McTighe, J., & O'Connor, K. (2005). Seven practices for effective learning. *Educational Leadership, 63,* 10–17.

Means, B., Bakia, M., & Murphy, R. (2014). *Learning online: What research tells us about whether, when and how.* New York, NY: Routledge.

Mezeske, B. (2009). *The Graduate* revisited: Not "plastics" but "metacognition." *Teaching Professor, 23*(9), 1.

Miller, G. (1956). The magical number seven, plus or minus two: Some limits on our capacity for processing information. *Psychological Review, 63*(2), 81–97.

MiniMatters: The best video length for different videos on YouTube. [web log]. Retrieved from https://www.minimatters.com/youtube-best-video-length/

Moreno, R. (2006). Does the modality principle hold for different media? A test of the method affects learning hypothesis. *Journal of Computer Assisted Learning, 22,* 149–158.

Murphy, R., Gallagher, L., Krumm, A. E., Mislevy, J., & Hafter, A. (2014, March 7). *Research on the use of Khan Academy in schools: Research brief.* Retrieved from https://www.sri.com/sites/default/files/publications/2014–03–07_implementation_briefing.pdf

Najafi, F., Giovannucci, A., Wang, S., & Medina, J. F. (2014). Coding of stimulus strength via analog calcium signals in Purkinje cell dendrites of awake mice. *eLife, 3,* e03663. Retrieved from http://dx.doi.org/10.7554/eLife.03663

Nilson, L. B. (2003). Improving student peer feedback. *College Teaching, 51*(1), 34–38.

Nilson, L. B. (2013). *Creating self-regulated learners: Strategies to strengthen students' self-awareness and learning skills.* Sterling, VA: Stylus.

Nilson, L. B. (2016). *Teaching at its best: A research-based resource for college instructors* (4th ed.). San Francisco, CA: Jossey-Bass.

Northrup, P. T. (2011). Online learners' preferences for interaction. In A. Orellana, T. L. Hudgins, & M. Simonson (Eds.), *The perfect online course: Best practices for designing and teaching* (pp. 463–473). Charlotte, NC: Information Age Publishing.

Nuhfer, E. B., & Knipp, D. (2003). The knowledge survey: A tool for all reasons. In C. Wehlburg & S. Chadwick-Blossey (Eds.), *To improve the academy: Vol. 21. Resources for faculty, instructional, and organizational development* (pp. 59–78). Bolton, MA: Anker.

Online Learning Consortium. (2016). *Teaching through feedback.* (website). Retrieved from http://olc.onlinelearningconsortium.org/effective_practices/teaching-through-feedback

Parry, M. (2013, March 24). You're distracted. This professor can help. *Chronicle of Higher Education.* Retrieved from http://chronicle.com/article/Youre-Distracted-This/138079/

Pashler, H., McDaniel, M., Rohrer, D., & Bjork, R. (2009). Learning styles: Concepts and evidence. *Psychological Science in the Public Interest, 9*(3), 105–119.

Patterson, M. C. (2017). A naturalistic investigation of media multitasking while studying and the effects on exam performance. *Teaching of Psychology, 44*(1), 51–57.

Persellin, D. C., & Daniels, M. B. (2014). *A concise guide to improving student learning: Six evidence-based principles and how to apply them.* Sterling, VA: Stylus.

Pintrich, P. R. (2002). The role of metacognitive knowledge in learning, teaching, and assessing. *Theory into Practice, 41*(4), 219–225.

Rhode Island Diploma System. (2005). *Exhibition toolkit: Support student self-management and reflection.* Retrieved from http://www.ride.ri.gov/highschoolreform/dslat/exhibit/exhact_1003.shtml#t

Rockinson-Szapkiw, A. J., Courduff, J., Carker, K., & Bennett, D. (2013, April). Electronic versus traditional print textbooks: A comparison study on the influence of university students' learning. *Computers and Education, 63,* 259–266.

Roediger, H. L. III, & Butler, A. C. (2010). The critical role of retrieval practice in long-term retention. *Trends in Cognitive Sciences, 15*(1), 20–27. doi:10.1016/j.tics.2010.09.003.

Roediger, H. L. III, & Karpicke, J. D. (2006). The power of testing memory: Basic research and implications of the educational practice. *Perspectives on Psychological Science, 1*(3), 181–210. doi:10.1111/j.1745–6916.2006.00012.x

Roediger, H. L. III, & Marsh, E. J. (2005). The positive and negative consequences of multiple-choice testing. *Journal of Experimental Psychology: Learning, Memory, and Cognition, 31,* 1155–1159.

Rohrer, D., & Pashler, H. (2010). Recent research on human learning challenges conventional instructional strategies. *Educational Researcher, 39*(5), 406–412. doi:10.3102/0013189X10374770

Rohrer, D., Taylor, K., & Sholar, B. (2010). Tests enhance the transfer of learning. *Journal of Experimental Psychology: Learning, Memory, and Cognition, 36*(1), 233–239.

Rosenfield, M., Jahan, S., Nuñez, K., & Chan, K. (2015). Cognitive demand, digital screens, and blink rate. *Computers in Human Behavior, 51,* 403–406.

Rosenshine, B., Meister, C., & Chapman, S. (1996). Teaching students to generate questions: A review of the intervention studies. *Review of Educational Research, 66,* 181–221.

Salter, A. (2015, September 21). Three tips for handling discussions in online courses. *Chronicle of Higher Education.* Retrieved from http://chronicle.com/blogs/profhacker/3-tips-online-discussion/61107?cid=at&utm_source=at&utm_medium=en

Samrejrongroj, P., Boonsiri, T., Thunyaharn, S., & Sangarun, P. (2014). The effectiveness of implementing an e-book: Antigen and antibody reaction for diagnosis of diseases in microbiology learning. *Journal of College Teaching and Learning (Online), 11*(1), 35. doi:http://dx.doi.org/10.19030/tlc.v11i1.8395

Sanchez, C. A., & Wiley, J. (2005). To scroll or not to scroll: Scrolling, working memory capacity, and comprehending complex texts. *Human Factors, 51*(5), 730–738. doi:10.1177/0018720809352788

Schell, J. (2012, September 4). How one professor motivated students to read before a flipped class, and measured their effort. *Turn to Your Neighbor blog.* Retrieved from http://blog.peerinstruction.net/2012/09/04/how-one-professor-motivated-students-to-read-before-a-flipped-class-and-measured-their-effort/

Shaaban, K. (2006). An initial study of the effects of cooperative learning on reading comprehension, vocabulary acquisition, and motivation to read. *Reading Psychology, 27*(5), 377–403.

Shams, A., & Seitz, L. (2008). Benefits of multisensory learning. *Trends in Cognitive Science, 12*(11), 411–417.

Shaw, M. (2013, March). An evaluation of instructor feedback in online courses. *Journal of Online Higher Education, 4*(3), 1–15.

Shute, V. (2006). *Focus on formative feedback.* Unpublished manuscript, Educational Testing Service, Princeton, NJ.

Spence, L. D. (2001). The case against teaching. *Change, 33*(6), 11–19.

Stage, F. K., Kinzie, J., Muller, P., & Simmons, A. (1999). *Creating learning centered classrooms: What does learning theory have to say?* Washington, DC: ERIC Clearinghouse on Higher Education.

Suskie, L. (2009). *Assessing student learning: A common sense guide* (2nd ed.). San Francisco, CA: Jossey-Bass.

Svinicki, M. (2004). *Learning and motivation in the post-secondary classroom.* Bolton, MA: Anker.

Swiderski, S. (2005, September). *Active learning: A perspective from educational psychology.* Presented at the annual Lilly Conference on College Teaching North, Traverse City, MI.

Szupnar, K. K., McDermott, K. B., & Roediger, H. L., III. (2007). Expectation of a final cumulative test enhances long-term retention. *Memory and Cognition, 35*(5), 1007–1013.

Tanner, M. J. (2014). Digital vs. print: Reading comprehension and the future of the book. *SJSU School of Information Student Research Journal, 4*(2). Retrieved from http://scholarworks.sjsu.edu/slissrj/vol4/iss2/6

Taylor, A. K., & Kowalski, P. (2014). Student misconceptions: Where do they come from and what can we do? In V. A. Benassi, C. E. Overton, & C. M. Hakala (Eds.), *Applying science of learning in education: Infusing psychological science into the curriculum* (pp. 259–273). Washington, DC: Division 2, American Psychological Association, Society for the Teaching of Psychology.

Tigner, R. B. (1999). Putting memory research to good use: Hints from cognitive psychology. *College Teaching, 47*(4), 149–152.

Tindell, D. R., & Bohlander, R. W. (2012). The use and abuse of cell phones and text messaging in the classroom: A survey of college students. *College Teaching, 60*(1), 1–9.

Tulving, E. (1967). The effects of presentation and recall of material in free-recall learning. *Journal of Verbal Learning and Verbal Behavior, 6,* 175–184.

Tulving, E. (1985). How many memory systems are there? *American Psychologist, 40,* 385–398.

US Department of Education, Office of Planning, Evaluation, and Policy Development. (2010). *Evaluation of evidence-based practices in online learning: A meta-analysis and review of online learning studies.* Washington, DC: Author. Retrieved from http://www2.ed.gov/rschstat/eval/tech/evidence-based-practices/finalreport.pdf

Van Voorhis, S. N. V., & Falkner, T. M. R. (2004). Transformation of student services: The process and challenge of change. In J. E. Brindley, C. Walti, & O. Z. Richter (Eds.), *Learner support in open, distance, and online learning environments* (pp. 231–240). Oldenburg, Denmark: Center for Lifelong Learning, Carl von Ossietzky University of Oldenburg.

Vekiri, I. (2002). What is the value of graphical displays in learning? *Educational Psychology Review, 14*(3), 261–312.

Wästlund, E., Reinikka, H., Norlander, T., & Archer, T. (2005). Effects of VDT and paper presentation on consumption and production of information: Psychological and physiological factors. *Computers in Human Behavior, 21*(2), 377–394.

Wickens, C. D. (2002). Multiple resources and performance prediction. *Theoretical Issues in Ergonomic Science, 3*(2), 159–177.

Wickens, C. D. (2008). Multiple resources and mental workload. *Human Factors, 50*(3), 449–455.

Wieman, C. E. (2007). Why not try a scientific approach to science education? *Change, 39*(5), 9–15.

Wiggins, G. (2012, September). Seven keys to effective feedback. *Educational Leadership, 70*(1), 11–16.

Williams, J. J. (2013, December). *Applying cognitive science to online learning.* Paper presented at the Data Driven Education Workshop at Conference on Neural Information Processing Systems, Lake Tahoe, NV. Retrieved from https://papers.ssrn.com/sol3/papers.cfm?abstract_id=2535549

Winne, P. H., & Nesbit, J. C. (2010). The psychology of academic achievement. *Annual Review Psychology, 61,* 653–678.

Wired: How long should you make that YouTube video? [web log]. Retrieved from http://www.wired.com/2011/08/how-long-should-you-make-that-youtube-video/

Wirth, K. R. (n.d.). Reading reflections. *The role of metacognition in teaching geoscience: Topical resources.* Retrieved from http://serc.carleton.edu/NAGTWorkshops/metacognition/activities/27560.html

Yuan, J., & Kim, C. M. (2015). Effective feedback design using free technologies. *Journal of Educational Computing Research, 52*(3), 408–434.

Zander, R. S., & Zander, B. (2000). *The art of possibility: Transforming professional and personal life.* Cambridge, MA: Harvard University Business Press.

Zhang, H., Yan, H-M., Kendrick, K., & Li, C. (2012). Both lexical and non-lexical characters are processed during saccadic eye movements. *PLoS ONE, 7*(9). doi:10.1371/journal.pone.0046

Zimmerman, B. J. (2001). Theories of self-regulated learning and academic achievement: An overview and analysis. In B. J. Zimmerman & D. H. Schunk (Eds.), *Self-regulated learning and academic achievement: Theoretical perspectives* (pp. 1–38). Mahwah, NJ: Erlbaum.

Zimmerman, B. J. (2002). Becoming a self-regulated learner: An overview. *Theory into Practice, 41*(2), 64–70.

Zimmerman, B. J., Moylan, A., Hudesman, J., White, N., & Flugman, B. (2011). Enhancing self-reflection and mathematics achievement of at-risk students at an urban technical college. *Psychological Test and Assessment Modeling, 53*(1), 141–160.

Zimmerman, B. J., & Schunk, D. H. (2001). *Self-regulated learning and academic achievement: Theoretical perspectives.* Mahwah, NJ: Erlbaum.

Zull, J. E. (2002). *The art of changing the brain: Enriching the practice of teaching by exploring the biology of learning.* Sterling, VA: Stylus.

Zull, J. E. (2011). *From brain to mind: Using neuroscience to guide change in education.* Sterling, VA: Stylus.

CHAPTER 5

Motivating Elements
Course Policies, Communications, Assessments, and More

This chapter assembles the evidence about the role that motivation plays in determining how much effort students invest in a course, as well as whether they complete it and achieve its outcomes. It also summarizes the research on the relationship between intrinsic and extrinsic motivators. The literature on both classroom and online teaching identifies a list of course policies and grading practices, as well as types of communication, activities, assignments, assessments, and feedback that enhance student motivation, but the overlap between the two lists is minimal. We bring the two lists together to create a powerful collection of motivating factors and ways to build these into online courses. We also link these factors to theories of motivation.

The more that instruction supports a positive attitude and maintains student interest and utility value for course goals and student self-efficacy for the course by convincing students that they are capable of achieving the learning and performance goals of the course, the more students will persist when environmental events distract them.

— **R. E. Clark (2004)**

■ MOTIVATION, EFFORT, AND ACHIEVEMENT

Recall that one of the seven learning principles that Ambrose, Bridges, DiPietro, Lovett, and Norman (2010) proposed focuses on student motivation, specifically on how it determines how much effort and perseverance students will invest in their learning. The online learning literature emphasizes motivation just as much for its impact on course completion and outcomes achievement (Clark, 1999, 2004; Noesgaard & Ørngreen, 2015; Stöter, Bullen, Zawacki-Richter, & Prümmer, 2011). After all, instructional materials make no difference if the student is not motivated to use them and learn (Ally, 2004). Unmotivated students are more likely to drop out, but you can change their attitudes by using intentional motivation strategies (Hartnett, St. George, & Dron, 2011; Woodley & Simpson, 2014). Do not assume you will not have to motivate your online students just because they are more mature than traditional-age classroom students. We have no evidence that online students have greater self-motivation.

The impact of motivation in online learning has remained strong over many years. In fact, in a web-based learning study by Shih and Gamon (2001), students' motivation explains more than 25 percent of their achievement. Many other studies show how motivation factors into success (or failure), as well as persistence, in online courses. For example, Lee and Choi's (2011) meta-analysis of the research from 1999 through 2009 reveals that covariants of motivation—including self-efficacy, goal commitment, and satisfaction—affect online course completion. Hart's (2012) review of twenty studies published between 2001 and 2011 finds that motivated students persist in online courses in spite of obstacles. The mediating variables she identifies include student satisfaction and a sense of belonging to the learning community. Many studies confirm that faculty can enhance student motivation and improve student performance by adding particular motivation strategies to online courses (Chang & Chen, 2015; Chang & Lehman, 2002; Chyung, Winiecki, and Fenner, 1999; Hu, 2008; Keller & Suzuki, 2004; Kim & Keller, 2007; Marguerite, 2007; Park & Choi, 2014; Robb & Sutton, 2014; Visser, Plomp, & Kuiper, 1999; Zammit, Martindale, Meiners-Lovell, & Irwin, 2013; additional studies cited by Keller, 2016).

Mediating between motivation and academic success are the choices students make and the effort they exert in pursuing a goal (Hu, 2008). In predicting success, Firmin et al. (2014) find that "measures of student effort eclipse all other variables examined, including student demographic descriptions, course subject matter, and student use of support services" (p. 189). Fortunately, most of the motivators overlap with some of the principles of learning that the previous chapter addressed and the quality of student-content, student-instructor, and student-student interactions that we address in the next chapter. Thus, many facets of good teaching serve both to motivate and facilitate cognitive processing and memory.

This chapter examines the research on how course policies, communications, activities, assignments, assessments, feedback, and grading can enhance student motivation (Hoskins & Newstead, 2009; Nilson, 2016). Furthermore, it links the motivating factors to various theories of motivation:

- Behaviorist; goal setting (Locke & Latham, 1990)
- Goal expectancy (Wigfield & Eccles, 2000)
- Self-determination (Deci & Ryan, 1985, 2002)
- Social belonging (see chapter 6)
- ARCS—Attention, Relevance, Confidence, and Satisfaction (Keller, 2000, 2008a, 2008b, 2010, 2011, 2016)

ARCS incorporates elements of other theories, such as Bandura's self-efficacy (1977a, 1977b), Berlyne's curiosity and arousal (1960, 1965, 1978), Maslow's needs hierarchy (1954), McClelland's achievement motivation (McClelland & Burnham, 1976), Rotter's locus of control (1975), and Seligman's learned helplessness (1975). We will mention relevant causes of persistence in online courses because it is a by-product of motivation.

Setting Meaningful Goals

A second approach is to help students identify or select useful and meaningful goals. Some of your students will not have goals, and you may have to help them focus their attention on their future, identify a goal, organize their effort toward it, and develop and follow strategies to reach it (Koballa & Glynn, 2007). You can offer examples of goals and explain their value to students' lives in the real world. Having students set a goal increases their motivation to attain it, according to goal-setting theory (Locke & Latham, 1990). Certainly, mastering some definable body of material and earning a good grade qualify as possible goals for students. This motivation in turn increases the energy, work, persistence, and thought they will give toward achieving their goals.

For this motivational approach to work, a few conditions must hold:

1. Students must believe that they have freely chosen the goal, and they might not always think they have in what they perceive to be required courses. However, you can incorporate choices into your courses, such as different ways to satisfy course requirements and choices among assignments, topics, media used, and the like. Giving students options cultivates that sense of free will. We know that volition (self-regulation) helps students persist with goal-driven behaviors, like studying and completing course activities (Zammit, Martindale, Meiners-Lovell, & Irwin, 2013).
2. They have to see the goal as specific and measurable; these are the qualities typically found in a good assessment, rubric, or a grade.
3. They must get feedback about their progress toward the goal and ways they improve in their course work.
4. Students must size up the goal as challenging, but achievable. Difficulty does not necessarily discourage; in fact, the higher the difficulty (up to a reasonable point), the more effort a student will put toward the goal.

The research on online learning upholds the value of goal-driven activities in increasing student motivation. For example, in their study of preservice teachers in online distance learning, Hartnett, St. George, and Dron (2011) found it most important to help students clearly see the relevance and value of the learning activities and the connections between those activities and both the learning outcomes and students' personal goals and aspirations in the short- and long-term.

When students have group goals, as they do in problem-based learning, they are more motivated to work with each other to turn out a good product. When the group completes its project, it can post its results in a whole-class forum, which also motivates high-quality work (Dennen & Bonk, 2007). Of course, such motivation depends on the students' degree of preparation and your design of the group and discussion assignments. In any case, developing goal-oriented activities makes it less likely that other things competing for their attention will distract students.

Using Student Interests

A third strategy is to adapt the course topics, course policies, content organization, and assessments to student preferences, interests, and needs as much as possible. This increases students' sense of free choice over their goals. People want to pursue their interests and use their capabilities (Koballa & Glynn, 2010). This preference ties in with their desire for self-determination—that is, the ability to have choice and some control in what they do and how they do it (Dennen & Bonk, 2007; Koballa & Glynn, 2010).

Therefore, let students select how to organize what they learn—for instance, to use concepts maps, diagrams, flowcharts, or outlines—and how they want to be assessed—by a paper, report, treatment plan, business plan, portfolio, website, a video, audio presentation, or something else. What would be most useful to individual students? The student's control over the sequence of learning is also known to increase persistence (Chyung, Winiecki, & Fenner, 1999; Hu, 2008).

Several course examples illustrate this strategy:

- With motivation in mind, Anna Gibson gives her students in her online organizational leadership course the opportunity to choose the topic of the weekly discussion they will lead based on their interests (Goodson, 2016a). Using this approach might seem like an obvious strategy because of her subject matter, but you can apply it broadly whenever students can assume responsibility for leading a discussion (Anderson, 2004).
- InSook Ahn gives her students topical choices each week of her aesthetics of fashion design online course. For each discussion, she provides links to resources illustrating distinctively different types of art and fashion design. Students can choose one type as the focal point of the discussion (Goodson & Ahn, 2014). In later offerings of this course, Ahn can change the names of the artists and the links while keeping the same discussion structure and directions. In another learning activity, she lets her students find any fashion designs they like, analyze their choices, and determine the sources of their inspirations.
- In art history, Debbie Morrison offers students choices in an assignment that uses social media (Online Learning Insights, 2016). Her directions allow students to take and post photos of any art form that represents any one of seven art movements (Renaissance, Baroque, Romanticism, Realism, Impressionism, Post-Impressionism, or Modernism) from any location in their everyday lives, and she lets them post their images however they choose (such as Instagram, for which she provides instructions). She asks students to describe what movements their images represent and challenges them to post partial images with enough information that other students can identify the movements they represent.
- Integrating students' photos into a course activity also has worked well in John LaMaster's online math course at Purdue University Fort Wayne. He has his students find and photograph local examples of mathematical concepts as one of their online learning activities. LaMaster receives the photos by e-mail to make sure the examples are correct before adding them to the course site for all to view (Goodson, 2016c).

Explaining Your Methods

A fourth and final way to enhance the relevance of your course is to explain why you designed, organized, and developed the course the way you did. Tell students why you chose or designed the activities, readings, videos, podcasts, assignments, teaching methods, policies, and assessment strategies that you did. Students do not assume that everything you do is well considered or for their own good (Nilson, 2016), and they have no idea of the research behind your choices. In fact, their perceptions of course quality and utility have an impact on their motivation and entire online experience (Sun, Tsai, Finger, Chen, & Yeh, 2008).

Veronika Ospina-Kammerer's course on psychopathology illustrates the power of explanation (Goodson, 2016d). After her students complained about the heavy workload, she acknowledged it and explained her reasons for the depth of work on the course topics each week and the need for students to practice high-level analysis and judgment in this field. Without missing a beat, the students continued with their hard work and fully participated in the online discussions. Their final course evaluations revealed that they had developed such a high degree of community that they had exchanged names and contact information in the student lounge area and planned to stay in touch after the semester ended.

■ ENCOURAGING GOAL EXPECTANCY AND SELF-EFFICACY

Helping students set goals gives them a good start, but they also must have the self-confidence to achieve them. Expectancy theory rests on a pragmatic premise: Why aspire to achieve something you know you cannot achieve? Students will not even try to learn something that seems impossibly difficult. To set and pursue a goal, they need to believe that they have the agency and the capability. Agency depends on their sense of self-efficacy and their beliefs about the malleability of their intelligence and their locus of control. Students with low self-confidence, the fixed mind-set that their intelligence is determined by heredity, or the fatalist belief in an external locus of control have a weak sense of agency and a low expectancy of challenging goal achievement. They may also not understand what they are expected to do—a condition you change by providing clear learning outcomes, directions, and models of what you expect (Keller, 2000).

Students feel capable, confident, and self-efficacious when they view the learning task as doable within the scope of their abilities, academic background, and resources, such as time, encouragement, and assistance (Wigfield & Eccles, 2000)—that is, when they can expect success (Keller, 2000; Liao & Wang, 2008). In one study, self-efficacy, along with good time management and study strategies, distinguished students who persisted beyond three courses from those who did not persist (Holder, 2007).

The following strategies will contribute to your students' sense of self-efficacy and their expectations for success:

- Explicitly fostering self-efficacy
- Making the path for success visible
- Providing multiple opportunities for success
- Sending motivational messages
- Sharing strategies for success
- Explaining the value of errors

Explicitly Fostering Self-Efficacy

You can explicitly foster students' beliefs that they have the agency and capabilities to achieve. While many of today's students have high self-esteem, they still may have a weak sense of self-efficacy. Some sailed through the K–12 system and never had to meet an academic challenge before coming to college (Ripley, 2013). They may even sabotage their own success by not studying in order to protect their self-esteem because if they do poorly, they can blame their lack of studying rather than their lack of ability. Such students may also believe that they cannot increase their intelligence.

Others may doubt that they have any real control over their academic fate. In their experience, studying and working hard seem to make little difference in their grades. They feel that they just get lucky when they encounter readings they can understand, test questions they can answer, and assignments they can handle. In their view, most of the control resides in you. They do not perceive themselves *earning* a letter grade; rather, they believe that you *give* it to them on some basis that they do not fully understand.

Moreover, students often underestimate the effort and time that a high-quality product or performance requires. Because attributing one's success to effort is associated with high achievement, you should give praise for effort (Ley & Gannon-Cook, 2014) and encourage a growth mind-set (Dweck, 2007). A growth mind-set endorses an internal locus of control, a sense of personal responsibility for one's own success or failure, and a belief that one's effort and perseverance determine one's success. Furthermore, telling students the learning outcomes of the lesson, encouraging their success, and giving them the option to use different strategies to complete it can help build student confidence (Ally, 2004).

Online students typically report their own limitations, such as getting behind in a course and not being able to get caught up, running into scheduling and time problems, and having poor computer skills or low confidence in using technology (Fetzner, 2013; Ilgaz & Gülbahar, 2015; Lee & Choi, 2011; Sun et al., 2008). For these students, you may find that motivation improves with clear start and due dates for activities and assignments, encouragement and reminders between those dates, clear directions and guidelines, and technology training and support, such as just-in-time online tutorials and access to a campus help desk.

Making the Path for Success Visible

Students must be able to see that the learning path is achievable and meaningful (Ally, 2004). You help them see their progress or lack thereof and evaluate their success when you do the following:

- Set clear goals, standards, requirements, and evaluative criteria for the assigned tasks
- Provide explicit, assessable, measurable learning outcomes (see chapter 3)
- Make assignments that ask students to reflect on their progress

You can encourage reflection by using these strategies:

- Having students write a learning analysis of their first test in which they appraise how they studied and can improve their studying
- Giving them second chances by letting them drop the lowest quiz or test score, earn back some of their lost points, or write explanations for their wrong answers to objective quiz or test items
- Telling your students about their peers from prior course offerings who have succeeded
- Preparing students for tests with practice tests containing the same types of items that will appear on the actual test and by giving them a list of the learning outcomes that they will have to perform on the test
- Designing rubrics with specific descriptions of different quality levels of the work and distributing these along with the assignments
- Providing constructive feedback emphasizing how to improve—that is, giving confirmatory, corrective, informative, or analytical feedback rather than social praise
- Specifying the criteria for success in future performance (Chyung et al., 1999)

Providing Multiple Opportunities for Success

Create plenty of opportunities for students to experience some measure of success and achievement, especially early in the course. As Benjamin S. Bloom once recalled, all of the great teachers have distinguished assessment for learning from assessment for evaluation (Brandt, 1979). After all, learning is a process. Strategies to support this approach include these (Nilson, 2016):

- Sequence your course outcomes, content, and skills from simple to complex or from known to unknown.
- Assign activities and tasks that build in some challenge and desirable difficulty—not too easy but not overwhelming—adjusted to the experience and aptitude of the class. Finding the right balance can be challenging, but experience will help a great deal.
- Give students the chance to reflect on their success at a challenging task to foster their self-confidence and a growth mind-set (Müller, 2008).
- Pace the course to accommodate students' needs to help ensure their persistence (Müller, 2008).
- Give students multiple chances to practice performing your learning outcomes before you grade them on their performance.
- Use criterion-referenced grading instead of norm-referenced grading; the former system gives all the students in a course the opportunity to earn high grades.
- Provide many and varied opportunities for graded assessment so that no single assessment counts too much toward the final grade.
- Test early and often.

Sending Motivational Messages

Research on online courses shows that your strategic encouragement increases motivation, persistence, and completion rates (Chyung et al., 1999; Kim & Keller, 2008; Visser, 1998; Robb, 2010; Robb & Sutton, 2014). In an early online learning study, students' motivation scores improved when each module ended with positive language, each correct answer yielded a congratulatory message, and each test closed with encouraging words (Chyung et al., 1999). Another study reported a variety of tactics that significantly improved student confidence, satisfaction, performance, and perception of the relevance of the material: an introductory letter expressing a personal interest in and expectation of the students' success; shared personal information to build community and lower anxiety; clear learning requirements; reminders of success opportunities; and the assignment to design a study plan, which instills a sense of personal control and responsibility (Huett, Young, Huett, Moller, & Bray, 2008).

A related study (Huett et al., 2008) obtained similar results when the instructor sent students motivational e-mails with the following features (pp. 167–168):

Introduction. The beginning of the message contained a brief paragraph with an enthusiastic tone of introduction. For instance, "I hope you are doing great! I sent a letter out last week introducing myself and reminding you of what is expected in this class. If you are anything like me, you might have a tendency to procrastinate or a tough time getting started. Don't worry—there is still time." The intent of the opening paragraph was to get the learners' attention and convey assurances of the instructor's personal interest in learner success.

Goal Reminders. The intent of the next few paragraphs was to offer goal reminders. For instance, "Ideally, by the end of these first few weeks, you will have completed at least three or four of the *SAM Office 2003* assignments" and "Don't forget the deadline for. . ."

Words of Encouragement. The next paragraph was devoted to general words of encouragement. For instance, "As you complete the assignments this week, I would like to extend hearty congratulations to all of you for your hard work" and "You are almost done with this section of the class, so run for the finish. I have great faith in your continued success. You can do it!"

Multiple Points of Contact. The final paragraph served to assure learners and offer multiple contact points for feedback opportunities. For instance, "I am very sure you will be successful. If you ever need my help or have any questions or concerns, please do not hesitate to contact me via e-mail at XXXXX@xyz.edu. If it is an emergency, I can be reached on my cell at 555–1234."

In this study, the same course was taught on campus and online, with one online section receiving the motivational messages (treatment class) every two weeks and the other online section and the campus class not receiving them. In the online treatment class, students attained motivation scores equal to those of the on-campus class and significantly higher than those of the other online class. Relatedly, the failure rate in the online treatment class matched up with the campus class at about 6 percent, whereas that in the other online class approached 19 percent. The withdrawal rate in the treatment class was nearly 5 percent versus 16 percent in the other online class. These statistics show the power of simple, biweekly motivational e-mails.

In another study, Robb and Sutton (2014) used five motivational e-mail messages based on the ARCS model. These messages boosted students' motivation to continue with the course, their perception of the instructor as caring about their success, their comfort in communicating and asking questions, and the course completion rate. Robb and Sutton sent out the first message ten days into the course with the title "Class Success" and an embedded graphic relating a goal to success. After the fourth week, they sent an online greeting card that had animation, humor, music, and a text message with advice for students who might be struggling. They sent the third message after the sixth week with an embedded graphic and text telling students how important it was for them to review the instructor's comments on their work. Targeting the midterm date for the fourth message, they congratulated students for reaching the halfway point and added a motivational quote and a colorful graphic. Finally, they sent a fifth message after the eleventh week containing a variety of photos, congratulating students for making it so far through the course, encouraging them to work hard to finish, and reminding them of the final date for submitting their work. Here is a description of the fourth-week message:

Image on the left side: monkey with a thumbs-up signal, broad smile, holding a bunch of bananas, under a tall tree with broad green leaves.

Text next to image: Life's detours are never easy… But hang in there… Your efforts will surely lead you to SUCCESS!

Message on right: Are you experiencing roadblocks with the assignments? If so, keep going… Don't give up. Take time to review the posted course instructions and syllabus to overcome any detours and to get on the right track.

Cook, Bingham, Reid, and Wang (2015, p. 7) provide other examples of brief motivational messages:

Welcome: "Welcome! Taking part in this course is a great way to improve your already impressive English language skills and to share your thoughts and ideas about academic integrity with others. We hope you find the course useful and the community of learners supportive."

Recognize and encourage: "Thank you everyone for sharing your tips and techniques for time management. Some fantastic ideas coming through here. They will be really beneficial to others on the course."

Give further information: "You may also find the following helpful: http://www.aquinas.edu/library/pdf /ParaphrasingQuotingSummarizing.pdf."

Clarify confusion: "The term 'academic integrity' is one that some people find confusing, especially if they've grown up hearing about 'plagiarism' or 'cheating.' The move from those phrases to a more comprehensive term such as 'academic integrity' is born out of a desire to describe the subject in a more positive way."

Summarize key points: "I've noticed that the thing that most people are neutral or not confident about are the values that underpin academic integrity. This isn't surprising and is one of the reasons we created this course!"

Make connections: "… and you will learn more in Week 3 about how to acknowledge sources you use in your work."

Troubleshoot: "Sorry to hear you can't play the video. There is a link underneath the video where you can report any problems."

Do not underestimate the influence of your expressing confidence in your students' abilities and efforts. In addition, you can urge students along by sending out reminders of upcoming due dates and situated prompts to encourage their timely progress on major assignments.

Sharing Strategies for Success

Share strategies and tips on the most effective and efficient ways to learn your material, including reading, studying, problem solving, time management, metacognitive, and self-regulated learning strategies (McGuire, 2015; Nilson, 2013, 2016). Many students lack basic skills such as how to focus, read carefully, take decent notes, approach problems, think critically, study effectively, and write clearly. They also underestimate the effort, concentration, and perseverance that learning and higher-level thinking involve. Without knowledge of cognitive psychology, they have little familiarity with how their minds learn, and they will tend to rely on the ineffective techniques they learned in their K–12 schooling (e.g., memorizing, practicing in one block of time, rereading text over and over, and cramming). You might wait until after the first test or graded homework assignment to bring up these learning strategies because the disappointed students will be amenable to changing their habits.

For study habits, Inkelaar and Simpson (2015) reported success using an early study tip system. After introducing the system in the first e-mail, they issued a dozen more motivational tips every week or two on topics such as how to learn, get organized, manage time, and catch up. This system, grounded in the style of Keller's ARCS motivation model, not only helped students but also increased retention rates enough to give the campus a "positive financial return" (p. 152).

At the very least, point students to some websites that give solid, research-based advice on academic reading, note taking, studying, writing, and other college skills, such as these:

- Getting Ready, Taking In, Remembering, Output, and How to Study by Discipline: http://www.howtostudy.org
- Study Skills Guide from Education Atlas: http://www.bestfreetraining.net/?p=1309
- How to Study.com: http://www.how-to-study.com/
- Mind Tools: https://www.mindtools.com/
- Study Guides and Strategies: http://www.studygs.net/
- Study Skills Information (Checklist and Strategies): https://ucc.vt.edu/academic_support/study_skills_information.html
- How to Get the Most Out of Studying (videos from Samford University): http://www.samford.edu/departments/academic-success-center/how-to-study

Students who put the recommended strategies into practice are likely to see the positive results quickly.

Explaining the Value of Errors

Finally, explain the value of errors in learning, and try to help students overcome their mistaken view of errors as failures. Not only are errors a natural part of learning, but students tend to remember what they learn through correcting their mistakes (see chapter 4).

■ CREATING SATISFACTION

Satisfaction encompasses several related motivators: a sense of achievement, perceived autonomy, felt competency, and being rewarded. Research tells us that students' satisfaction with an online course increases their learning and their likelihood of completing the course (Hart, 2012; Ivankova & Stick, 2007; Kuo, Walker, Belland, & Schroder, 2013; Levy, 2003, 2007; Müller, 2008; Park & Choi, 2009). This makes sense. Apart from circumstances beyond anyone's control, why wouldn't a student stay with a course that gives him or her a sense of satisfaction?

As a motivating factor, satisfaction has roots in self-determination theory, which posits a set of built-in human needs that motivate action and achievement (Deci & Ryan, 1985, 2002). People have an innate need to grow, develop, and attain fulfillment as a person. But in order to grow and be fulfilled, they must believe they have these three qualities:

Competence, which requires that they master new knowledge and skills and live through new experiences

Relatedness, which means feeling attached to others, valued by them, and integrated into a social group

Autonomy, which is the sense that they can freely choose and are in control of their own goals, outcomes, and behavior

Therefore, the conditions that help students meet these needs should foster motivation. The many course characteristics and instructor behaviors described in the rest of this section help create these favorable conditions (Keller, 2000, 2008a, 2008b, 2010, 2011, 2016; Nilson, 2016).

Let us consider now all of the factors that we know increase student satisfaction with an online course. Students must feel that the work they have invested in the course is appropriate and worthwhile, which is more likely when the course gives them opportunities to apply what they learn in real-life situations, offers significant learning (see chapter 2), and is coherently aligned (see chapter 3) (Ally, 2004; Kauffman, 2014). The relevance of the content and skills they are learning contributes to their sense of competency and achievement. Therefore, you should do the same things that ensure the relevance of your content (see the previous section):

- Explain the hidden value of learning tasks that are not obviously interesting, useful, and worth the effort.
- Bring learning into the real world with practical examples, simulations, and activities that focus on application and real problem solving.
- Design authentic, useful assignments and activities that give students practice in their future occupational and citizenship activities, such as conducting research, crafting business-related plans and reports, constructing a persuasive argument, and developing a new product.

- Encourage students to share practical ideas and real-life examples, and provide testimonials from previous students about the value of your course.
- Offer options and choices, which both foster your students' sense of autonomy and increase the relevance of the material. Consider allowing a choice of activities, assignments, and content organization and even some input into course content and policies.
- Request and pay attention to their feedback about the course and your teaching.

Other factors that contribute to student satisfaction include these:

- The quality of the content, the course design, and the use of a variety of assessment methods (Barbera, Clara, & Linder-Vanberschot, 2013; Ilgaz & Gülbahar, 2015; Park & Choi, 2009; Sun, Tsai, Finger, Chen, & Yeh, 2008), all of which augment students' feelings of competence
- Instructor-generated video content (Draus, Curran, & Trempus, 2014), which builds relatedness
- The quantity and quality of communication and the variety of interaction tools and activities (Ilgaz & Gülbahar, 2015), which also foster relatedness
- The instructor's attitude toward online learning and the flexibility built into the course (Sun et al., 2008), which enhance a sense of competence
- Student comfort and perceived efficacy with the technology (Alshare, Freeze, Lane, & Wen, 2011; Chang et al., 2014; Henson, 2014; Liaw, 2008; Sun et al., 2008), which also increase feelings of competence

In addition, students are more likely to experience satisfaction under these conditions:

- When they receive recognition (positive feedback) from their instructor and peers, which enhances their sense of competence and relatedness
- When they feel that they have been treated fairly, which increases their sense of autonomy
- When they have evidence of their success, which makes them feel competent

Not surprisingly, some of the opposite conditions are known to undermine satisfaction: poor computer skills, poor time management strategies, and family stressors (Park & Choi, 2009; Willging & Johnson, 2009), as well as a lack of access to the instructor, insufficient feedback, and the instructor's low expectations of students (Hawkins, Graham, Sudweeks, & Barbour, 2013; Herbert, 2006; Müller, 2008). Clearly, some factors under the instructor's control can mitigate against these satisfaction detractors, including explicit, just-in-time directions; a week-by-week organization of topical units and modules; posting of due dates and reminders about activities and assignments; and situated prompts to encourage students' timely progress on major assignments (Park & Choi, 2009; Willging & Johnson, 2009). All of these make students feel more competent. We explore relatedness in the next section on social belonging and do so in much greater detail in the next chapter.

■ FOSTERING SOCIAL BELONGING

Online learning can be lonely. Students can feel isolated when they spend hours studying all alone and interacting only with a computer (Kauffman, 2015). We must help them overcome these feelings by integrating well-designed, meaningful interactions with us and other students. Social belonging, relating to others, and feeling part of a community are so critical to student success and persistence (Croxton, 2014) that most of the next chapter recommends ways to build social interaction and community into a course. Therefore, we touch only briefly on the topic here.

At the start of the online learning process, student-instructor interactions correlate with higher learner satisfaction, and students with weak skills need more individual attention (Funk, 2005). Virtual online office hours, where the entire class can post questions and comments, also help students feel more connected (Major, 2015). Deliberately designed cohort- and team-based learning experiences foster a sense of belonging to a learning community (Bocchi, Eastman, & Swift, 2004). The positive effects of social support have proven particularly strong among ethnic minorities and first-generation students (Cox, 2011; Dennis, Phinney, & Chuateco, 2005; Jackson, Smith, & Hill, 2003).

However, students must be able to perceive this support for the benefits to accrue, so you must be explicit in expressing it (Dennis et al., 2005). When they don't perceive this support or when the interactions seem forced rather than meaningful, such as when an instructor requires an arbitrary number of discussion board postings, they feel a loss of community and are more likely to drop out of the course (Biesenbach-Lucas, 2003; Grandzol & Grandzol, 2013).

One of the most powerful strategies for building your students' sense of social belonging and their relationship with you is to personalize your course as much as you can. Make an effort to get to know your students by asking them about their majors, interests, and backgrounds. This information will help you tailor the material to their concerns and professional goals, which in turn will make them feel a part of a learning community (Müller, 2008). In large classes, you can foster this kind of sharing in small groups.

Let your students get to know you. Share some professional and personal information about yourself. Foster open lines of communication in both directions. Explain your expectations and assessments, but also invite your students' feedback on ways you can help them learn more effectively. Monitor your students' participation in discussion boards and chats and their submission of assignments. Contact those who have been missing from course-related activities, expressing your concern and encouragement. Finally, help your students get to know each other by planning online icebreakers at the beginning of the course and some group activities throughout. Chapter 6 contains many more strategies.

■ MOTIVATING AS OUR MAJOR TASK

While we can place students in situations and offer them experiences that foster learning, the actual process of learning ultimately goes on inside their minds. Students have to make themselves focus and reflect on these situations and experiences, sometimes for long, effortful periods of time. From this perspective, motivating students to do this is our primary job and one just as critical as creating engaging learning situations and experiences. We have clear evidence of what works to motivate online students, we know to make a balanced use of our motivational strategies, and we have models and resources to support our choices. Here are some additional resources that may help your course planning:

- (My) Three Principles of Effective Online Pedagogy, Bill Pelz (2004), a Sloan-C award for Excellence in Online Teaching recipient: https://www.ccri.edu/distancefaculty/pdfs/Online-Pedagogy-Pelz.pdf
- Speaking to Students with Audio Feedback in Online Courses, Debbie Morrison: https://onlinelearning insights.wordpress.com/2013/04/06/speaking-to-students-with-audio-feedback-in-online-courses/
- Learning to Teach Online Episodes, University of New South Wales (short, topic-focused videos): http://online.cofa.unsw.edu.au/learning-to-teach-online/ltto-episodes.

Reflections

For Instructors

- About student attention
  - What elements of course design, website design, and content presentation can you incorporate to capture and maintain your students' interest and attention? To arouse their curiosity?
  - What content and activities can you add to your course to stimulate an attitude of inquiry?
  - How can you vary the content presentations, course materials, and activities to maintain student attention?
  - How will you convey to students your personal enthusiasm and passion for what you are teaching?
- About student goals and values
  - What do students in your course value? What are their interests?
  - What do your students aspire to become? What do they want? What do they *not* want?
  - How will you ensure that your course activities and assignments are goal driven?
  - What strategies can you use to help students set their own goals?
- About relevance to students
  - How can you relate the course content, activities, and assignments to the needs, goals, and interests of your students?
  - Where can you give students choices in topics, activities, and assignments? What content and policies can you invite your students to select or modify?
  - How can you explain to students the reasons behind the course decisions you have made?
- About student confidence
  - What degree of self-regulation, self-confidence, and self-efficacy do you anticipate your students having?
  - How can you help them become more self-regulating and feel more confident and in control of their success?
  - What time management challenges do you think your students may have in your course? How can you help them make more efficient use of their limited time?
  - How can you build your students' positive expectations for success in your course?
  - How can you encourage or affirm your students' confidence in their own abilities?
  - How will your students know that they are being treated fairly?
  - How will your students know that their accomplishments in your course come from their own efforts, behaviors, and abilities?
  - How do you plan to recognize your students' effort?
  - What kinds of motivational messages will you develop ahead of time to send out biweekly or at critical times during your course?
- About student satisfaction
  - What will you do to set and communicate high expectations for your students?
  - How will you give your students opportunities to apply what they are learning?
  - How will you reinforce (reward) students for their participation and accomplishments?
  - How will you challenge your students?
  - How can you help your students feel that their investment of time in your course content, activities, and assignments has been worth it?

For Instructional Designers

- What do you know about the instructor's answers to the questions just listed?
- What elements of course design will support the instructor's strategies for motivation?
- What interface features can be adjusted to add visual appeal to the course site?
- What image resources can you provide to enhance the visual instructional integrity of the course?
- What technology applications will complement the instructor's teaching and motivational strategies and technological capabilities?
- What technology applications will be easy for the students to use and at the same time optimize the instructor's teaching strategies?
- What tutorials or other resources can support effective use of the technology?
- What free media support sites can you identify for the instructor?
- What just-in-time tips can you build into the course to help students use the technology and media?
- What additional strategies can you identify to create the optimal degree of motivation in the course (avoiding too little as well as too much of a good thing)?

For Administrators

- What instructional technology support can your institution furnish so that instructors and instructional designers can easily integrate multimedia into their courses?
- What tutorials can your institution develop or purchase to train instructors and students to use the online-course technology?

■ REFERENCES

Ally, M. (2004). Foundations of educational theory for online learning. In T. Anderson & F. Elloumi (Eds.), *Theory and practice of online learning* (pp. 3–31). Edmonton, Alberta, Canada: Athabasca University Press.

Alshare, K. A., Freeze, R. D., Lane, P. L., & Wen, H. J. (2011). The impacts of system and human factors on online learning systems use and learner satisfaction. *Decision Sciences Journal of Innovative Education, 9*(3), 437–461. doi:10.1111/j.1540–4609.2011.00321.x

Ambrose, S. A., Bridges, M. W., DiPietro, M., Lovett, M. C., & Norman, M. K. (2010). *How learning works: Seven research-based principles for smart teaching.* San Francisco, CA: Jossey-Bass.

Anderson, T. (2004). Teaching in an online context. In T. Anderson & F. Elloumi (Eds.), *Theory and practice of online learning* (pp. 273–294). Edmonton, Alberta, Canada: Athabasca University.

Bandura, A. (1977a). Self-efficacy: Toward a unifying theory of behavioral change. *Psychological Review, 84*(2), 191–215. doi:10.1016/0146–6402(78)90002–4

Bandura, A. (1977b). *Social learning theory.* New York, NY: General Learning Press.

Barbera, E., Clara, M., & Linder-Vanberschot, J. A. (2013, September). Factors influencing student satisfaction and perceived learning in online courses. *E-Learning and Digital Media, 10*(3), 226–235. doi:10.2304/elea.2013.10.3.226

Berlyne, D. E. (1960). *Conflict, arousal, and curiosity.* New York, NY: McGraw-Hill.

Berlyne, D. E. (1965). *Structure and direction in thinking.* New York, NY: Wiley.

Berlyne, D. E. (1978). Curiosity and learning. *Motivation and Emotion, 2*(2), 97–175.

Biesenbach-Lucas, S. (2003). Asynchronous discussion groups in teacher training classes: Perceptions of native and non-native students. *Journal of Asynchronous Learning Networks, 7*(3), 24–46.

Bocchi, J., Eastman, J., & Swift, C. (2004). Retaining the online learner: Profile of students in an online MBA program and implications for teaching them. *Journal of Education for Business*, *79*(4), 245–253.

Bolliger, D. U., Supanakorn, S., & Boggs, C. (2010). Impact of podcasting on student motivation in the online learning environment. *Computers and Education*, *55*, 714–722.

Brandt, R. (1979, November). A conversation with Benjamin S. Bloom. *Educational Leadership*, *37*(2), 157–161.

Cameron, J., & Pierce, W. D. (1994). Reinforcement, reward, and intrinsic motivation: A meta-analysis. *Review of Educational Research*, *64*, 363–423.

Chang, C-S., Liu, E. Z., Sung H-Y., Lin, C-H., Chen, N-S., & Cheng, S-S. (2014). Effects of online college students' Internet self-efficacy on learning motivation and performance. *Innovations in Education and Teaching International*, *51*(4), 366–377.

Chang, M. M., & Lehman, J. (2002). Learning foreign language through an interactive multimedia program: An experimental study on the effects of the relevance component of the ARCS model. *CALICO Journal*, *20*(1), 81–98.

Chang, N., & Chen, H. (2015). A motivational analysis of the ARCS model for information literacy courses in a blended learning environment. *International Journal of Libraries and Information Services*, *65*(2), 129–142. doi:10.1515/libri-2015-0010

Chyung, Y., Winiecki, D., & Fenner, J. A. (1998, August). A case study: Increase enrollment by reducing dropout rates in adult distance education. In *Proceedings of the Annual Conference on Distance Teaching and Learning*, 97–101. ERIC (ED 422 848).

Clark, R. C., & Lyons, C. (2011). *Graphics for learning: Proven guidelines for planning, designing, and evaluating visuals in training materials*. San Francisco, CA: Jossey-Bass.

Clark, R. E. (1999). Yin and yang cognitive motivational processes operating in multimedia learning environments. In J. van Merriënboer (Ed.), *Cognition and multimedia design* (pp. 73–107). Herleen, Netherlands: Open University Press.

Clark, R. E. (2004). What works in distance learning: Motivation strategies. In H. O'Neil (Ed.), *What works in distance learning: Guidelines* (pp. 89–110). Greenwich, CT: Information Age Publishers.

Cook, S., Bingham, T., Reid, S., & Wang, L. (2015). Going massive: Learner engagement in a MOOC environment. *Higher Education Technology Agenda*. Retrieved from https://www.caudit.edu.au/system/files/Media%20library/Resources%20and%20Files/Presentations/THETA%202015%20Learner%20engagement%20in%20a%20MOOC%20environment%20-%20S%20Cook%20T%20Bingham%20S%20Reid%20and%20L%20Wang%20-%20Full%20Paper.pdf

Cox, R. D. (2011). *The college fear factor: How students and professors misunderstand one another*. Cambridge, MA: Harvard University Press.

Croxton, R. A. (2014, June). The role of interactivity in student satisfaction and persistence in online learning. *MERLOT Journal of Online Learning and Teaching*, *10*(2), 314–325.

Deci, E. L., & Ryan, R. M. (1985). *Intrinsic motivation and self-determination in human behavior*. New York, NY: Plenum.

Deci, E. L., & Ryan, R. M. (Eds.). (2002). *Handbook of self-determination research*. Rochester, NY: University of Rochester Press.

Dennen, V. P., & Bonk, C. J. (2007). We'll leave the light on for you: Keeping learners motivated in online courses. In B. H. Khan (Ed.), *Flexible learning in an information society* (pp. 64–76). Calgary, Alberta, Canada: Idea Group.

Dennis, J. M., Phinney, J. S., & Chuateco, L. I. (2005). The role of motivation, parental support, and peer support in the academic success of ethnic minority first-generation college students. *Journal of College Student Development*, *46*, 223–236.

Draus, P. J., Curan, M. J., & Trempus, M. S. (2014). The influence of instructor-generated video content on student satisfaction with and engagement in asynchronous online classes. *Journal of Online Learning and Teaching*, *10*(2), 240.

Dweck, C. S. (2007). *Mindset: The new psychology of success.* New York, NY: Random House.

Eisenberger, R., & Cameron, J. (1996). Detrimental effects of reward: Reality or myth? *American Psychologist, 51,* 1153–1166.

Fahy, P. J. (2004). Media characteristics and online learning technology. In T. Anderson & F. Elloumi (Eds.), *Theory and practice of online learning* (pp. 137–171). Edmonton, Alberta, Canada: Athabasca University Press.

Fetzner, M. (2013). What do unsuccessful online students want us to know? *Journal of Asynchronous Learning Networks, 17*(1), 13–27. Retrieved from http://sloanconsortium.org/publications/jaln_main

Firmin, R., Schiorring, E., Whitmer, J., Willett, T., Collins, E. D., & Sujitparapitaya, S. (2014). Case study: Using MOOCs for conventional college coursework. *Distance Education, 35*(2), 178–201. doi:10.1080/01587919.2014.917707

Funk, J. T. (2005). At-risk online learners: Reducing barriers to success. *eLearning Magazine.* Retrieved from http://elearnmag.acm.org/featured.cfm?aid=1082221

Funk, J. T. (2007). *A descriptive study of retention of adult online learners: A model of interventions to prevent attrition* (Order No. 3249896). Available from ProQuest Dissertations and Theses Global (304723480. Retrieved from http://search.proquest.com/openview/e6183a94ca54e333bab714da3b8d6870/1?pq-origsite=gscholar&cbl=18750&diss=y

Goodson, L. A. (2016a). *Course review: BUS W430 Organizations and Organizational Change: Leadership and Group Dynamics.* Instructor: A. Gibson, Indiana University-Purdue University Fort Wayne.

Goodson, L. A. (2016b). *Course review: FNN 30300 Essentials of Nutrition.* Instructor: L. L. Lolkus, Indiana University-Purdue University Fort Wayne.

Goodson, L. A. (2016c). *Course review: MA 15300 Algebra and Trigonometry I.* Instructor: J. LaMaster, Indiana University-Purdue University Fort Wayne.

Goodson, L. A. (2016d). *Course review: SOW 5125 Psychopathology.* Instructor: V. Ospina-Kammerer, Florida State University.

Goodson, L. A., & Ahn, I. S. (2014). Consulting and designing in the fast lane. In A. P. Mizell & A. A. Piña (Eds.), *Real-life distance learning: Case studies in research and practice* (pp. 197–220). Charlotte, NC: Information Age Publishing.

Grandzol, C. J., & Grandzol, J. R. (2010). Interaction in online courses: More is not always better. *Online Journal of Distance Learning Administration, 13*(2), 1–18.

Hart, C. (2012). Factors associated with student persistence in an online program of study: A review of the literature. *Journal of Interactive Online Learning, 11*(1). Retrieved from http://www.ncolr.org/jiol/issues/pdf/11.1.2.pdf

Hartnett, M., St. George, A., & Dron, J. (2011, October). Examining motivation in online distance learning environments: Complex, multifaceted, and situation-dependent. *International Review of Research in Open and Distributed Learning, 12*(6). Retrieved from http://www.irrodl.org/index.php/irrodl/article/view/1030/1954

Hawkins, A., Graham, C., Sudweeks, R., & Barbour, M. K. (2013). Course completion rates and student perceptions of the quality and frequency of interaction in a virtual high school. *Distance Education, 34*(1), 64–83.

Henson, A. R. (2014). The success of nontraditional college students in an IT world. *Research in Higher Education Journal, 25.* Retrieved from http://www.aabri.com/manuscripts/141911.pdf

Herbert, M. (2006). Staying the course: A study in online student satisfaction and retention. *Online Journal of Distance Learning Administration, 9*(4). Retrieved from http://www.westga.edu/~distance/ojdla/winter94/herbert94.htm

Hew, K. F. (2015). Promoting engagement in online courses: What strategies can we learn from three highly rated MOOCs? *British Journal of Educational Technology, 47*(2), 320–341. doi:10.1111/bjet.12235

Holder, B. (2007). An investigation of hope, academics, environment, and motivation as predictors of persistence in higher education online programs. *Internet and Higher Education, 10*(4), 245–260.

Hoskins, S. L., & Newstead, S. E. (2009). Encouraging student motivation. In H. Fry, S. Ketteridge, & S. Marshall (Eds.), *A handbook for teaching and learning in higher education: Enhancing academic practice* (3rd ed., pp. 27–39). London, UK: Routledge.

Hu, Y. (2008). *Motivation, usability and their interrelationships in a self-paced online learning environment.* (Order No. DP19570). Available from ProQuest Dissertations and Theses Global (1030135967). Retrieved from http://search .proquest.com.ezproxy.library.ipfw.edu/docview/1030135967?accountid=11649

Huett, J., Kalinowski, K., Moller, L., & Huett, K. (2008). Improving the motivation and retention of online students through the use of ARCS-based emails. *American Journal of Distance Education, 22*(3), 159–176.

Huett, J. B., Young, J., Huett, K. C., Moller, L., & Bray, M. (2008). Supporting the distant student: The effect of ARCS-based strategies on confidence and performance. *Quarterly Review of Distance Education, 9*(2), 113–126.

Ilgaz, H., & Gülbahar, Y. (2015). A snapshot of online learners: E-readiness, e-satisfaction, and expectations. *International Review of Research in Open and Distributed Learning, 16*(2), 171–187.

Inkelaar, T., & Simpson, O. (2015). Challenging the "distance education deficit" through "motivational emails." *Open Learning, 30*(2), 152–163.

Intrinsic motivation doesn't exist, researcher says. (2005, May 17). PhysOrg.com. Retrieved from http://www.physorg .com/news4126.html

Ivankova, N. V., & Stick, S. L. (2005). Collegiality and community-building as a means for sustaining student persistence in the computer-mediated asynchronous learning environment. *Online Journal of Distance Learning Administration, 8*(3). Retrieved from http://www.westga.edu/~distance/ojdla/fall83/ivankova83.htm

Jackson, A. P., Smith, S. A., & Hill, C. L. (2003). Academic persistence among Native American college students. *Journal of College Student Development, 44*, 548–565.

Kauffman, H. (2015). A review of predictive factors of student success in and satisfaction with online learning. *Research in Learning Technology, 23*. Retrieved from http://www.researchinlearningtechnology.net/index.php/rlt /article/view/26507

Keller, J. M. (2000). *How to integrate learner motivation planning into lesson planning: The ARCS model approach.* Paper presented at VII Semanario, Santiago, Chile. Retrieved from http://apps.fischlerschool.nova.edu/toolbox /instructionalproducts/ITDE_8005/weeklys/2000-Keller-ARCSLessonPlanning.pdf

Keller, J. M. (2008a). An integrative theory of motivation, volition, and performance. *Technology, Instruction, Cognition and Learning, 6*, 79–104. Retrieved from http://www.oldcitypublishing.com/FullText/TICLfulltext/TICL6.2fulltext /TICLv6n2p79–104Keller.pdf

Keller, J. M. (2008b). First principles of motivation to learn and e-learning. *Distance Education, 29*(2), 175–185.

Keller, J. M. (2010). *Motivational design for learning and performance: The ARCS model approach.* New York, NY: Springer Science and Business Media.

Keller, J. M. (2011). *Five fundamental requirements for motivation and volition in technology-assisted distributed learning environments.* doi:10.5216/ia.v35i2.12668.

Keller, J. M. (2016). *ARCS design process.* [website]. Retrieved from http://www.arcsmodel.com/?utm _campaign=elearningindustry.com&utm_medium=link&utm_source=%2Farcs-model-of-motivation

Keller, J. M., & Suzuki, K. (2004). Learner motivation and e-learning design: A multinationally validated process. *Journal of Educational Media, 29*(3), 229–239. doi:10.1080/1358t65042000283084

Kim, C., & Keller, J. M. (2007). Effects of motivational and volitional email messages (MVEM) with personal messages on undergraduate students' motivation, study habits and achievement. *British Journal of Educational Technology, 39*(1), 36–51. doi:10.1111/j.1467–8535.2007.00701.x

Koballa, T. R., & Glynn, S. M. (2007). Attitudinal and motivational constructs in science learning. In S. K. Abell & N. G. Lederman (Eds.), *Handbook for research in science education* (pp. 75–102). Mahwah, NJ: Erlbaum.

Kohn, A. (1993). *Punished by rewards.* Boston, MA: Houghton Mifflin.

Kuo, Y., Walter, A. E., Belland, B. R., & Schroder, K. E. (2013). A predictive study of student satisfaction in online education programs. *International Review of Research in Open and Distance Learning, 14*(1). Retrieved from http://www.irrodl.org/index.php/irrodl/article/view/1338/2416

Lee, Y., & Choi, J. (2011). A review of online course dropout research: implications for practice and future research. *Educational Technology Research and Development, 59*(5), 593–618. doi:10.1007/s11423–010–9177–y

Levy, Y. (2003). *A study of learners' perceived value and satisfaction for implied effectiveness of online learning systems.* (Doctoral dissertation). Arizona State University. *Dissertation Abstracts International, 65*(3), 1014A.

Levy, Y. (2007). Comparing dropouts and persistence in e-learning courses. *Computers and Education, 48*(2), 185–204.

Lewes, D., & Stiklus, B. (2007). *Portrait of a student as a young wolf: Motivating undergraduates* (3rd ed.). Pennsdale, PA: Folly Hill Press.

Ley, K., & Gannon-Cook, R. (2014). Learner-valued interactions: Research into practice. *Quarterly Review of Distance Education, 15*(1), 23–32. Retrieved from http://www.aect.org/pdf/proceedings13/2013/13_16.pdf

Liaw, S-S. (2008). Investigating students' perceived satisfaction, behavioral intention, and effectiveness of e-learning: A case study of the Blackboard system. *Computers and Education, 51*, 864–873.

Liao, H., & Wang, Y. (2008). Applying the ARCS motivation model in technological and vocational education. *Contemporary Issues in Education Research, 1*(2), 53–58.

Lidwell, W., Holden, K., & Butler, J. (2010). *Universal principles of design.* Beverly, MA: Rockport Publishers.

Lin, Y., McKeachie, W. J., & Kim, Y. C. (2001). College student intrinsic and/or extrinsic motivation and learning. *Learning and Individual Differences, 13*(3), 251–258.

Liu, J., & Tomasi, S. D. (2015). The effect of professor's attractiveness on distance learning students. *Journal of Educators Online, 12*(2), 142–165.

Locke, E. A., & Latham, G. P. (1990). *A theory of goal setting and task performance.* Englewood Cliffs, NJ: Prentice Hall.

Lysakowski, R. S., & Walberg, H. J. (1981). Classroom reinforcement and learning: A quantitative synthesis. *Journal of Educational Research, 75*(2), 69–77.

Major, C. H. (2015). *Teaching online: A guide to theory, research, and practice.* Baltimore, MD: Johns Hopkins University Press.

Marguerite, D. (2007). *Improving learner motivation through enhanced instructional design.* (Master's thesis). Athabasca University Governing Council, Edmonton, Alberta, Canada.

Maslow, A. H. (1954). *Motivation and personality.* New York, NY: Harper and Row.

Mayer, R. E. (2014). Incorporating motivation into multimedia learning. *Learning and Instruction, 29*, 171–173.

McClelland, D. C., & Burnham, D. H. (1976). Power is the great motivator. *Harvard Business Review, 54*(2), 100.

McGuire, S. Y., with McGuire, S. (2015). *Teach students how to learn: Strategies you can incorporate into any course to improve student metacognition, study skills, and motivation.* Sterling, VA: Stylus.

Moore, J. (2014). Effects of online interaction and instructor presence on students' satisfaction and success with online undergraduate public relations courses. *Journalism and Mass Communication Educator, 69*(3), 271–288.

Müller, T. (2008). Persistence of women in online degree-completion programs. *International Review of Research in Open and Distance Learning, 9*(2), 1–18.

Norman, D. A. (2005). *Emotional design: Why we love (or hate) everyday things.* New York, NY: Basic Books.

Nilson, L. B. (2013). *Creating self-regulated learners: Strategies to strengthen students' self-awareness and learning skills.* Sterling, VA: Stylus.

Nilson, L. B. (2016). *Teaching at its best: A research-based resource for college instructors* (4th ed.). San Francisco, CA: Jossey-Bass.

Noesgaard, S. S., & Ørngreen, R. (2015). The effectiveness of e-learning: An explorative and integrative review of the definitions, methodologies, and factors that promote e-learning effectiveness. *Electronic Journal of E-Learning, 13*(4), 278–290.

Online Learning Insights. (2016, July 23). *How and why to use social media to create meaningful learning assignments* [web log]. Retrieved from https://onlinelearninginsights.wordpress.com/

Park, J-H., & Choi, H. J. (2009). Factors influencing adult learners' decision to drop out or persist in online learning. *Educational Technology and Society, 12*(4), 207–217.

Pelz, B. (2004, June). (My) three principles of effective online pedagogy. *Journal of Asynchronous Online Learning Networks, 8*(3). Retrieved from https://www.ccri.edu/distancefaculty/pdfs/Online-Pedagogy-Pelz.pdf

Rigby, C. S., Deci, E. L., Patrick, B. C., & Ryan, R. M. (1992). Beyond the intrinsic-extrinsic dichotomy: Self-determination in motivation and learning. *Motivation and Emotion, 16*(3), 165–185.

Ripley, A. (2013). *The smartest kids in the world and how they got that way.* New York, NY: Simon & Schuster.

Robb, C. (2010). *The impact of motivational messages on student performance in community college online courses.* (Order No. 3430898). Available from ProQuest Dissertations and Theses Global (778224030). Retrieved from http://search.proquest.com/openview/5f95506841cb3ccf43d440986d2af02e/1?pq-origsite=gscholar&cbl=18750&diss=y

Robb, C. A., & Sutton, J. (2014). The importance of social presence and motivation in distance learning. *Journal of Technology, Management, and Applied Engineering, 31*(2), 2–10.

Rotter, J. B. (1975). Some problems and misconceptions related to the construct of internal versus external control of reinforcement. *Journal of Consulting and Clinical Psychology, 43*, 56–67.

Ryan, R. M., & Deci, E. L. (2000). Intrinsic and extrinsic motivations: Class definition and new directions. *Contemporary Education Psychology, 25*(1), 54–67.

Sankey, M. D. (2002). Considering visual literacy when designing instruction. *e-Journal of Instructional Science and Technology, 5*(2). Retrieved from http://ascilite.org/archived-journals/e-jist/docs/Vol5_No2/Sankey-final.pdf

Schunk, D. H. (2012). *Learning theories: An educational perspective* (6th ed.). Boston, MA: Pearson Education.

Seligman, M.E.P. (1975). *Helplessness: On depression, development, and death.* New York, NY: Freeman.

Shih, C., & Gamon, J. (2001). Web-based learning: Relationships among student motivation, attitude, learning styles, and achievement. *Journal of Agricultural Education, 42*(4), 12–20. (ERIC EJ638591.)

Stöter, J., Bullen, M., Zawacki-Richter, & Prümmer, C. (2011). From the back door into the mainstream: The characteristics of lifelong learners. In O. Zawacki-Richter & T. Anderson (Eds.), *Online distance education: Towards a research agenda* (pp. 421–457). Edmonton, Alberta, Canada: Athabasca University Press.

Sun, P., Tsai, R. J., Finger, G., Chen, Y., & Yeh, D. (2008). What drives a successful e-learning? An empirical investigation of the critical factors influencing learner satisfaction. *Computers and Education, 50*(4), 1183–1202.

Svinicki, M. (2004). *Learning and motivation in the postsecondary classroom.* San Francisco, CA: Jossey-Bass/Anker.

Tomita, K. (2015). Principles and elements of visual design: A review of the literature on visual design studies of instructional materials. *Educational Studies, 56*, 165–173.

Urdan, T. (2003). Intrinsic motivation, extrinsic rewards, and divergent views of reality. [Review of the book *Intrinsic and extrinsic motivation: The search for optimal motivation and performance*]. *Educational Psychology Review, 15*(3), 311–325.

Visser, L. (1998). *The development of motivational communication in distance education support.* Retrieved from http://www .learndev.org/People/LyaVisser/DevMotCommInDE.pdf

Visser, L., Plomp, T., & Kuiper, W. (1999). Development research applied to improve motivation in distance education. In *Annual Proceedings of Selected Research and Development Papers Presented at the National Convention of the Association for Educational Communications and Technology.* Houston, TX. Retrieved from http://files.eric.ed.gov/fulltext/ED436169 .pdf

Wigfield, A., & Eccles, J. (2000). Expectancy-value theory of achievement motivation. *Contemporary Educational Psychology, 25*, 68–81.

Willging, P. A., & Johnson, S. D. (2009). Factors that influence students' decision to drop out of online courses. *Journal of Asynchronous Learning Networks, 13*(3), 115–127.

Woodley, A., & Simpson, O. (2014). Student dropout: The elephant in the room. In O. Zawacki-Richter & T. Anderson (Eds.), *Online distance education: Towards a research agenda* (pp. 459–484). Edmonton, Alberta, Canada: Athabasca University Press.

Zammit, J. B., Martindale, T., Meiners-Lovell, L., & Irwin, R. (2013). Strategies for increasing engagement and information seeking in a multi-section online course: Scaffolding student success through the ARCS-V model. In *Proceedings of Selected Research and Development Papers Presented at the Annual Convention of the Association for Educational Communications and Technology, 1.* Anaheim, CA. Retrieved from http://eric.ed.gov/?id=ED546877

CHAPTER 6

Developing Interactivity, Social Connections, and Community

This chapter addresses one set of high-impact practices over which faculty have complete control: student-instructor, student-content, and student-student interaction. It opens with a review of the literature on the effects of these interactions. Next we show how online technologies, used wisely, can foster interactivity, social connectedness, and community in online courses, starting with student-instructor interaction. Of the three types of interaction, this one makes the biggest difference in student success. Student-content interaction encompasses various media presentations, discussion formats, group work, interactive technologies, study aids, and connections with subject librarians. Meaningful student-student interactions can involve discussions, collaboration, peer review, or group work on any of several whole-class and small-group communication platforms. One final type of student interaction is with the technology, and in this section we will focus on your best uses of the learning management system, course management strategies, the meaning of contact hours in online courses, and ways to determine and boost student engagement.

The forcing of interaction can be as strong a detriment to effective learning [as is] its absence.

—M. Simonson (2000)

■ THE EFFECTS OF INTERACTIONS ON LEARNING

For several decades, we have known the value of student interactions with the instructor, the course content, classmates, and technology in online courses (Anderson, 2003; Educause Learning Initiative, 2005; Moore, 1989; Moore, 2014; Reisetter & Boris, 2009; Rhode, 2009; Simonson, 2000; Sorensen & Baylen, 2009;

Wang, Chen, & Anderson, 2014; Wanstreet, 2009). When these interactions develop instructor, cognitive, and social presence, they help students feel part of a community, which sustains their persistence in online courses (Angelino, Williams, & Natvig, 2007; Estes, 2016; Luyegu, 2016; Semingson & Smith, 2016). Online students vary in their desired degree of community, and researchers vary in how they define it, yet across the board, well-designed interactions keep students from feeling the sense of isolation that often leads them to withdraw (Drouin & Vartanian, 2008).

In a face-to-face classroom, interactions usually occur spontaneously, but in an online class, you must design productive interactions in advance. Student interactions with content and the instructor matter most. The principles for good practice in undergraduate education offer strategies for building high-quality interactions in an online course (Chickering & Ehrmann, 1996; Chickering & Gamson, 1987; Sorensen & Baylen, 2009; Zhang & Walls, 2009):

- Student-faculty contact, such as e-mail communications, online discussions, student conferences, and sharing introductions at the start of a course
- Student reciprocity and cooperation, such as study group discussion areas, group problem solving, and project teams
- Active learning through assignments, such as research projects, simulations, and creating relevant deliverables
- Prompt feedback on learning, such as automated feedback on quizzes or practice tests and instructor feedback on ways to improve student work
- Time on task, such as recommending time spent on an assignment and underscoring student commitment to schedules and steady progress in the class
- Communication of high expectations, such as explaining requirements, assigning significant real-life problems, and giving clear criteria for grading of assignments
- Opportunities for students to express their diverse talents and ways of learning, such as encouraging self-reflection, providing choices for projects, and allowing different ways of fulfilling assignments

In online learning, we also focus on student interactions specifically with the instructor, content, fellow students, and technology. Getting the balance of these interactions right, aligned with learning outcomes and student interests, yields the following benefits (Anderson, 2003; Angelino, Williams, & Natvig, 2007; Croxton, 2014; Drouin & Vartanian, 2008; Estes, 2016; E. Moore, 1989; J. Moore, 2014; Reisetter & Boris, 2009; Simonson, 2000; Sorensen & Baylen, 2009; Wang, Chen, & Anderson, 2014; Wanstreet, 2009; Zhang & Walls, 2009):

- Creates teaching, cognitive, and social presence
- Develops a feeling of community
- Raises student engagement and satisfaction with online learning
- Improves student learning
- Increases student persistence and retention (reduces withdrawals)

Online students are more willing to minimize interactions with other students (Morris, 2016), but planning for some student-student interactions such as a study buddy in the class can foster informal social connections (Madland & Richards, 2016). Not all interactions need to be formally structured or graded, as students like room for informal interaction too (Rhode, 2009). Build in some space for them, such as open-topic discussion areas, a student lounge, informal blogs, or a social media forum.

In practice, the types of interactions overlap. For example, familiarity with the content prepares students for reflections, critical thinking, teamwork, assignments, discussions, and tests. Morris (2016) identifies some of the most interactive technologies, including messages to students that invite a reply, construction of discussion forums with meaningful problems and questions, collaboration tools such as wikis and blogs, social media such as Facebook and Twitter, website building tools such as Ning, and labs and interactive homework tools. For determining how to use such tools, make sure to invite, if not require, meaningful student interactions (Dixson, 2010) and consider the following steps for planning (Hirumi, 2009):

- Identify the essential experiences for achieving your goals and learning outcomes.
- Use a research-based instructional strategy suitable for your students.
- Organize and describe how each interactive event will be used during the course.
- Define the type of interaction, and plan both the quality and the quantity expected.
- Select the tools for interactions, such as e-mail, chat, discussion board, or other technologies.
- Review and analyze the appropriateness of your planned interactions, and revise them to make improvements.

Finally, specify technologies that are easy to use, at least after you provide or direct students to some training. Students value the quality and type of interactions more than the quantity or the variety of technology tools. Focusing on a required number of responses in a discussion rather than quality can actually decrease student participation (Jeong, 2014). So can failure to furnish clear guidelines for participation, give feedback, explain criteria for evaluating participation, and ensure that students can work with the courseware and technology (Zheng & Smaldino, 2009). Thus, be sure to let pedagogy drive your technology choices and your interaction design, and do not overload your students with either too much technology or too many interactions (Hirumi, 2009).

In the following sections, we explore what we know about effective strategies for student-instructor, student-content, and student-student interactions.

■ STUDENT-INSTRUCTOR INTERACTION

Research studies show that student-instructor interactions produce positive outcomes and matter more than other kinds of interactions (Battalio, 2009; Cho & Cho, 2014; J. Moore, 2014; Thurmond & Wambach, 2004). But contrived interactions can do more harm than good (Sorensen & Baylen, 2011; Thurmond & Wambach, 2004). Interactions must have a clear purpose and hold value for students. Do they clarify meaning, deepen student understanding, or encourage and support the student? Factors that contribute to quality include these:

- A visible instructor presence and a well-prepared course (Liu, Magjuka, Bonk, & Lee, 2009; Tsiotakis & Jimoyiannis, 2016)
- Organization of content, clarity of your directions, provision of examples of exemplary work, and timely feedback (Estes, 2016)
- Appropriate use of communication tools (Pavlis-Korres & Leftheriotou, 2016)
- Frequent and personalized interactions (Thurmond & Wambach, 2004)

Some interactions can be formally organized and others informally. For example, an online office within the course allows questions and answers about course schedules, changes in due dates, directions for assignments, and other general course issues. A personal introduction and course orientation video add to personal presence. Virtual office hours (usually held weekly) do the same. The telephone, e-mail, or conferencing tools also have a role.

These research findings on online learning may also apply to others who have a role in your course such as a teaching assistant or subject-area librarian, and they parallel related principles of learning from cognitive science (see chapter 4). Exhibit 6.1 lists guidelines based on these findings for setting communication tone and style, with an emphasis on early scaffolding for course communications.

Exhibit 6.1: Communication Tone and Style

- Create a safe, low-stress, supportive, welcoming environment.
- Set the tone for the style of communication you expect.
- Express clear communication policies from the outset, including expected netiquette protocols.
- Share your professional background, your interest in the course content, and your enthusiasm about teaching it.
- Communicate the personal relevance of the material.
- From the outset, send students a positive, motivating message. Let them know that you care about their welfare, their success in your course, and their opinions about how the course is going.
- Show sensitivity to cultural diversity. For example, use gender-neutral language and deal appropriately with sensitive and controversial issues.
- Send periodic motivating messages in announcements or e-mails.
- Respond quickly to offensive communication and signs of harassment early on. If you find insulting comments, unfounded attacks on student work or ideas, or netiquette violations such as "flaming," privately counsel offenders in an e-mail, phone call, or other technology, such as FaceTime or Skype. If you decide to remove the student's comments, explain why, or move them to a private discussion forum or journal area.
- If an offender does not cooperate, enforce consequences as stated in your syllabus and in your institution's policies against harassment.

Visible presence goes beyond a preliminary introduction. Gaining a sense of your personality matters to students (Reisetter & Boris, 2009). It is a good idea to include a link to your home web page or vita and respond to frequently asked questions in a personalized way. Students care about your knowledge, helpfulness, response time, encouragement, support for their time management, and expectations of quality work. After all, students do change their approach to learning when they understand the nature of the task (Stöter, Zawacki-Richter, & von Prümmer, 2014). They need the same kinds of routines they experience in face-to-face classes (Estes, 2016). For example, a beginning-of-the-week introductory, conversational e-mail message such as "Welcome to Week 1," "Welcome to Week 2," and so on, can give students a quick overview of your expectations for the week. A list of learning activities in a weekly or module folder supplies a convenient checklist of their progress. A weekly wrap-up message can pull together students' contributions, highlighting how they relate to the past week's content and concepts as well as the next week's.

Like the scaffolding that supports construction, timely scaffolding in an online course saves students time and effort and actively supports their success. It should help students learn not only the content but also organizational and time management strategies, ways to succeed, and institutional resources for trouble-shooting technology problems, writing papers, and resolving other course-related issues (Liu & Kaye, 2016; Sorenson & Baylen, 2009). Students drop out when the reality of the academic demands of online learning clashes with their prior misconceptions of online learning being easier than classroom (Zawacki-Richter & Anderson, 2014). They usually hold jobs and often have parenting demands and need the time flexibility that online courses allow (Ertmer et al., 2007; Pavlis-Korres & Leftheriotou, 2016; Woods, 2016). Early frequent contact can get students on track and reduce future interaction workload (Angelino et al., 2007; Estes, 2016).

Without feedback, students can feel disconnected from the course (Ertmer et al., 2007). If they do not get quick feedback, many will send repeated e-mails asking for it (Sorensen & Baylen, 2011). Timely responses cut back on those kinds of e-mails, keep students more engaged in learning, and guide them in how to improve. So give timely, meaningful, positive, nonthreatening, and constructive feedback to students on their assignments, e-mails, postings, and tests to scaffold their learning (Sorensen & Baylen, 2011; Grandzol & Grandzol, 2006; Kelly, 2014). Common time frames for feedback include forty-eight hours for e-mails and a week for assignments, but they may vary with the type of assignment and schedule changes.

In discussions, formative feedback informs students where they hit the mark and what requires improvement (Knowlton, 2009). For example, Michelle Drouin e-mails her students privately right after their first and subsequent academic discussion (Drouin & Van Gorder, 2015). She prepares ahead of time the messages that she will send to the top performer, the bottom performer, and those in between and then adapts each message to the quality of each student's posting. In this way, top performers receive affirmation that they are on track, and the bottom and in-between performers receive guidance on what to do to improve their future posts. For quizzes and tests, you usually can preset automated feedback in the learning management system (LMS) for correct and incorrect responses, or use flash cards and crossword puzzles where students can self-check their responses on their own.

Exhibit 6.2 provides recommendations for providing feedback to students based on principles of learning from cognitive science (see also chapter 4).

Exhibit 6.2: Instructor Feedback to Students

- Give feedback through multiple technology channels.
- Preload feedback for quizzes and tests for correct and incorrect answers and set the timing for delivery to the students. What you write in the feedback for correct versus incorrect answers will guide the students in their learning. You can set up reflective feedback for free-response quizzes, too, such as, "If your answer includes _____, then you are on track. If you left out any of these, then review _____."
- Praise effort, and guide students on how to close the gap between current and desired performance.
- For essays and papers, concentrate on major writing issues such as content, reasoning, and organization and less on style and grammar. You may need to provide further clarification and examples of desired products. Consider making a follow-up assignment in which students paraphrase or summarize your feedback back to you.
- When giving feedback in discussion forums, use your messages to stimulate further discussion and guide student thinking. Stick with the role of facilitator, and avoid dominating the discussion. Too many of your words can shut down the students' words.

Prompt students to self-assess their responsiveness, participation, and performance. Reverse the feedback loop by asking students to formatively evaluate the course design and teaching. Their feedback carries tremendous value, especially when launching a course for the first time. You gain insight from their perspective into what works well, what does not work so well, and what they would want to change in some way. (You need not make every change they ask for, but do explain why you will not make it.) In addition, it is another way for you to interact with them. Questionnaires, surveys, discussion forums, and reflective logs can help collect student feedback (Goodson, 2004c). Limit options to those that guarantee students' anonymity. For a new course, check the web pulse between the third and the sixth weeks. Ask questions as simple as, "What do you like most?" "What do you like least?" and "What would you change?" Or solicit students' perceptions about and reactions to what they are learning.

■ STUDENT-CONTENT INTERACTION

Interaction with content paves the way for successful learning (Liu & Kaye, 2016; Sadik & Reisman, 2009), and some evidence indicates it is as important as, or more important than, student-instructor interaction (Ekwunife-Orakwue & Teng, 2014; Ramos & Yudko, 2008; Zimmerman, 2012). But students place a high value on their time and will not access content that they think they do not need (Murray, Pérez, Geist, & Hedrick, 2013). The LMS offers many pathways to a content source, but a single, clear path works best (see chapter 3). Students' interaction with content through various technologies (e.g., publisher online materials, an e-textbook, discussion forums, or other online software) needs to be clean and lean, or they will be less likely to use it. Strategic selection of content to keep content lean will allow more time for meaningful interactions. Content must be relevant, accurate, useful, and complete enough to address the learning outcomes in the course, and no more (Murray et al., 2013). If certain content does not map directly onto the outcomes, leave it out.

Content Guidance for Students

While students themselves must interact with and process the content, they need guidance—for example (Reisetter & Boris, 2009; Sadik & Reisman, 2009):

- A chance to browse and see the organization of the lesson or module before tackling it
- Explicit expectations for what they have to learn how to do with the content
- A readable and understandable textbook
- Links to previous related lessons or materials
- Interactive visuals
- Access to relevant library materials
- Links to supplemental information available within a lesson or weekly folder rather than outside the folder
- Automated feedback in interactive practice sessions and quizzes to inform them of their progress

The following example illustrates the implementation of most of these strategies. For her nutrition course at Purdue University Fort Wayne, Linda Lolkus selected a quality textbook with interactive, visually rich publisher materials that provided automated feedback, followed by a discussion allowing for additional feedback. She aligned student learning activities with the textbook structure (Goodson, 2016b), as illustrated in one of the study guides:

READ IT
- Access and read Chapter 2 of your textbook.
- Review the learning objectives for the chapter.
- Review the *Top Ten Points to Remember*.

SEE IT
- Nutrition Animations
- Review *Overview of Digestion and Absorption*.

STUDY IT
- Review Study Guide for Chapter 3.

DO IT
- NutriTools
- Review *Build a Sandwich* then complete *Build a Sandwich Assignment*.
- Review *Digestion and Absorption* then complete the *Overview of Digestion and Absorption Assignment*.

DISCUSS IT
- Complete Week 2A *Probiotics* discussion.

Lolkus gave her students the choice of using the print textbook or the e-textbook of *MyNutritionLab* with *MyDietAnalysis*. She gave details on each edition (author, title, ISBN) and the option for purchasing only the access code for the lab if a student preferred to buy a used textbook. Both textbook formats were well designed to engage students in highly relevant active learning for achieving the course outcomes.

Other possible activities that foster content interaction include virtual labs and field trips, role playing, problem and project-based learning, debates, expert panels, structured discussions, writing assignments, and website building (Sorenson & Baylen, 2009). We list online resources for some of these activities in the "Web Resources for Content Interaction" section in this chapter.

The following conditions also support student interactions with content (Helms et al., 2011; Murray et al., 2013; Rourke & Lewer-Fletcher, 2016; Thurmond & Wambach, 2004).

- Ongoing interactions with the content such as just-in-time content for certain assignments or discussions rather than large chunks of content dumping
- Consistent course content structure, similarity of format for content presentation, and simple access to content
- Enough time for students to study the content before asking them to use it
- Explicit alignment of content with learning outcomes to make its purpose and value clear to students
- Opportunities for analysis and critical thinking about content, as in reflective journals and analyses of the blog postings of others
- Points or grades for recalling and using content, such as a graded quiz, discussion, or assignment

Content Presentation

Interactive content presentation encompasses various media representations, interactive technologies, carefully chosen social media, study aids, and connections with subject librarians. A straight presentation, no matter how beautiful, is not an interaction, and students can easily turn it off or skip it. Make your short lectures interactive by interspersing student activities and holding students accountable for completing them by showing or submitting some kind of work. When students must do research, try to embed a link to the library and the librarian for your specialty area so they have easy, convenient access to the materials they will need and scheduled appointments with the librarian.

Exhibit 6.3 shows the best strategies for content presentation based on the principles of learning from cognitive science (see also chapter 4).

Exhibit 6.3: Content Presentation and Interactions

- Present online content cleanly and simply in whatever medium you use. Get right to the point, and do not elaborate more than is necessary. Highlight the main points, and avoid extraneous audio, graphics, and text.
- To reduce cognitive load, reduce the number of pieces of new information by collapsing them into categories or logical groups; also see chapter 3 on coherence. Whenever possible, try to help your students categorize material.
- Build a complex lesson in shorter segments rather than as one long, continuous lesson.
- Launch new topics with a graphic organizer of their sequenced components. (See the "Visuals and Media" section in this chapter.)
- For the content files you build, use headings and subheadings to organize content.
- For readings, avoid assigning too much text at one time.
- Model procedures or methods you want students to use, such as in a video or podcast.
- Show students examples of exemplary and unacceptable student work.
- Explain abstract content with practical examples.
- Encourage positive emotions about the content by finding ways to display enthusiasm and drama.
- Use stories and examples, such as illustrative anecdotes, case studies, and problem-based learning. Include different contexts, conditions, disciplines, and levels of abstraction to help students arrive at the most robust and useful generalizations and conclusions.
- Show students worked examples (problem solutions) to start and only partially worked examples as they progress.
- When choosing the textbook, whether print or electronic, evaluate the quality of content, the fit to your learning outcomes, the ease of use, the format and layout, and the quality of interactivity. Personally verify a publisher's marketing claims for the functionality and ease of use.

Visuals and Media

Following the principles of learning from cognitive science (see chapter 4), present content and have students interact with it in more than one modality whenever appropriate. Students value and learn more from engaging, media-rich content presentations (Brewer & Brewer, 2015; Clark & Mayer, 2011). However, keep in mind that "media mix is not mind rich" (Mayer & Clark, 2013), and often less is more. Kilburn, Henckell, and Starrett (2016) provide examples of productive ways to use images and media:

- Short text posts, such as status updates (twitter.com, blogger.com, edublogs.org, classblogmeister.com)
- Long text messages, such as reports, research, papers, or reflections (mediawiki.org, facebook.com, wordpress.com)
- Photos, such as those of field trips, live research, or depictions of topics of study (flickr.com, instagram .com, facebook.com, pinterest.com)
- Video, such as short clips from a smartphone or camera (youtube.com, vimeo.com, vine.co, instagram.com)
- Audio, such as recordings of a talk, interview, or podcast (audioboom.com)
- Portfolios, such as those to display one's work for future employers (linkedin.com)

Images enliven content and enhance immediate learning as well as long-term memory (Nilson, 2007). Create your own or use images from your library or free image collections such as these:

- EveryStockPhoto: http://www.everystockphoto.com/
- PublicDomainPictures: http://www.publicdomainpictures.net/
- Free Images: http://www.freeimages.co.uk/
- Free Images: http://www.freeimages.com/
- 4Free Photos: http://4freephotos.com/
- Free Digital Photos: http://www.freedigitalphotos.net/
- Public Domain: http://www.public-domain-photos.com/
- Flckr Creative Commons: https://www.flickr.com/creativecommons/

Videos are also powerful learning tools when you give students opportunities to engage with them. Make your own videos, or pull them from your library or other sources such as YouTube (E. Moore, 2013). Here are some activities to make them active learning vehicles:

- Distribute questions for students to answer before, during, and after the viewing.
- Use a video to present a controversy for a discussion in which students must choose a position and explain their reasoning.
- Provide links to multiple videos, and have students compare their strengths and weaknesses or choose one for analysis.
- Send students on a web hunt for videos to support different points of view and post them with annotations on a class or group discussion forum.

Many course materials with dynamic student-content interactions are readily available. For example, college algebra courses use plenty of open educational resources (OERs) (Hilton, Gaudet, Clark, Robinson, & Wiley, 2013). (You can read about the OER university and their creators at https://oeru.org/.) These course materials include tutorials, quizzes, audio and video materials, images, lessons, textbooks, scenarios and case studies, software, games, animations, and maps—for example:

- Introductory Algebra: Open Educational Resource Project, Fall 2015: https://sccmath.wordpress.com /mat09x-fall-2015/
- MAT12x—Intermediate Algebra, Spring 2015, Open Educational Resource Project: https://sccmath .wordpress.com/mat12x-fall-2014/

- Arithmetic, Algebra, and Trigonometry, Open Educational Resource Materials: https://sccmath .wordpress.com/oers16/
- Internet Mathematics Assessment System (homework delivery and automatic grading): http://www .imathas.com/
- Arithmetic and Algebra Workbooks and Exams: https://sccmath.wordpress.com/

The last section of this chapter lists other OERs available for free in different disciplines.

Exhibit 6.4 furnishes guidelines for using visuals and media based on the principles of learning from cognitive science (see also chapter 4).

Exhibit 6.4: Visuals and Media

- Do not rely only on text-based presentations and readings. Instead, find or create media, varying them among videos, audio, graphics, and text. Give students the opportunities to process your online content in at least two or three modalities involving multiple senses. Allow them to read, hear, talk, write, see, draw, think, act, and feel new material, involving as many parts of the brain in their learning as you can. Look for what can engage students emotionally as well as cognitively. (Accessibility guidelines require you to make text material available in both audio and text formats as well as visual whenever possible; see chapter 7.)
- Display graphics (e.g., pictures, photographs, diagrams, flowcharts, animations, videos, concept maps, mind maps) as much as possible to illustrate phenomena, principles, examples, processes, procedures, and causal and conceptual relationships. Accompany them with relevant labels and descriptions.
- Avoid dense text in slides. Reserve slides for what the students need to see, such as pictures, photographs, diagrams, flowcharts, and other visuals. Use relevant and interesting images.
- Explain graphics with audio narration or written text but not both. Encourage students to either listen to the audio recording or read the text, but not both at the same time. (Make both formats available.)
- Create or find presentations with a visible speaker using an informal, conversational style.
- In your personal recordings, vary your facial expressions, vocal intonations, speaking pace, and movements as far as the technology allows.
- Produce videos or podcasts of your lectures in short installments, and select similarly short presentations from other sources (students view up to six minutes), reserving longer ones for powerful, authentic, and professional videos (such as TED Talks, which run no more than eighteen minutes).

Content Misconceptions

Faulty mental models interfere with learning because, as "prior knowledge," they cannot accommodate the correct content. Many instructors face the challenge of convincing students to give up their misconceptions and replace them with valid models. Exhibit 6.5 recommends ways to help them get past those faulty mental models in consonance with the principles of learning from cognitive science (see chapter 4).

Exhibit 6.5: Faulty Mental Models

- If you do not know your students' mental models of your content, find out. For example, ask about how they think some phenomenon emerges or works, or give them a multiple-choice test with distracters that reflect possible or likely misconceptions.
- Once you know your students' faulty mental models, explain or demonstrate how your discipline's models provide better explanations. Help students question their misconceptions with demonstrations, animation, videos, and simulations. Integrate challenges to create impasses in their current mental models—that is, contradictions, conflicts, anomalies, uncertainties, and ambiguities, which in turn stimulate curiosity, inquiry, questioning, problem solving, and deep reasoning to restore "cognitive equilibrium." Give students opportunities to test out their misconceptions against your discipline's models.
- Once you know that your students have a valid mental model, relate new knowledge to it as much as possible.

Content Practice

Teaching involves not only presenting content but also giving students practice working with it. Some kinds of practice are more effective than others (Dunlosky, Rawson, Marsh, Nathan, & Willingham, 2013):

- *Highly effective:* practice testing and distributed (spaced) practice
- *Moderately effective:* elaborative interrogation, self-explanation, and interleaved practice
- *Modestly effective:* writing of summaries from text, highlighting or underlining the text while reading, associating key words and images as aids to remembering the text, rereading text

Incorporating the highly and moderately effective techniques into student-content interactions should advance student learning across platforms:

- *Practice testing:* Self-testing or taking practice tests over new material. *Examples:* Free-recall-based self-testing, flash cards, low-stakes pop quizzes, open- or closed-book retrieval of information, free or cued recall, short-answer questions, multiple-choice inference-based questions, and practice testing with feedback.
- *Distributed (spaced) practice:* Following a schedule of practice that spreads out study activities over time. *Examples:* Multiple repetitions after initial learning, opportunities to go beyond recall to deeper, conceptual levels of learning.
- *Elaborative interrogation:* Generating an explanation for why a stated fact or concept is valid. *Examples:* Why does it make sense that . . . ? Why is this true?
- *Self-explanation:* Explaining how new information is related to known information or explaining the steps taken during problem solving. *Example:* Explain what the sentence means to you. That is, what new information does the sentence contain for you? And how does it relate to what you already know?
- *Interleaved practice:* Following a schedule of practice that integrates previously learned material with new material (e.g., "old" problems with new ones) in a single study session; alternating practice on different kinds of problems.

In another type of practice, students reflect on and self-assess their learning. This has high impact when it prompts students to think critically about their learning process (Nilson, 2013). It also supports the student's cognitive presence, which is so important in an online course (Luyegu, 2016). Since most students are unfamiliar with reflection, providing criteria for and models of what you expect will improve results. Use course tools such as journals and practice tests, or make productive use of microblogging tools such as Twitter, Jaikku, Tumblr, MySay, Hictu, and Edmodo (Kilburn et al., 2016).

Exhibit 6.6 lists ways to build effective practice into course activities based on the principles of learning from cognitive science (see chapter 4).

Exhibit 6.6: Practice Activities

- Give quizzes and exams as often as you can. Taking a test is a powerful form of practice (Karpicke & Roediger, 2008) that helps students evaluate their learning progress and become self-regulating (Nilson, 2013; Soderstrom & Bjork, 2014).
- Integrate the right level of challenge into practice activities. When students have to work harder to learn material, they generate multiple retrieval paths and stretch their abilities. Asking students to take a quiz, solve "old" problems along with new ones, generate explanations, or relate new to previously learned knowledge supply that challenge.
- Ask reflective free-response questions, such as, "What is the most important thing you learned?" or, "What is the most surprising?"
- Ask students to describe their preparation, process, or steps for doing assignments.
- After a simulation or role play, ask students to describe and evaluate their goals, decisions, strategies, and responses to the actions of other students. Grade their analyses pass/fail with nominal points for passing.
- Give students informal opportunities for self-assessment, such as flash cards or crossword puzzles with answer keys in Respondus (http://www.respondus.com/).
- Give step-by-step hints and feedback to guide students' early practice.
- Create opportunities for reflective writing about a topic's importance, deeper meaning, and connection to what students already know or believe to be true. Collect and give feedback on student responses.
- Have students review and retrieve previously learned content at spaced intervals and in the process of learning new material.
- Guide students in retrieval practice. Have them read, listen to, or watch the assignment, then free-recall as much as they can by writing it down or reciting it aloud, and finally review the assignment to find what they forgot, missed, or recalled incorrectly.
- Give students the opportunity to correct their errors and redo the problem or exercise.

Content Discussions

While you may think of discussion forums as only a student-to-student interaction format—and they are indeed a major focus of the next section on student-student interaction—they can also engage students in the content. You just need to set up clear expectations from the beginning that students will have to supply sound evidence and reasoning for their claims (Brewer & Brewer, 2015; Gilbert & Dabbagh, 2005; Helms et al., 2011; Woods, 2016). You can guide them by asking the following types of questions to advance their thinking (MacKnight, 2000):

- *Clarification:* "Would you put it another way?" "Would you give an example?"
- *Query about initial question or topic:* "What does this question assume?"
- *Probe assumptions:* "What could we assume instead?" "Why do you think the assumption holds here?"
- *Probe reasons and evidence:* "What are the reasons for your position?" "What is the evidence to support your claim?"
- *Probe origin or source:* "Where did you get this idea?" "What caused you to feel this way?"
- *Probe implications and consequences:* "If this is the case, what else must be true?" "What would be the effects?"
- *Probe viewpoints or perspectives:* "What is an alternative opinion?" "How would other groups of people respond? Why?" "What would someone who disagrees say?"

Content Assessments

Chapter 3 addressed assessment in depth, so our treatment of the topic here will be brief. Assessments should indeed be a learning experience for students in which they interact with the content. Of course, when you assess students' mastery of content, you are really interested in assessing what students can *do* with it. This doing is built into the learning outcomes. Before you design a test or assignment, review the learning outcomes because they should dictate your assessments. As we stated in chapter 3, if you want your students to be able to do X, Y, and Z, assess their ability to do X, Y, and Z. Therefore, at least some of the questions and tasks in your assessments should require explanatory, inferential, analytical, evaluative, or creative thinking depending on the course outcomes.

Consider having students develop high-level thinking questions on a reading, video, or other content presentation. Teach them the higher-level cognitive operations, and show them model questions. When they know you might use them on a quiz or test or fashion them into an assignment or discussion prompt, they will be motivated to submit good questions.

Exhibit 6.7 lists best practices for effective assessments based on the principles of learning from cognitive science (see chapter 4).

Exhibit 6.7: Effective Assessment

- Plan on giving a comprehensive final integrative assignment or exam, and tell your students from the beginning that you will do so. This strategy will discourage students from forgetting the content you presented earlier in the course.
- Provide plenty of assessment opportunities, including low-stakes quizzes and exams, practice tests, and homework assignments that can tell students how much they are really learning and give them retrieval practice.
- Ask students to explain what the content means on a deeper level and why it is important.
- For the most important material, create test questions that require free recall, such as short-answer items, essay questions, and problems to solve. But ask students to do more than just recall. Ask them to do whatever your learning outcomes specify they should be able to do with the content. Tell

---

students in advance what material merits short answers, essays, complete problem solutions, and the like so they will study accordingly.

- Make assessment criteria explicit and specific. Delineate what a student product should accomplish, what elements it should contain, and what questions it should answer. Furnish them with models of excellent, fair, and unacceptable work. You might set up a discussion forum to allow students to ask about the criteria and models you provide.
- Remind students to space their pre-exam study sessions over several days and get a good night's sleep the night before a test instead of cramming.
- For assessing group work, have some kind of peer performance evaluation in which students assess their own contributions as well as those of their teammates. (See chapter 3.)

Design one or two assignments to take advantage of available technology—for example (adapted from Kirsner, Teem, & Underwood, 2011; Pérez & Hurysz, 2011; Stowell, 2011; Yandell & Bailey, 2011):

- Invite students to review existing wikis, edit existing articles, post new ones to a wiki site, create wikis with the tool built into your LMS, or with Wikispaces: http://www.wikispaces.com/
- Create your own podcasts; then have students create their own podcasts using a free audio recorder and editor such as Audacity: https://sourceforge.net/projects/audacity/
- Submit podcasts to the iTunes directory for your course; also see Apple's podcast resources: http://www.apple.com/podcasting
- Have students find relevant videos using search tools such as:
  - Google video: http://video.google.com/
  - YouTube: https://www.youtube.com/
- Select and assign screencasts (recordings of activities on computer screen, often with audio added) with tools such as these:
  - Screencast.com: http://www.screencast.com/
  - Mathcasts: http://www.mathcasts.org/
  - Create your own screencasts to highlight content, address concepts or problems, show demonstrations, or answer student questions. Students generally enjoy screencasts and find them helpful. Follow up with written assignments in which students explain what they learned from the screencasts.
- Have students create blogs on the content with tools such as these:
  - Blogger: http://www.blogger.com
  - Wordpress: http://www.wordpress.com
- Design an assignment, possibly a group assignment, that makes use of Google Docs, sheets, or slides: https://support.google.com/docs/answer/49008?hl=en
- Create and send students on a competitive knowledge hunt, scavenger hunt, treasure hunt, or webquest: http://www.webquest.org/
- Select a cluster of websites to prompt students to write an analysis or reflection on an issue related to the content.
- Have students use search engines to find and analyze blogs related to the content such as Find Blogs: http://www.findblogs.com/

- Assign simulations that assess students' facility applying the content, such as PHET at University of Colorado: https://phet.colorado.edu/en/simulations/category/physics/
- Give digital photography or video assignments in which students can show their ability to apply or demonstrate the content, and store their photographs on sites such as Flickr: http://www.flickr.com/
- Have students design concept maps using tools such as these:
  ○ Inspiration: http://www.inspiration.com/Inspiration/ (modestly priced)
  ○ Bubbl.us: http://www.bubbl.us/ (free)
- Guide students in creating their personal websites that link to content-relevant sites with tools such as My Yahoo: https://my.yahoo.com

  For more ideas, explore these:

- Edutools: http://www.edu-tools.info/
- Google tools: http://www.google.com/about/products/
- Google Hangouts: https://hangouts.google.com/
- teachweb2.0: http://teachweb2.wikispaces.com/

Web Resources for Content Interaction

Whether for content presentations, visuals, media, practice, or assignments, the web offers an amazing array of free digital teaching and learning resources. This section and Shank (2014) list those of exceptional value. The following types of resources are available:

- Course materials, including podcasts and videos of lectures
- Realistic demonstrations, animated or on video
- Performances (musical, dramatic, dance, and sport)
- Virtual science laboratories for hazardous or costly procedures and experiments
- Virtual field trips
- Case studies and problem-based learning problems
- Simulations for many subjects (e.g., business, management, history, sociology, urban planning, political science, environmental studies, and biology)
- Science, technology, engineering, and mathematics (STEM) problems for students to solve
- Drills and exercises for remediation, practice, or review (e.g., mathematics, reading, and foreign languages)
- Teacher resources for K–12 and special education (presentations, exercises, and other activities)
- Tests of greater or lesser validity on temperament and personality, aptitudes, career preferences, political ideology, leadership style, team member style, and other human dimensions, many free
- Multimedia materials useful for research

Instructional Podcasts, Videos, and Text Materials

Below are some free instructional resources, the first few for podcasts and the rest for videos and text:

- iTunes: https://itunes.apple.com/us/genre/podcasts/id26?mt=2/
- iTunesU—thousands of podcasts of varying length on hundreds of subject: https://itunes.apple.com/us/genre/itunes-u/id40000000?mt=10/

- Learn Out Loud—a podcast search tool: http://www.learnoutloud.com/
- American Rhetoric—hundreds of speeches mainly from real-world politics and movies: http://www.americanrhetoric.com/
- Anneberg Media—specializing in the arts, literature, language, history, math, social and natural sciences: http://www.learner.org/
- Artbabble—specializing in art and architecture: http://www.artbabble.org/partner/national-gallery-art-washington/
- Khan Academy—over three thousand lessons, mostly in the STEM fields: http://www.khanacademy.org/
- MITOpenCourseware—lectures and materials from over twenty-two hundred courses: https://ocw.mit.edu/index.htm
- Online Books Page—free access to over 2 million books: http://www.digital.library.upenn.edu/books/
- OpenYale—lectures and materials from selected introductory courses: http://oyc.yale.edu/
- TED Talks—many hundreds of highly polished lectures of about twenty minutes or less on a wide range of subjects: http://www.ted.com/
- TEDEd—TED talks with short lessons ("flips"): http://ed.ted.com/
- Videolectures—full-length faculty lectures on many subjects at http://videolectures.net/
- YouTube sites:
  - YouTube Home: https://www.youtube.com/
  - YouTube EDU: http://www.youtube.com/edu/
  - TeacherTube: http://www.teachertube.com/
  - Utubersity—lessons, lectures, sports, media broadcasts, interviews, and performances (musical, dance, opera, drama, and comedy): http://utubersidad.com/en/
  - YouTube CrashCourse—fifteen- to eighteen-minute videos on physics, astronomy, anatomy and physiology, economics, philosophy, literature, history, political science, and computer games: https://www.youtube.com/user/crashcourse/videos/
- Access to free textbooks in every major academic and professional disciplines at these sites:
  - Open-Course Library, Creative Commons—free to download and edit: http://opencourselibrary.org/
  - Open Textbook Content: http://www.collegeopentextbooks.org/textbook-listings/
  - Open Education Consortium: http://www.openedconsortium.org/
  - Open Stax: http://openstaxcollege.org/books/
  - Open Stax small modules: http://cnx.org/
  - Open Stax CNS Library: https://cnx.org/browse
  - Open Textbook Library: http://open.umn.edu/opentextbooks/
  - Saylor Academy Open Textbooks: http://www.saylor.org/books/
  - Open Culture, cultural and educational media: http://www.openculture.com/free_textbooks/
  - BookBoon: http://www.bookboon.com/
  - The Global Text Project: http://globaltext.terry.uga.edu/books/
  - IOER Research Search: http://ioer.ilsharedlearning.org/search/

Multimedia Research Collections

Your institution may have a library collection of multimedia materials or licensed access to such collections, such as Artstor. In addition, here are some extensive cross-disciplinary collections of well-established, research-worthy multimedia sites that you can use for lesson planning and send your students to use:

- Calisphere—a huge collection of websites, scholarly materials, images, electronic books, data, and statistics: https://calisphere.org/
- Creative Common CC Search—a searchable collection of millions of images, music, and videos: http://search.creativecommons.org/
- CSERDA Metadata Catalog—a searchable repository of web-based teaching materials for mathematics, computer science, and the sciences: http://www.shodor.org/refdesk/Catalog/
- Google Custom Search (University Learning=OCW+OER=Free): https://cse.google.com/cse/home?cx=009190243792682903990:e40rcqv1bbo
- Internet Archive—millions of websites, software, and digitized cultural artifacts (images, audio files, animations); also courses, study guides, assignments, books, and recorded lectures under Education (aka the WayBack Machine): https://archive.org/
- Lumen Learning—access to almost sixty academic online courses: https://courses.lumenlearning.com/catalog/lumen/
- MERLOT (Multimedia Educational Resource for Learning and Online Teaching)—tens of thousands of annotated links to free learning materials, most of them peer reviewed, including entire courses, databases, presentations, and collections: http://www.merlot.org/
- National Science Foundation Internet Library—rich and technologically sophisticated instructional materials for the sciences, engineering, mathematics, public health, economics, and other fields: https://nsdl.oercommons.org/
- Open Learning Initiative—access to over two dozen online courses and course materials in a wide range of academic fields: http://oli.cmu.edu/
- New York Public Library Digital Collections—a vast collection of culturally significant images, audio files, videos, print and audio books, articles, maps, DVDs, menus, and research-worthy databases and archives: http://www.nypl.org/collections/
- Notre Dame University's OpenCourseWare—lecture transcripts, syllabi, and other instructional materials in history and the social sciences: http://online.nd.edu/ocw/
- Smithsonian Institution—virtual access to the world's largest museum (actually over a dozen museums), nine research centers, and the National Zoo: http://www.si.edu/
- Temoa OER Portal—hundreds of thousands of online educational materials of all types in all subjects: http://www.temoa.info/
- The Valley of the Shadow—primary sources (letters, diaries, census and government records, newspapers, and speeches) documenting the lives of Northerners and Southerners in two counties during the Civil War and Reconstruction eras: http://valley.lib.virginia.edu/

Learning Objects

These are self-contained, reusable digital lessons on specific topics, the best of which are animated, interactive, and truly multimedia. Students can learn on their own and at their own pace by playing or running them any number of times. Both faculty and students perceive learning objects to be powerful teaching and learning tools (Ip, Morrison, & Currie, 2001; Moore, 2003–2004; Shank, 2014), and one study reports that they most benefit students who need the most help (Biktimirov & Nilson, 2007).

Learning objects are housed in open learning object repositories, many of them searchable by discipline. In some cases, you must join an online community, but this entails no cost. The last one listed even provides annotated links to additional repositories:

- MERLOT (Multimedia Educational Resource for Learning and Online Teaching)—many thousands of interactive case studies, simulations, games, and animations for every discipline: http://www.merlot.org/
- OER (Open Educational Resources) Commons—close to thirty thousand materials, many interactive and animated, for college level and above (much more for K–12) for every discipline: http://www.oercommons.org/
- JORUM—close to twenty thousand materials, many interactive and animated, for college-level and continuing education, almost all unique to this site: http://www.jorum.ac.uk/
- Brock University—twenty high-quality simulations, games, animations, and exercises for English, finance, German, management, mathematics, and psychology: http://www.brocku.ca/learningobjects/flash_content/
- University of Wisconsin, Milwaukee Center for International Education—learning objects for global studies and a few more for the social sciences, plus an annotated listing of dozens of learning object repositories across the disciplines: https://www4.uwm.edu/cie/learning_objects.cfm?gid=47

Websites for STEM Activities

STEM disciplines often require laboratory and problem-solving experiences that are difficult to transfer to the online environment. The sites listed here offer the best virtual alternatives:

Physics

- PhET—physics simulations at Colorado University: https://phet.colorado.edu/
- AP Physics site by Delores Gende with links to many virtual labs: http://apphysicsb.homestead.com/
- Technology Enabled Active Learning (TEAL), MIT iCampus: https://icampus.mit.edu/projects/teal/
- Online Labs in Physics: http://onlinelabs.in/physics

Chemistry

- Resources to Teach and Learn Chemistry: http://www.chemcollective.org/
- Online Labs in Chemistry: http://onlinelabs.in/chemistry
- Chemistry Education Applets, University of California: http://www.chem.uci.edu/undergrad/applets/

Biology

- Biointeractive Virtual Labs: http://www.hhmi.org/biointeractive/explore-virtual-labs
- Online Labs in Biology: http://onlinelabs.in/biology
- McGraw-Hill Biology Lab: http://www.mhhe.com/biosci/genbio/virtual_labs_2K8/
- General Biology Labs, Rutgers: http://bio.rutgers.edu/~gb102/virtuallabs_102.html
- The Virtual Biology Labs, Rutgers: http://bio.rutgers.edu

- Pearson, The Biology Place: http://www.phschool.com/science/biology_place/labbench/
- The Molecular Workbench Database: http://workbench.concord.org/database/

Zoology

- iExploreSTEM: Zoology Activities: https://iexplorestem.org/zoology-activities

Human Anatomy

- Online Labs in Anatomy: http://onlinelabs.in/anatomy/
- NOVA Map of the Human Heart: http://www.pbs.org/wgbh/nova/body/map-human-heart.html

Geography

- Make Your Own Virtual Field Trip: http://www.nmgeoed.org/google-earth-virtual-field-trips.html
- Discovery Education Virtual Field Trips: http://www.discoveryeducation.com/Events/virtual-field-trips/explore/
- Virtual Field Trips, iLearn Technology: http://ilearntechnology.com/?tag=virtual-field-trips

Geology

- Online Learning Labs in Geology: http://onlinelabs.in/geology

Engineering

- Virtual Lab, Johns Hopkins University: http://pages.jh.edu/~virtlab/virtlab.html
- UVA Virtual Lab Website: http://www.virlab.virginia.edu/VL/contents.htm

Statistics

- Random: Probability, Mathematical Statistics, Stochastic Processes: http://www.math.uah.edu/stat/
- Rice Virtual Lab in Statistics: http://onlinestatbook.com/rvls.html

Multidisciplinary STEM sites

- Planet Seed: https://www.pinterest.com/pin/55943220348648276/
- MERLOT: https://www.merlot.org/merlot/index.htm
- Virtual Laboratory, Colorado: http://virtuallaboratory.colorado.edu/
- Interactive Experiments, University of Oregon: http://jersey.uoregon.edu/
- Interactivate, Shodar: http://www.shodor.org/interactivate/
- SERC Pedagogy in Action: http://serc.carleton.edu/sp/library/pogil/examples.html
- Instructor's guide to POGIL (Process Oriented Guided Inquiry Learning): http://www.pogil.org/resources/implementation/instructors-guide/

■ STUDENT-STUDENT INTERACTION

Meaningful student-student interactions can involve sharing, discussion, debate, collaboration, peer review, or peer instruction on any of several whole-class or small-group communication platforms. These interactions and the sense of class community do not depend on whether communication is asynchronous, as in discussion forums, or synchronous, as with chats and videoconferencing (Liu et al., 2009; Orellana, 2009). Factors that *do* make a difference are (Cho & Cho, 2014; Sadik & Reisman, 2009; Zheng & Smaldino, 2009):

- Students' preparation for the interaction
- Number of respectable responses to the questions
- Guidelines for participation
- Alignment of the activity with the learning outcomes
- Clarity of deadlines for posting
- Stability of the technology

To help students develop their own learning community, encourage them to post personal profiles, meet and greet in an online café, reflect on and evaluate their discussions, create their own special interest and study groups, and participate in group projects that require use of content and negotiation. Shallow interactions do not support such community (Ertmer et al., 2007; Liu et al., 2009; Peterson, 2016). Online students in small groups develop more sociability, commitment, and closeness to classmates (Akcaoglu & Lee, 2016), so consider dividing large classes into smaller groups (Peterson, 2016). A "study buddy" strategy also works well (Madland & Richards, 2016). In addition, make thoughtful use of technologies within and outside the course LMS, such as GoogleDocs, wikis, blogs, and Twitter, to promote a sense of online community (Abdelmalak, 2015). Such tools allow students to benefit from others' perspectives.

The rest of this section examines the various forms of student-student interaction and how best to set them up and, where appropriate, grade them.

Peer Review

Peer review can deepen learning and help students improve their work when you follow these recommendations (Ertmer et al., 2007):

- Explain how the peer review process works and why it is worthwhile.
- Give models and examples of effective feedback.
- Provide guidelines on how to give clear, constructive feedback, such as giving positive feedback first.
- Ensure that the peer review process is easy to use.

In chapter 3 we mentioned a few more guidelines for effective peer review and will elaborate here. Do not ask students to actually evaluate each other's work the way we evaluate it. They are uncomfortable doing this as well as ill equipped because they have not yet acquired professional judgment. In addition, their attempts at evaluation tend to be too brief and disconnected from the author's text. Rather, ask students to analyze or react to their peers' work: to find the thesis statement, the evidence, and the main conclusion, or to identify the "strongest sentence," a particularly persuasive piece of evidence, and a sentence or two that the reviewer had to read more than once to understand. The responses provide the author with the most useful information possible: how the reviewers received and experienced the piece of work. If they did not pick out the intended thesis statement or conclusion, the author then realizes the need to communicate more clearly (Nilson, 2003). At the same time, the author does not feel criticized or discredited.

Class Discussions

The purpose of discussion is to generate a fruitful, constructive exchange of different ideas and points of view, all backed by an argument or evidence and leading to a decision, judgment, recommendation, or solution. Therefore, the questions should be open-ended and have multiple respectable answers. To motivate sufficient student participation in an online discussion, Helms et al. (2011) suggest these strategies:

- Create unique topics across the course.
- Create topics relevant to assignments, such as discussing ideas for upcoming papers.
- Make it easy and clear for students to get into the discussion area and make their contributions.
- Make only some of the postings compulsory.
- Provide detailed instructions and exemplars of productive contributions.
- Develop and use clear, simple rubrics to grade the quality of contributions. One criterion should be posting contributions by your deadline.
- Facilitate the discussion to guide it, but avoid prominence.
- Show that you welcome open debate on any relevant contributions, even if they are controversial.
- Set up a system for responsible critique of contributions.
- For some discussions, require students to work together.

Here are some additional ways to get students to participate. Give them enough lead time to familiarize themselves with the content needed for the discussion. Ask them to give examples of concepts from their own experiences or examples from people they know. In this way, they add to the repertoire of examples. Give them a topic, and ask them to generate questions about it, requiring that no student duplicate any question already asked. Or assign only certain students to ask questions and others to answer. A student who asks a question becomes the leader of the discussion, offers resources such as web links, and at the end of the week gives the summary of the discussion (Sorensen & Baylen, 2011). Other students may send private e-mails with their personal reflections. Or require all students to answer at least one question with evidence added. Whether any of these strategies make sense depends on your purpose.

For one or more discussions, you can develop an expert panel for your course. Recruit a few colleagues and enroll them in a special discussion forum for two to three weeks (Bonk, 2013). Have students complete the appropriate readings, videos, or podcasts and discuss some of the issues in advance. Then have them prepare questions for the visiting experts. Afterward, post a summary of the important issues in the discussion. Veronika Ospina-Kammera used this technique in her course, Family Violence across the Lifespan (Goodson, 2004a). She posted six forums to capture important themes from a panel discussion for her students to review. Alternatively, you can have students identify and post such themes. Or set up the guest speakers' visit for a single session and use a conferencing tool that allows recording of the session to make it available for students in future semesters (Bonk, 2013).

To sustain discussions, direct students' attention as necessary to earlier relevant messages or current events (Ghadirian, Ayub, Bakar, & Hassanzadeh, 2016). In addition, encourage students to express themselves (Ross et al., 2013), summarize the discussion, and add knowledge resources to advance further reflection and learning (Hirumi, 2009; Liu et al., 2009). You may need to guide the interactions to better support problem solving and critical thinking (Kolloff, 2011). Without guidance and the right amount of intellectual challenge, students are more likely to engage in shallow discussions (Ramos & Yudko, 2008). But keep in mind that too much instructor presence will diminish student interactions.

To encourage deep learning, questions should require students to connect content and concepts beyond simple factual responses (Leflay & Groves, 2013). For example, Lolkus wanted her students to connect their discussion to the preparation activities she had assigned for the following week (Goodson, 2016b):

Week 2A Probiotics Discussion

WHAT TO DO: Click the title link above (*Week 2A Probiotics*). Then click the *Directions* "Thread." After selecting *Directions*, scroll down to view the directions. Click *Reply* and then post your answers to the discussion questions.
DUE: No later than 11:59 PM July 8. Postings after the deadline will not be counted.

After following those directions, students would then see the following directions:

Week 2A Probiotics Directions Thread

Probiotics: Do You Need Them? Probiotics are live microorganisms, usually bacteria, mainly found in cultured dairy foods. Some research indicates that probiotics can have health benefits. However, the research is not conclusive, and some experts feel adding probiotics to the diet is ineffective at best and possibly harmful at worst. Should you seek out fortified yogurt or probiotic supplements, or can you get along fine without them? Read the arguments in the textbook, then consider the critical thinking questions and decide for yourself.
1. Which is the most compelling argument for taking probiotics?
2. Which is the most compelling reason not to take them?
3. Do you think we know enough about probiotics to recommend them to the public? (Adapted from Blake, 2012)

In the classroom you may or may not grade discussions, but giving some points for online posts recognizes student effort and contributions. You may not want to require and rely on just the number of postings and replies. Instead, craft guidelines to focus student attention on what quality means (Abawajy, 2012; Jeong, 2014; Ramos & Yudko, 2008). For example, Jeong (2004) integrates self-reflection by requiring students to label the type of messages they post and allowing them to return at any time to correct errors in their labels. Jeong uses these symbols:

+ = support for a claim or statement

− = opposition to a claim or statement

ARG# = one argument (only one)

EXPL = additional support, clarification, elaboration

BUT = question or challenge to logic, validity, accuracy, plausibility

EVID = proof or evidence for validity of a claim, argument, or challenge

In deciding what to grade, consider whether an activity is something you would also grade in a face-to-face classroom. This can help determine whether to give just a few points or assign only "complete" or "incomplete" status, or whether an activity should be graded at all. For example, students' recording of notes in a journal area makes sense, especially if dealing with potentially sensitive issues, but they may merit only a few points when completed each week.

An efficient way to grade students' contributions to discussion is a participation portfolio (Division of Information Technology, University of Maryland Baltimore County, 2013), which has worked very well across the disciplines. At the beginning of the course, post a rubric defining quality contributions and replies; the web contains dozens of them. Students submit examples (specify how many) of their highest-quality contributions or replies every two to four weeks and "grade" them as a whole. Then accepting, raising, or lowering the grade and assessing student participation takes a fraction of the time that it would take to evaluate every post. (For more detailed instructions and a demonstration, go to http://doit.umbc .edu/itnm/managing-discussions/.)

To assess how far a discussion advances students' understanding of the content, you can ask them to post at the end of a discussion their answers to reflective questions like these (Herman & Nilson, in press): What are your five major take-aways from the discussion? What new or deeper understanding of the content did you gain from the discussion? How would you evaluate the quality of the contributions in general? What about your contributions specifically?

Group Work

Group discussions and projects work best when you make explicit what actions you expect from the members and the whole group (Wang, Chen, & Anderson, 2014); students will follow where you lead them. For group discussions, tell students what you want them to do. Do you want them to illustrate or apply concepts? Do you want them to connect the material to local issues, use reasoning, apply rules, solve problems, or make logical, evidence-based decisions? Guide them in finding their way through your topics and questions.

A simple group discussion requires very little setup on your part. But when you assemble groups for projects, you need to plan group membership, define group roles, incorporate individual and group accountability measures, and develop a strategy for assigning individual grades (Hirumi, 2009; McLaren, 2009; Sorensen & Baylen, 2011), including a peer performance evaluation process (see chapter 3).

When setting up teams or groups, try to build heterogeneity into each group. Members can vary on academic background, relevant skills, or points of view depending on the group task. Consider giving meaningful names or having team members name themselves (such as Four Girls and a Guy, Insomniacs, Green Beans, Thinkers, Seekers). Give each team member a specific role to start out (such as leader, encourager, critic, summarizer, or reporter), and let the group rotate roles weekly. Allocate discussion space for the groups to develop their own rules for interaction and responsibilities. Make sure the project is challenging enough to demand synergy among the group members, and carefully specify the product you expect from them (Goodson, 2004a; Heo, Lim, & Kim, 2010).

For example, in her organizational leadership course at Purdue University Fort Wayne, Anna Gibson places her students in leadership roles in the discussion forums (Goodson, 2016a):

> Discussion leaders need to sign up during Modules 01 and 02 and select the module they would like to lead for their team. The discussion topics for each module may be current leadership issues, required readings, or an assigned case study for the current module. Alternatively, the forum leader may choose the topic.

Current leadership issues: Using current news, choose a leadership concept that is related to the topic covered during the current module. The discussion should be on a leader/manager and the current situation that appeared in the news (e.g., print, television, radio, internet, etc.) within the last six months. Sources you might draw from include, but are not limited to: *Bloomberg Businessweek, The Economist, Fortune, Forbes, Black Enterprise, Wall Street Journal, New York Times*, CNN, etc.

Required Readings: Video(s) assignments or readings should be used to guide forum discussions.

Case study: Case studies assigned in the current module should be used to guide forum discussions.

Forum leader's choice: If no case study is assigned for the module, the forum leader may choose the topic.

Forum participant: When you are a discussion forum participant and someone else is the leader of your group, you are to contribute a minimum of one meaningful response within your assigned team (Skidmark, Smoove Move, or White Shadow) discussion forum.

- The forum participation points will be assessed starting with Module 03, January 24, 2015, 8:01 p.m.
- Forum discussions are the equivalent to classroom discussions and are a critical part of the online learning experience.
- Active forum participation will be one measure of your ability to lead, effectively communicate, make and communicate sound decisions, and contribute to everyone's learning.
- The forum discussions close on Saturdays at 8:00 p.m. You will not be able to post additional discussions for the module.

Similarly, think about the purpose of team projects to decide how to set up the group space. If you want teams to work "in secret" to produce, for example, competing designs, give each group a private discussion space. If you want teams to share, set up threads in whole-class discussion forums. For example, you can have a forum titled "Research Ethics" and set up separate threads for each group but with the same purpose and directions:

Forum: Research Ethics

Threads:

- ◦ Team 1 Area
- ◦ Team 2 Area
- ◦ Team 3 Area
- ◦ Team 4 Area

Or you could designate subtopics for each team—for example:

Forum: Research Ethics

Threads:

- ◦ Team 1 Tuskegee Case
- ◦ Team 2 Nuremberg Code
- ◦ Team 3 Thalidomide
- ◦ Team 4 Stanley Milgram

As long as the task is challenging, you can give all kinds of assignments to groups, such as a complex case study analysis or a fuzzy problem to solve. Give all the groups the same case or problem, or distribute different ones across the groups. If you choose the latter, consider what layers of interaction will most benefit the class. Where do you want each group to record its summary or conclusions, and what kinds of review and comments do you want each group to give to the other? Or do you want them to follow a rotation, such as having team 4 review team 1, team 1 review team 2, team 2 review team 3, and team 3 review team 4? Such a rotation can shift for the next team assignment. Just make sure to align your choices with a learning outcome; do not have students review each other's work just for the sake of review.

Another approach is to assign roles for different members to play in analyzing and interpreting a case, such as Investigator, Patient, Family Member of a Patient, or Institutional Review Board. In the case of an international economic conflict, each group member could represent a different country's perspective. At the local level, as in a case about water pollution, the roles may include Commissioner, Parent of Ill Child, Grant Funding Agency, and so on. To prepare for their roles, individual students should conduct scholarly research reviews, provide citations, and include the reasoning for their perspectives. This strategy builds individual accountability within the group process.

In his Media Legalities Course at Florida State University, Pat Hadley privately made his own list of hot topics for possible team investigations, but he also used the first week of class to invite students to develop and submit their own lists. He then distributed a complete blended list from which students could choose initial research topics (Goodson, 2004b). Similarly, you may invite students to pose questions to investigate.

Discussion forums also can provide space for a well-structured debate that fosters critical analysis and evaluation. Set up opposing teams on an issue for which students individually conduct and write up research to send to their team members before they all discuss the issue and possible sides. You might require each student to submit three articles, an abstract for each, a correct citation, and a position statement on the issue. Then direct students to discuss their findings within their team, reach a consensus, and post their team's position statement. This activity can occur over several weeks in preparation for final team debates. Here are sample directions that explain the activity's purpose and grading criteria (Goodson, 2004b, p. 103):

Purpose: You will be one of three to five students in an assigned team. Individually and as a group, you are assigned a topic or issue of controversy. Your purpose is to prepare for online debates with your classmates. All of these controversy topics will be related to issues you have been preparing for the whole term, so you should be able to articulate positions and counter-positions using sound reasoning, logic, and evidence. . . .

Grading: Points will be awarded based on the quality of the presentations made this week and the following week. These are the criteria for quality:

Clearly stated position
- Argument or response, using sound reasoning
- Supporting evidence from readings or resources
- Analysis of issues that explains your position on the controversy
- Courteous and professional communication style
- Compliance with debate instructions

You have individual and team responsibilities, and the quality of your work and participation as an individual and as a team member will influence your grade. You must complete a form evaluating the level of participation of each individual member.

For determining individual grades based on major projects, consider peer performance evaluations in which each group member assesses her or his own and the others' contributions, distributes points among the members, or gives them ratings. Chapter 3 explains your options.

■ INTERACTIONS WITH TECHNOLOGY

As with any other access, being able to open a door allows passage into a room. Students who do not know how to open the door will have trouble. For this reason, a number of colleges and universities provide students with the opportunity to self-assess their readiness for online learning. Requirements include daily access to a computer, connection to the Internet, and technology skills such as keyboarding, use of browsers, e-mail, file management, and downloading and running of software that may be needed in a course. Inexperience with such technologies may be frustrating and inconvenient, but an orientation can help students quickly pick up enough skills to make it through a course (Ekwunife-Orakwue & Teng, 2014; Liu & Kaye, 2016; Thurmond & Wambach, 2004). Students also benefit from just-in-time reminders of how to operate technology, like how to submit an assignment in the LMS or how to enter a discussion. Lack of access to a computer and the Internet is a more serious matter that can force students to quickly drop a course.

Five areas or tools in the LMS play a particularly important role in fostering student interactions (Sorensen & Baylen, 2011, p. 73):

- *Announcement space:* brief instructor messages to students such as reminders, additional resources, class schedule changes
- *Question and answer space:* like a virtual office where students can ask for clarifications or assistance (Online Office, Ask the Prof, News 'n' Notes, or other name)
- *Content discussion space:* areas with topics and questions for students to discuss or private journal space (time limited, such as weekly; graded or ungraded)
- *Social space:* an area for informal student-student interactions that you might entitle the Student Lounge, Cybercafé, Coffee Shop, Water Cooler, Venn Den (math course), or Jazz Lounge (music course)
- *Team space:* areas for small-group discussions (ungraded or graded)

Time and student workload do not transfer easily from a classroom to an online course. The student workload and contact hours should be equivalent to those in an on-the-ground course. But in a face-to-face course, contact hours means face time with the instructor in the classroom, typically forty-five hours for a three-credit course, plus two to three times as many hours for out-of-class readings, studying, and other assignments. In an online class, you might count the contact hours as the time it takes students to view a lecture or video or listen to a podcast, as well as take notes and participate in discussions. Students will need your help with time management, and you can give it in the form of organizational strategies, online calendars, file management tips, reminder announcements and e-mails, and periodic checkpoints on their progress (Sorensen & Baylen, 2009).

For the teaching workload, the question is how much time the different types of student-instructor interactions will demand. Planning many one-on-one interactions creates a heavy load. The following practices can help (Mandernach, Holbeck, & Cross, 2016):

- Complete all the basic course components before the course launch date.
- Integrate resources into the course for online guidance, technical support, writing, tutoring, and academic advising, as well as links to the library and subject matter librarian.

- Prebuild a personal introduction and orientation to the course.
- Use a consistent format and structure for course materials and expectations (e.g., assignments always due on Wednesday by 11:59 p.m.).
- Make deliberate use of technology for a particular purpose, and limit supplemental technology.
- Prebuild all quizzes, tests, and self-checks (e.g., flash cards), making use of automated feedback features.
- Develop alternative learning activities and assessments so that students can select those of greatest individual interest.
- Develop your own instructor's manual for the course with documents that will save you time while teaching—for example, concept maps to guide students' interaction with the content, just-in-time resources some of your students may need, and feedback banks or templates for replying to different student situations.
- Create an automated way to solicit anonymous feedback from your students on their learning and course design, such as surveys or polls with scheduled release dates.
- Set priorities for teaching tasks versus grading tasks.
- Create clear boundaries. For example, set and enforce definite due dates, and redirect individual e-mails to your online office when the issue relates to the whole class. Create a repository of course announcements, sets of questions and answers, and anticipated summaries of discussions that you can later customize.
- Create your own templates for e-mails and redundant questions.

Mandernach et al. (2016) also recommend time management and technology tools to support different functions:

- Time management: electronic to-do lists such as Tasks in Microsoft Office or Reminders in Apple
- Short messages: screen-capture apps for recording messages such as screencast-o-matic.com or techsmith.com/jing-features
- Personalized mini-lessons with tools such as creately.com or sliderocket.com
- Communication tools in addition to what might be in your LMS: wimba.com, voicethread.com, powwownow.com, skype.com, and join.me
- Blog and miniblog tools: wordpress.com and twitter.com
- Wiki applications: wiki.com, pbworks.com, and wikispaces.com
- Social networking: facebook.com, linkedin.com, ning.com, myspace.com, and pinterest.com
- Digital repositories: door.sourceforge.net/, Ariadne-cms.org, and trac.cnx.org, as well as many other education areas

Finally, because we know that active participation in the course influences student performance (Coldwell, Craig, Paterson, & Mustard, 2008), take advantage of student tracking and grading tools in your LMS. For example, the Evaluation tool in the Control Panel of Blackboard Learn offers a choice of reports on the frequency of student participation in different course areas. The Performance Dashboard view of Users shows who has made it into the course site, when, and how often. Such tools provide early alerts to send inquiries and encouraging messages to the slow starters. This kind of early intervention can put students on the right track and let them know that the course is not just an inhuman computer-managed system.

Reflections

For Instructors

- How do you want to create your initial online presence? What links to information about yourself do you want to make available to your students? Where in your course site do you want to post these links? In what stages do you want to reveal your online presence? What persona do you want to express? What style of communication do you want to use?
- Looking back over your course map and the planning you have done so far for your course, what content or exercises could you reduce to leave more time for interactions?
- Are others going to provide support for your course? If so, what strategy do you and they want to use for establishing and sustaining their presence in the course?
- What response times do you want to set for different types of communication and assignments from your students?
- What materials do you want to place in your instructor's manual to save you future time in responding to students?
- If students send you e-mails concerning issues of interest to the class, how will you redirect them to your reply in your virtual online office?
- What name and personality do you want to give your virtual online office? The name "Online Office" is fine, but you may be able to give it a more inviting or colorful label.
- What name and personality do you want to give your students' social space? The name "Online Café" is fine, but consider a more creative name like "Firefly Café" or one related to your subject matter like "Green Room."
- In what ways can you interact with your online students without getting into a deep time sink?
- What kinds of practice exercises, quizzes, or tests can you build ahead of time with automated feedback for your students?
- What are your highest priorities for student-content interactions, and how can you implement them?
- What are your highest priorities for student-student interactions in your course, and how can you implement them?
- How and when do you want to ask students for feedback about how the course is going?

For Instructional Designers

- What models or templates can you provide to help the instructor establish an online presence? If the instructor has little professional and personal content to share, what places and stages for revealing an online presence can you recommend?
- What perspectives can you share about the "overstuffed" versus the "lean-and-targeted" content planned so far? What other resources can you direct the instructor to consider to accomplish the same goals with less material or a lighter student workload?
- How can you help others involved in the course, such as a librarian and teaching assistants, develop a presence in the course?
- What kinds of preplanned responses do you think might be useful for anticipated student questions?
- For the materials to go into the instructor's manual, what templates or examples might you suggest?
- What potential time sinks do you see in the planned grading and interactions that may require too much time or take away from appropriate interactions?
- What kinds of practice exercises, quizzes, or tests can the instructor build ahead of time with automated feedback?

- For formative student feedback, what templates or items can you recommend? How can you adapt them to accommodate the instructor's interests in knowing what is working well for the students and what is not?

For Administrators

- Where can resources be visibly posted and readily available to support faculty in their student-instructor, student-content, and student-student interactions?
- What interface with the specialty librarian can be integrated into the online course sites?
- What policies guide the role of support staff such as the librarian and teaching assistants in ensuring an online course goes well for the students and the instructor? If no such policies exist, who can be recruited to create them?

■ REFERENCES

Abawajy, J. (2012). Analysis of asynchronous online discussion forums for collaborative learning. *International Journal of Education and Learning, 1*(2). Retrieved from http://www.sersc.org/journals/IJEL/vol1_no2/2.pdf

Abdelmalak, M.M.M. (2015). Web 2.0 technologies and building online learning communities: Students' perspectives. *Online Learning Journal, 19*(2). Retrieved from http://olj.onlinelearningconsortium.org/index.php/olj/article/view/413

Akcaoglu, M., & Lee, E. (2016). Increasing social presence in online learning through small group discussions. *International Review of Research in Open and Distributed Learning, 17*(3). Retrieved from http://www.irrodl.org/index.php/irrodl/article/view/2293/3680

Anderson, T. (2003). Getting the mix right again: An updated and theoretical rationale for interaction. *International Review of Research in Open and Distance Learning, 4*(2). Retrieved from http://www.irrodl.org/index.php/irrodl/article/view/149/230

Angelino, L. M., Williams, F. K., & Natvig, D. (2007). Strategies to engage online students and reduce attrition rates. *Journal of Educators Online, 4*(2), 1–14.

Battalio, J. (2009). Interaction online: A reevaluation. In A. Orellana, T. L. Hudgins, & M. Simonson (Eds.), *The perfect online course: Best practices for designing and teaching* (pp. 443–462). Charlotte, NC: Information Age Publishing.

Biktimirov, E. N., & Nilson, L. B. (2007). Adding animation and interactivity to finance courses with learning objects. *Journal of Financial Education, 33*, 35–47.

Blake, J. S. (2012). *Nutrition and you* (2nd ed.). San Francisco, CA: Benjamin-Cummings.

Bonk, C. (2013). *Bringing experts from around the world into your class.* Indiana University Bloomington. [website]. Retrieved from http://citl.indiana.edu/innovations/spotlights/bonk.php

Brewer, P. E., & Brewer, E. C. (2015). Pedagogical perspectives for the online education skeptic. *Journal on Excellence in College Teaching, 26*(1), 29–52.

Chickering, A. W., & Ehrmann, S. C. (1996). Implementing the seven principles: Technology as lever. *AAHE Bulletin, 49*(2), 3–6. Retrieved from https://www.aahea.org/articles/sevenprinciples.htm

Chickering, A. W., & Gamson, Z. F. (1987). Seven principles for good practice in undergraduate education. *AAHE Bulletin, 39*(7), 3–7. Retrieved from http://files.eric.ed.gov/fulltext/ED282491.pdf

Cho, M., & Cho, Y. (2014). Instructor scaffolding for interaction and students' academic engagement in online learning: Mediating role of perceived online class goal structures. *Internet and Higher Education, 21*, 25–30.

Clark, R. C., & Mayer, R. E. (2011). *E-learning and the science of instruction: Proven guidelines for consumers and designers of multimedia learning.* San Francisco, CA: Pfeiffer/Wiley.

Coldwell, J., Craig, A., Paterson, T., & Mustard, J. (2008). Online students: Relationships between participation, demographics and academic performance. *Electronic Journal of e-Learning, 6*(10), 19–30.

Croxton, R. A. (2014, June). The role of interactivity in student satisfaction and persistence in online learning. *MERLOT Journal of Online Learning and Teaching, 10*(2), 314–325. Retrieved from http://jolt.merlot.org/vol10no2/croxton0614.pdf

Division of Information Technology, University of Maryland Baltimore County. (2013). *Managing discussions using a "participation portfolio."* Retrieved from http://doit.umbc.edu/itnm/managing-discussions/

Dixson, M. D. (2010). Creating effective student engagement in online courses: What do students find engaging? *Journal of the Scholarship of Teaching and Learning, 10*(2), 1–13. Retrieved from http://josotl.indiana.edu/article/download/1744/1742

Drouin, M., & Van Gorder, K. (2015). *Implementing an online student success program on campus.* Presented at Educause Annual Conference, Orlando, FL. Retrieved from http://www.educause.edu/annual-conference/2014/implementing-online-student-success-program-campus

Drouin, M., & Vartanian, L. R. (2008). Students' feelings of and desire for sense of community in face-to-far and online courses. *Quarterly Review of Distance Education, 11*(3), 147–149.

Dunlosky, J., Rawson, K. A., Marsh, E. J., Nathan, M. J., & Willingham, D. T. (2013). Improving students' learning with effective learning techniques: Promising directions from cognitive and educational psychology. *Psychological Science in the Public Interest, 14*, 4–58. doi:10.1177/1529100612453266

Ekwunife-Orakwue, K. C. V., & Teng, T. (2014). The impact of transactional distance dialogic interactions on student learning outcomes in online and blended environments. *Computers and& Education, 78*, 414–427.

Ertmer, P. A., Richardson, J. C., Belland, B., Camin, D., Connolly, P., Coulthard, G., … Mong, C. (2007). Using peer feedback to enhance the quality of student online postings: An exploratory study. *Journal of Computer Mediated Communication, 12*(2), 412–433.

Estes, J. S. (2016). The pivotal role of faculty in online student engagement and retention. In L. Kyei-Blankson, J. Blankson, E. Ntuli, & C. Agyeman (Eds.), *Handbook of research on strategic management of interaction, presence, and participation in online courses* (pp. 65–87). Hershey, PA: IGI Global.

Ghadirian, H., Ayub, A. F. M., Bakar, K. B. A., & Hassanzadeh, M. (2016). Growth patterns and e-moderating supports in asynchronous online discussions in an undergraduate blended course. *International Review of Research in Open and Distributed Learning, 17*(3). Retrieved from http://www.irrodl.org/index.php/irrodl/article/view/2397/3692

Gilbert, P. K., & Dabbagh, N. (2005). How to structure online discussions for meaningful discourse: A case study. *British Journal of Educational Technology, 36*(1), 5–18.

Goodson, L. A. (2004a, June). Constructive controversy in asynchronous time. In *Proceedings of the Association for Educational Communications and Technology Conference* (pp. 94–108). Retrieved from http://www.aect.org/pdf/AECT_UNT_Proceedings_2004.pdf

Goodson, L. A. (2004b, June). Face-to-face with an online expert panel. In *Proceedings of the Association for Educational Communications and Technology Conference* (pp. 124–137). Retrieved from http://www.aect.org/pdf/AECT_UNT_Proceedings_2004.pdf

Goodson, L. A. (2004c, June). Formative evaluation in online courses. In *Proceedings of the Association for Educational Communications and Technology Conference* (pp. 109–123). Retrieved from http://www.aect.org/pdf/AECT_UNT _Proceedings_2004.pdf

Goodson, L. A. (2016a). Course review: BUS W430 Organizations and Organizational Change: Leadership and Group Dynamics. Instructor: A. Gibson, Indiana University–Purdue University Fort Wayne.

Goodson, L. A. (2016b). Course review: FNN 30300 Essentials of Nutrition. Instructor: L. L. Lolkus, Indiana University-Purdue University Fort Wayne.

Grandzol, J., & Grandzol, C. (2006). Best practices for online business education. *International Review of Research in Open and Distance Learning, 7*(1), 1–18. Retrieved from http://www.irrodl.org/index.php/irrodl/article/view/246/475

Helms, J. L., Marek, P., Randall, C. K., Rogers, D. T., Taglialatela, L. A., & Williamson, A. L. (2011). Developing an online curriculum in psychology. In J. H. Wilson, D. S. Dunn, J. R. Stowell, & J. Freeman (Eds.), *Best practices for technology-enhanced teaching and learning* (pp. 53–71). New York, NY: Oxford University Press.

Heo, H., Lim, K. Y., & Kim, Y. (2010). Exploratory study on the patterns of online interaction and knowledge co-construction in project-based learning. *Computers and Education, 55*(3), 1383–1392.

Herman, J. H., & Nilson, L. B. (in press). *Avoiding crickets: Strategies for creating engaging discussions.* Sterling, VA: Stylus.

Hilton III, J. L., Gaudet, D., Clark, P., Robinson, J., & Wiley, D. (2013). The adoption of open educational resources by one community college math department. *International Review of Research in Open and Distance Learning, 14*(4). Retrieved from http://www.irrodl.org/index.php/irrodl/article/viewFile/1675/2705

Hirumi, A. (2009). A framework for analyzing, designing, and sequencing planned e-learning interactions. In A. Orellana, T. L. Hudgins, & M. Simonson (Eds.), *The perfect online course: Best practices for designing and teaching* (pp. 201–228). Charlotte, NC: Information Age Publishing.

Ip, A., Morrison, I., & Currie, M. (2001). *What is a learning object, technically?* Retrieved from http://users.tpg.com.au /adslfrcf/lo/learningObject(WebNet2001).pdf

Jeong, A. J. (2004, October). *The effects of communication style and message function in triggering responses and critical discussion in computer-supported collaborative argumentation.* Paper presented at the 27th Annual Conference of the Association for Educational Communications and Technology. (ERIC ED485058)

Jeong, A. J. (2014). Quantitative analysis of interactive patterns in online distance education. In O. Zawacki-Richter & T. Anderson (Eds.), *Online distance education: Towards a research agenda* (pp. 403–420). Edmonton, Alberta, Canada: AU Press, Athabasca University.

Karpicke, J. D., & Roediger, H. L. III. (2008). The critical importance of retrieval for learning. *Science, 319*, 966–968.

Kelly, R. (2014, February 27). Feedback strategies for online courses. *Faculty Focus.* Retrieved from http://www .facultyfocus.com/articles/online-education/feedback-strategies-online-courses/

Kilburn, M., Henckell, M., & Starrett, D. (2016). Instructor-driven strategies for establishing and sustaining social presence. In L. Kyei-Blankson, J. Blankson, E. Ntuli, & C. Agyeman (Eds.), *Handbook of research on strategic management of interaction, presence, and participation in online courses* (pp. 305–327). Hershey, PA: IGI Global.

Kirsner, B., Teem II, C. L., & Underwood, L. B. (2011). To the Internet and beyond. In J. H. Wilson, D. S. Dunn, J. R. Stowell, & J. Freeman (Eds.), *Best practices for technology-enhanced teaching and learning* (pp. 253–270). New York, NY: Oxford University Press.

Knowlton, D. S. (2009). Evaluating college students' efforts in asynchronous discussion: A systematic process. In A. Orellana, T. L. Hudgins, & M. Simonson (Eds.), *The perfect online course: Best practices for designing and teaching* (pp. 311–326). Charlotte, NC: Information Age Publishing.

Kolloff, M. A. (2011). *Strategies for effective student/student interaction in online courses.* Paper presented at the 17th Annual Conference on Distance Teaching and Learning, Madison, WI. Retrieved from http://www.uwex.edu/disted /conference/resourcelibrary/proceedings/0110.pdf

Leflay, K., & Groves, M. (2013). Using online forums for encouraging higher order thinking and "deep" learning in an undergraduate Sports Sociology module. *Journal of Hospitality, Leisure, Sport and Tourism Education, 13*, 226–232.

Liu, J. C., & Kaye, E. R. (2016). Preparing online learning readiness with learner-content interaction: Design for scaf- folding self-regulated learning. In L. Kyei-Blankson, J. Blankson, E. Ntuli, & C. Agyeman (Eds.), *Handbook of research on strategic management of interaction, presence, and participation in online courses* (pp. 216–243). Hershey, PA: IGI Global.

Liu, X., Magjuka, R. J., Bonk, C. J., & Lee, S.-H. (2009). Does sense of community matter? In A. Orellana, T. L. Hudgins, & M. Simonson (Eds.), *The perfect online course: Best practices for designing and teaching* (pp. 521–543). Charlotte, NC: Information Age Publishing.

Luyegu, E. (2016). Ensuring presence in online learning environments. In L. Kyei-Blankson, J. Blankson, E. Ntuli, & C. Agyeman (Eds.), *Handbook of research on strategic management of interaction, presence, and participation in online courses* (pp. 350–376). Hershey, PA: IGI Global.

MacKnight, C. B. (2000). Teaching critical thinking through online discussions. *Educause Quarterly, 4*, 38–41.

Madland, C., & Richards, G. (2016). Enhancing student-student online interaction: Exploring the study buddy peer review activity. *International Review of Research in Open and Distributed Learning, 17*(3). Retrieved from http://www .irrodl.org/index.php/irrodl/article/view/2179

Mandernach, B. J., Holbeck, R., & Cross, T. (2016). More teaching in less time: Leveraging time to maximize teaching presence. In L. Kyei-Blankson, J. Blankson, E. Ntuli, & C. Agyeman (Eds.), *Handbook of research on strategic management of interaction, presence, and participation in online courses* (pp. 281–304). Hershey, PA: IGI Global.

Mayer, R. E., & Clark, R. C. (2013). *Ten brilliant design rules for e-learning.* [web log]. Retrieved from https://donaldclarkplanb .blogspot.co.uk/2013/01/mayer-clark-10-brilliant-design-rules.html

McLaren, A. C. (2009). Designing effective e-learning. In A. Orellana, T. L. Hudgins, & M. Simonson (Eds.), *The perfect online course: Best practices for designing and teaching* (pp. 229–248). Charlotte, NC: Information Age Publishing.

Moore, A. H. (2003–2004). Great expectations and challenges for learning objects. *Essays on Teaching Excellence, 1*(4), 1–2.

Moore, E. A. (2013, May 20). From passive viewing to active learning: Simple techniques for applying active learning strategies to online course videos. *Faculty Focus.* Retrieved from http://www.facultyfocus.com/articles /teaching-with-technology-articles/from-passive-viewing-to-active-learning-simple-techniques-for-applying -active-learning-strategies-to-online-course-videos/

Moore, J. (2014). Effects of online interaction and instructor presence on students' satisfaction and success with online undergraduate public relations courses. *Journalism and Mass Communication Educator, 69*(3), 271–288.

Moore, M. G. (1989). Three types of interaction. *American Journal of Distance Education, 3*(2), 1–7.

Morris, O. P. (2016). Web-based technologies for ensuring interaction in online courses: Faculty choice and student perception of web-based technologies for interaction in online economics. In L. Kyei-Blankson, J. Blankson, E. Ntuli, & C. Agyeman (Eds.), *Handbook of research on strategic management of interaction, presence, and participation in online courses* (pp. 244–279). Hershey, PA: IGI Global.

Murray, M., Pérez, J., Geist, D., & Hedrick, A. (2013). Student interaction with content in online and hybrid courses: Leading horses to the proverbial water. *Informing Science, 16*. Retrieved from http://www.inform.nu/Articles/Vol16 /ISJv16p099-115MurrayFT114.pdf

Nilson, L. B. (2003). Improving student peer feedback. *College Teaching, 51*(1), 34–38.

Nilson, L. B. (2007). *The graphic syllabus and the outcomes map: Communicating your course.* San Francisco, CA: Jossey-Bass.

Nilson, L. B. (2013). *Creating self-regulated learners: Strategies to strengthen students' self-awareness and learning skills.* Sterling, VA: Stylus.

Orellana, A. (2009). Class size and interaction in online classes. In A. Orellana, T. L. Hudgins, & M. Simonson (Eds.), *The perfect online course: Best practices for designing and teaching* (pp. 127–156). Charlotte, NC: Information Age Publishing.

Pavlis-Korres, M., & Leftheriotou, P. (2016). Building interaction in adults' online courses: A case study on training e-educators of adults. In L. Kyei-Blankson, J. Blankson, E. Ntuli, & C. Agyeman (Eds.), *Handbook of research on strategic management of interaction, presence, and participation in online courses* (pp. 185–215). Hershey, PA: IGI Global.

Pérez. J., & Hurysz, K. (2011). I didn't know I could do that: Using web-based tools to enhance learning. In D. S. Dunn, J. H. Wilson, J. Freeman, & J. R. Stowell (Eds.), *Best practices for technology-enhanced teaching and learning: Connecting to psychology and the social sciences* (pp. 207–222). New York, NY: Oxford University Press.

Peterson, A. (2016, December 12). Five ways to make your online classrooms more interactive. *Faculty Focus.* Retrieved from http://www.facultyfocus.com/articles/online-education/five-ways-make-online-classrooms-interactive/

Ramos, C., & Yudko, E. (2008). "Hits" (not "Discussion Posts") predict student success in online courses: A double cross-validation study. *Computers and Education, 50,* 1174–1182.

Reisetter, M., & Boris, G. (2009). What works: Student perceptions of effective elements in online learning. In A. Orellana, T. L. Hudgins, & M. Simonson (Eds.), *The perfect online course: Best practices for designing and teaching* (pp. 157–178). Charlotte, NC: Information Age Publishing.

Rhode, J. F. (2009). Interaction equivalency in self-paced online learning environments: An exploration of learner preferences. *International Review of Research in Open and Distance Learning, 10*(1). Retrieved from http://www.irrodl.org/index.php/irrodl/article/view/603/1179

Ross, J., Gallagher, M. S., & Macleod, H. (2013). Making distance visible: Assembling nearness in an online distance learning programme. *International Review of Research in Open and Distributed Learning, 17*(3), 51–65.

Rourke, A. J., & Lewer-Fletcher, A. (2016). Building interaction online: Reflective blog journals to link university learning to real world practice. In L. Kyei-Blankson, J. Blankson, E. Ntuli, & C. Agyeman (Eds.), *Handbook of research on strategic management of interaction, presence, and participation in online courses* (pp. 120–184). Hershey, PA: IGI Global.

Sadik, A., & Reisman, S. (2009). Design and implementation of a web-based learning environment: Lessons learned. In A. Orellana, T. L. Hudgins, & M. Simonson (Eds.), *The perfect online course: Best practices for designing and teaching* (pp. 179–200). Charlotte, NC: Information Age Publishing.

Semingson, P. L., & Smith, P. (2016). "I'm not simply dealing with some heartless computer": Videoconferencing as personalized online learning in a graduate literacy course. In L. Kyei-Blankson, J. Blankson, E. Ntuli, & C. Agyeman (Eds.), *Handbook of research on strategic management of interaction, presence, and participation in online courses* (pp. 160–184). Hershey, PA: IGI Global.

Shank, J. D. (2014). *Interactive open educational resources: A guide to finding, choosing, and using what's out there to transform college teaching.* San Francisco, CA: Jossey-Bass.

Simonson, M. (2000). Myths and distance education: What the research says (and does not). *Quarterly Review of Distance Education, 4*(1), 277–279.

Soderstrom, N. C., & Bjork, R. A. (2014). Testing facilitates the regulation of subsequent study time. *Journal of Memory and Language, 73,* 99–115. doi:10.1016/j.jml.2014.03.003

Sorensen, C. K., & Baylen, D. M. (2009). Learning online: Adapting the seven principles of good practice to a web-based instructional environment. In A. Orellana, T. L. Hudgins, & M. Simonson (Eds.), *The perfect online course: Best practices for designing and teaching* (pp. 69–86). Charlotte, NC: Information Age Publishing.

Stöter, J., Bullen, M., Zawacki-Richter, O., & von Prümmer, C. (2014). From the back door into the mainstream: The characteristics of lifelong learners. In O. Zawacki-Richter & T. Anderson (Eds.), *Online distance education: Towards a research agenda* (pp. 421–457). Athabasca, Edmonton, Canada: Athabasca University Press.

Stowell, J. R. (2011). Emerging technologies to improve teaching and learning in a digital world. In J. H. Dunn, J. H. Wilson, J. E. Freeman, & J. R. Stowell (Eds.), *Teaching and learning: Connecting to psychology and the social sciences* (pp. 299–316). New York, NY: Oxford University Press.

Thurmond, V., & Wambach, V. (2004). Understanding interactions in distance education: A review of the literature. *International Journal of Instructional Technology and Distance Education, 1*(1). Retrieved from http://www.itdl.org/journal/jan04/article02.htm

Tsiotakis, P., & Jimoyiannis, A. (2016). Critical factors towards analyzing teachers' presence in online learning communities. *Internet and Higher Education, 28,* 45–58.

Wang, Z., Chen, L., & Anderson, T. (2014). A framework for interaction and cognitive engagement in connectivist learning contexts. *International Review of Research in Open and Distance Learning, 4.* Retrieved from http://www.irrodl.org/index.php/irrodl/article/view/1709/2838

Wanstreet, C. E. (2009). Interaction in online learning environments: A review of the literature. In A. Orellana, T. L. Hudgins, & M. Simonson (Eds.), *The perfect online course: Best practices for designing and teaching* (pp. 425–442). Charlotte, NC: Information Age Publishing.

Woods, K. (2016). Encouraging and increasing student engagement and participation in an online classroom. In L. Kyei-Blankson, J. Blankson, E. Ntuli, & C. Agyeman (Eds.), *Handbook of research on strategic management of interaction, presence, and participation in online courses* (pp. 426–447). Hershey, PA: IGI Global.

Yandell, L. R., & Bailey, W. N. (2011). Online quizzes: Improving reading compliance and student learning. In J. H. Dunn, J. H. Wilson, J. E. Freeman, & J. R. Stowell (Eds.), *Teaching and learning: Connecting to psychology and the social sciences* (pp. 271–282). New York, NY: Oxford University Press.

Zawacki-Richter, O., & Anderson, T. (2014). Research areas in online distance education. In O. Zawacki-Richter & T. Anderson (Eds.), *Online distance education: Towards a research agenda* (pp. 1–35). Edmonton, Alberta, Canada: AU Press, Athabasca University.

Zhang, J., & Walls, R. T. (2009). Instructors' self-perceived pedagogical principle implementation in the online environment. In A. Orellana, T. L. Hudgins, & M. Simonson (Eds.), *The perfect online course: Best practices for designing and teaching* (pp. 87–104). Charlotte, NC: Information Age Publishing.

Zheng, L., & Smaldino, S. (2009). Key instructional design elements for distance education. In A. Orellana, T. L. Hudgins, & M. Simonson (Eds.), *The perfect online course: Best practices for designing and teaching* (pp. 107–126). Charlotte, NC: Information Age Publishing.

Zimmerman, T. D. (2012). Exploring learner to content interaction as a success factor in online courses. *International Review of Research in Open and Distributed Learning.* Retrieved from http://www.irrodl.org/index.php/irrodl/article/view/1302/2294

CHAPTER 7

Making Accessibility for Everyone Much Easier

All students deserve to participate equally in an online course. Yet some faculty look on universal design for learning as just another set of technical chores they have to do to stay out of trouble with instructional designers and the administration. This attitude runs contrary to the genuine care they typically have for their students and their desire for significant learning in their courses. To help understand this cognitive dilemma, this chapter takes a closer look at what gets in the way of developing accessible online course materials. In the broader context, it shows how students who do not have disabilities also reap benefits from accessibility design practices. Finally, to ensure learning for all students and to make access to course content easier for everyone, we provide time-saving, productive strategies for accessibility design and the use of accessibility tools, formats, processes, and resources.

It's just intelligent thinking about your design and just making sure that you've considered factors . . . all the needs people will have.

—**Wendy Chisholm**

■ WHY USE STUDENT-CENTERED DESIGN?

Some faculty look on universal design for learning as just another set of technical chores they have to do to stay out of trouble with instructional designers and the administration. This is no surprise when so many technical training sessions push compliance with laws. Indeed, equal access is mandated by laws, grounded in the hope that people actually will have equal access. A few years ago, Coombs (2010) pointed out that not providing equal access to course materials violates civil rights. The US Department of Education, Office of Civil Rights (2016) has brought home this reality with a number of suits, investigations, and settlements reached with colleges and universities (University of Washington: Accessible Technology). In fact, Section 508 of the Rehabilitation Act requires equal access to electronic information sources, Section 504 requires equal opportunity to participate in programs, and Title II of the Americans with Disabilities Act affirms these civil rights and prohibits discrimination in state and local government services (HHS.gov: What is section 504?; HHS.gov, Section 508; ADA).

Compliance, however, is hardly the most noble motive for student-centered design. Most faculty would not want to create barriers for their students to the course content, communication, and activities. We want our students with physical, sensory, or cognitive disabilities to be able to access the same quality of content and learning experiences. We know that technology itself does not present inherent barriers, but our choices for the use of this technology, particularly in online courses, might (Wentz, Jaeger, & Lazar, 2011). In this context, we cannot make informed choices without knowing how our best intentions and course materials can create barriers. For this reason, this chapter provides the needed guidelines and tools.

Students who do not have disabilities often need or want the same kinds of support as accessibility laws require for students who do have them (Bozarth, 2015). More accessible course materials also facilitate mobile learning. Features that help all students include striking color contrasts, clean and easy-to-read font styles, meaningful headings, well-organized narratives, and descriptive links to websites. Many people are not blind but simply have low vision or trouble distinguishing colors, often seeing a color as gray, yellow, or beige. Others juggle tasks such as reading e-mail on a laptop while making supper in the kitchen, replying to a discussion or e-mail while riding a bus, working under fluorescent lighting that causes jumpy text-on-screen, listening to a podcast while walking across campus or in a noisy space, or studying during a gym workout (Chisholm & May, 2008; Stachowiak, 2009). Besides hearing, visual, or physical limits on their abilities to access materials, some students have dyslexia or attention deficit hyperactivity disorder, and course formatting can hinder or help how well they can comprehend your course content.

In this chapter, we think of students' variations in abilities more like Wendy Chisholm@wendyabc: "Stairs make a building inaccessible, not the wheelchair." Similarly, a singular print format, not a student's blindness, makes a textbook inaccessible; an audio podcast without a transcript, not the loss of hearing, makes the content inaccessible; a synchronous conference that requires real-time conversation, not the speech impediment, makes the learning inaccessible. Clark (2002b, Chapter 4, ¶4) puts it this way: "A deaf person cannot stop being deaf . . . a blind person cannot stop being blind . . . a learning disabled person cannot reset the functions of the brain . . . [and] a person with a mobility impairment cannot suddenly be able to move." When we design courses to be accessible, we really will walk the talk of a fundamental principle of undergraduate education: respecting diverse ways and talents for learning (Chickering & Ehrmann, 1996; Chickering & Gamson, 1987).

Earlier chapters in this book provided the starting point for making your courses accessible: (1) coherence of course design (chapter 3), (2) principles of learning from cognitive science (chapter 4), (3) motivation strategies (chapter 5), and (4) interaction design (chapter 6). The guidelines in these chapters support the three major principles for universal design (CAST, 2008; Dell, Dell, & Blackwell, 2015; National Center on Universal Design for Learning; Ralabate, 2011; UDL Guidelines—Version 2.0):

1. Provide multiple ways to acquire the course content.
2. Provide multiple ways to assess what students learn.
3. Provide multiple motivations to learn and multiple opportunities for engagement, interaction, and challenge.

■ SOURCES OF OBSTACLES

Many students formerly taught in separate spaces, such as those with sensory disabilities or whose behaviors fall on the autism spectrum, now learn in the same classroom and online spaces as everyone else (Ralabate, 2011; Simpson, 2013). They often experience unreliable and inconsistent access to online materials (Coombs, 2010), even when they use the extra assistive technology designed to make content accessible. Obstacles sometimes reside in the learning management system (LMS). However, Blackboard and Angel have passed basic requirements of accessibility (Accessibility at Blackboard; Angel Learning; National Center on Disability and Access to Education Tips and Tools). Moodle continues to increase accessibility, and Desire2Learn is "committed to accessibility in education" (D2L, ¶1). Recently, WebAIM.org certified that Canvas substantially meets web accessibility guidelines (WebAIM Canvas Certification, 2015).

In spite of the viability of such platforms, instructors often block access when they prepare materials incorrectly (Lee, 2016). Ironically, the ease of using technology can contribute to such missteps. For example, instructors often reuse PowerPoint presentations from their brick-and-mortar classrooms for quick content uploads in their online courses. PowerPoint, however, was designed for large-group presentations, and while it may sometimes work for online learning, commonly used features actually block access for many students. Features like text boxes added over built-in slide design layouts, animations, slide transitions, and images without alternative text descriptions get in the way of readability, and assistive technologies typically cannot follow the structure and content of add-on treatments. So why do instructors use PowerPoints in this way for online learning? Most likely they expect the added ornamentation to increase engagement, they know how to use the add-in features, and they trust their reliability without realizing the fallout of their choices.

Formats of test items also can create stumbling blocks, especially when the student must use a screen reader to read the test information aloud. Screen readers can handle multiple-choice and short-answer items fairly well. But students struggle with making sense of matching questions even if they have no discernable disabilities. Other stumbling blocks include not receiving information on what you are testing ahead of time (such as a rubric) and getting tests in only one format when a student needs it in another (Simpson, 2013).

In addition, instructors may use *italics* or **bold** to emphasize a word or phrase in a Word document or insert a table with a visually appealing layout. But screen readers cannot read the emphasis or the table layout unless some underlying signals are added. Seeing what looks good, faculty may proceed with good intentions to upload the Word document as is or choose "Save As Adobe PDF" for a more attractive and easy-to-open format. This process takes little thought and time, and it works well enough for sighted students. Then one instructor may tell another, "Oh, it is easy. Just copy your Word file over to a PDF and post that in your course site. This will open faster and won't kick the student out of the course," which is true, but this does not provide enough access. Thus, the problem may grow like wildfire over the landscape of multiple course sites. However, both the Word document and the "Save As Adobe PDF" shortcut fail to provide the needed signals to a screen reader to transform text to audio.

■ OVERCOMING OBSTACLES

Legal complaints against universities are on the rise, including a few against online learning (Dolhansky & Paire, 2016; O'Rourke, 2013; Public Affairs, UC Berkeley, 2016; US Department of Justice, Civil Rights Division, 2016; University of Washington, 2016). The main consequence of such complaints is the creation of vigorous campus-driven accessibility initiatives and settlement agreements (Resolution Agreement, University of

Phoenix, 2015; Settlement between Penn State University and National Federation of the Blind, n.d.). However, other complaints have broader consequences. For example, the University of California at Berkeley will remove its existing educational content (PDFs, video, and audio) from public access and "invest in developing new online content with necessary accessibility features" rather than trying to retrofit materials (Cielo24, 2017; "Campus Announces Restriction of Public Access to Educational Content," 2017, ¶2).

Universities and colleges now face a backlog of inaccessible files (University Business, 2016). The efforts to undo the variety of compound barriers usually exceed those of building online courses to provide equal access from the start (Wentz et al., 2011). The costs of "undoing" go beyond high legal costs and may include hiring an external company (Goetze, 2016; University Business, 2016). As for other costs, imagine what it takes to go into and fix all the course files on a campus—institutional costs caused by instructor disregard or ignorance of what works. Retrofitting always costs more and tends to meet only minimum legal requirements, falling short of the higher quality that comes from intentional planning (Clark, 2002a; Wentz et al., 2011). For the most part, preparing accessible materials is fairly easy, although some steps do take extra effort (Clark, 2002a). But why wouldn't we make this commitment? When we care about students and significant learning in our courses, can there be any other choice?

Not only do college and university students need accessible content, but some may need certain accommodations, typically arranged through your campus disabilities services. Such accommodations include alternate exam formats, more exam time, support from readers or note takers, or sign language interpreters. They would never require a change in your course or learning outcomes.

All disabilities services units require documentation of a student's disability, but as many as two-thirds of students with disabilities simply do not report them (Grasgreen, 2014). As a result, they risk not getting the tools they need to succeed, particularly in the first year of college. Students often fly under the radar because they want to be independent and treated the same as other students (Rodgers, 2015). They may also fear the negative assumptions and perceptions faculty and staff may have about disabilities (Grasgreen, 2014).

Just as with other aspects of teaching online, communicating an instructor's personal support matters as much as the technology support—for example, saying in the syllabus something like, "Let me know in advance if you think you will need an accommodation for the exam or other activities in this course." Instructors can also list common tools that all students may use, such as browser settings, along with information about the available assistive technology for students who have disabilities (Stachowiak, 2009). Disabilities services can recommend protocols.

Adam Dircksen illustrates the value of the human touch in his Media Criticism and Analysis class at Purdue University Fort Wayne. A student notified him that although she could recognize colors, she was legally blind and wanted to know if the course requirements would accommodate her. Dircksen informed her that the readings and the Blackboard-based course site were accessible, and while the video lectures clearly used imagery, everything was verbally or orally explained. However, some of the assignment requirements would need modification to meet her needs, especially an assignment that called for students to pick a film and analyze the production techniques being used to help create meaning. These techniques typically encompass camera movements, angles, focus, lighting techniques, editing techniques, and so on. For her paper, she was able to complete the requirements by focusing on her chosen film's musical score, sound effects, and other post-dubbed sound such as voice-overs, and on how the filmmakers' color choices affected mood and correlated with the sound she analyzed. Dircksen reports that the student's paper was excellent and she did very well in the course (A. Dircksen, personal communication, September 15, 2016).

Because of the need for confidentiality, faculty and staff must take care in guiding nondisclosing students to the kinds of support they need. You can start out by listing in your syllabus and on your course site the academic support and disabilities services on campus and any handbook for students with disabilities. Later you can direct specific students toward these services. Whatever your strategy, do not call out a student as having a disability or decide on your own what the student needs. The job of diagnosis resides in the hands of those with expertise and official responsibility.

Working with partners on your campus is one of the best ways to advance greater access in online courses—your office of disability services, instructional design specialists, other faculty who design online courses, information technology specialists, and, if you are fortunate to have the opportunity, students who have disabilities and face challenges in online learning (Simpson, 2013). Regardless of ability or differences in abilities, "the goal for equal access is to make it accessible from the beginning" (Ingeno, 2013, ¶9, citing Denise Wallace, vice president of legal affairs and general counsel at Dillard University). Fortunately, this is generally easy to do.

GUIDELINES AND STANDARDS FOR DESIGNING ACCESSIBILITY

Students, faculty, and institutions all benefit when we design accessibility from the start. Some basic accessibility guidelines mirror our course design recommendations in chapters 2, 3, and 4, including these (Leavitt & Schneiderman, 2006):

- Start with statements of your learning outcomes or goals for students.
- Understand and meet students' needs.
- Provide usable content.
- Build with consistency of structure.
- Provide feedback when needed.
- Evaluate your course components for effectiveness.
- Design for human limitations on working memory.
- Create a positive first impression for the home page by ensuring it looks like a home page and includes all the major course components.

Let's first gauge your accessibility knowledge with a few true-or-false questions posed by Vasquez and Johnson (2016, frame 13).

T or F: "All online materials must be made accessible before being posted online." *False:* Just-in-time accommodations are acceptable to balance the load, but they require planning and communication.

T or F: "In the absence of a student with a disability, I don't need to make my course accessible." *False:* The emphasis is on advance preparation.

T or F: "Accessibility in online education is primarily a faculty issue." We hope you know this one is false. While you do need to make the content materials accessible, accommodations for your students may involve many units: your information technology support system, the student disabilities office, your professional development unit, and the library.

Certain features support accessibility and deserve special attention in online courses: consistent design, striking color contrasts, accessible graphics, a modular course structure, a text equivalent for every nontext element, use of captions for multimedia presentations, careful use of color so that color alone does not convey meaning, use of tables only when they are really necessary, and well-written headings and subheadings that meaningfully signal the content to come. You will raise the accessibility value of your materials when you include such features in an organized structure with clearly written documents and apply styles to your text materials, including any tables that you feel are truly needed (Coombs, 2010).

Many institutions call for these specific accessibility requirements, which include Coombs's features above (Bastedo, Sugar, Swenson, & Vargas, 2013; CAST, n.d.; Frey, Kearns, & King, 2012; GRCC Distance Learning Standards, 2015, section 8; IPFW Online Course Design Standards, 2016, Standard 7; Portland Community College, n.d.; Quality Matters, 2014; Quality Online Course Initiative, section 5; Quality Online Learning and Teaching (QOLT) instrument, section 8; Web Learning @ Penn State, standard 7):

- The campus accessibility policy statement in the syllabus
- An explanation of how the instructor supports diverse learning styles and abilities
- Guidance to students about how to obtain accommodations
- Ease of navigation within the course
- Formats that accommodate assistive technologies (such as electronic style names in documents)
- Meaningful links (embedding hyperlinks within the titles of the source and adding screen tips)
- Readable materials with a hierarchy of organized content and few, if any, distracting elements
- Readable fonts
- Multimodal course materials and multimedia content
- Information about accessibility of all technologies used in a course
- Links to software needed for course applications
- Text-equivalent language (alternative text descriptions) for nontext elements (images and graphs)
- Captioning for audio and multimedia
- Features in addition to color to signal emphasis (do not rely only on color)
- Information on time limits before a student begins an activity or test
- Appropriate style names identifying row and column headings when tables are used
- Accessible design for forms

These standards for accessibility align with the requirements in Section 508, 1194.22 Web-based intranet and Internet information and applications (Section508.gov, Quick reference; W3C® Web Accessibility Initiative, n.d.).

Another way of looking at standards and guidelines for accessibility begins with the barriers that students may face with online materials and the strategies that break down these barriers. As exhibit 7.1 shows, some of these strategies address multiple barriers.

Exhibit 7.1: Examples of Accessibility Barriers and Strategies

Auditory impairments, such as loss of hearing, deafness, or combined hearing and vision loss

Barrier: Audio content without transcripts or captions

Strategy: For non-text content, prepare text equivalent, such as a Word file.

Barrier: Multimedia or video without captioning

Strategy: Add captioning or other text-based ways to communicate content.

Visual impairments, such as color blindness, partial or complete loss of vision, or combined vision and hearing loss

Barrier: Images with no equivalent text alternatives

Strategy: Add alternative text descriptions, typically noted by an Alt Text or Alt Tag link in the Format Image or Format Picture option.

Barrier: Multimedia without text or audio alternatives

Strategy: Add screen-readable text equivalent; add audio alternative for images.

Barrier: Page navigation clutter or inconsistency

Strategy: Use simple, consistent organization and navigation (see chapter 3).

Barrier: Poor contrast and color combinations in foreground and background of text and images

Strategy: Print a sample page in gray scale to view contrast and increase contrast by using different colors suitable for individuals who have color blindness. Use black, dark brown, or dark blue on white, light beige, or pale yellow, or vice versa (Color blind, 2009).

Cognitive and neurological challenges such as autism, attention deficit disorder, learning disabilities, mental health disorders, or seizure disorders

Barrier: Complex, cluttered, or difficult-to-use layout or navigation

Strategy: Use simple, logical, and consistent organization and navigation (see chapter 3).

Barrier: Blinking, moving, or flickering content or background audio that the student cannot turn off

Strategy: Avoid animations that move, flicker, blink, or make sounds. Make sure the student has the option to turn off the audio and view the content without sound.

■ THE SPECIFIC HOW-TOs OF ENSURING ACCESSIBILITY

On the basic bedrock strategies we have just examined, we add three top priorities for building your online course materials: (1) make a clear path for access, (2) add useful signposts and tips within your files, and (3) use media wisely. We organize the specific ways to ensure accessibility around these goals.

A Clear Path for Access

To make a clear path for access, you need to present course materials in ways that students can perceive them, typically allowing them to see and hear the content. This may seem obvious, but there is more to consider. Ways of scanning documents, the addition of alternative text for images, the use of tables and graphics, and the creation of mathematical symbols can hinder or help a student's accessibility to course content.

Font Choice

Coombs (2010) recommends avoiding hard-to-read fonts. Exhibit 7.2 provides guidance for font choices.

Exhibit 7.2: Best Font Choices for Online Course Materials

Use a reasonable font size such as 10 to 12 point for most narrative, add space between lines of text such as one and a half line spaces, and avoid very long lines of text, which can pose problems for some readers (Coombs, 2010). The following fonts are easier on the eyes in computer displays because of their clean lines (WebAIM Fonts):

- Arial
- Tahoma
- Helvetica
- Verdana
- Geneva

For students with dyslexia, instructors and students can install a special font to reduce the difficulty in processing information: https://www.dyslexiefont.com/en/dyslexie-font/.

Whatever font you choose, do not type whole sentences in ALL CAPS or *italic,* because these are hard to read. Also avoid low-contrast, quirky treatments like shadowed or outlined letters and blinking text.

Organization and Writing Style

Coombs (2010), who has used assistive technology all his life, places additional strong emphasis on writing and style choices. Here are ways to provide readable structure and organization and facilitate students' use of assistive technologies:

- Clear organization
- Prominent placement of critical information
- Chunking of related content
- Inclusion of only the necessary content
- Clear and meaningful headings, titles, and labels
- Descriptive first sentences; use of active voice and familiar language; and avoidance of rarely used acronyms, abbreviations, or jargon
- Introductions for lists and placement of listed items in the correct sequence or order of importance
- Descriptive rows and column headings in tables
- Emphasis of critical information (avoid use of color alone; avoid screen flicker)
- 12-point font, familiar fonts, and white space between lines
- Enough contrast, such as black text on uncluttered, high-contrast background
- Visual consistency and synchronized multimedia

Scanning Documents

To scan a document to post at your course site, keep in mind that scanning will produce an image rather than readable text unless you have the correct settings on the scan machine.

Word and PowerPoint File Formats

Some common do's and don'ts of word processing begin with abandoning manual typewriter methods for entering text. Instead, learn how to use these tools (Sutton, 2002):

- Electronic formatting for hanging indents rather than hitting a space bar or tab
- Inserting hard page breaks rather than manually hitting an enter key repeatedly
- Using styles rather than manually formatting a word or phrase as bold or italicized (more on styles in the next section)
- Avoiding columns

If you are using older file formats, you may find it helpful to copy them over to a newer file format, such as .doc to .docx and .ppt to .pptx, or students may need to download a .docx converter (Microsoft Office Compatibility Pack). With text-based files such as Word, you can go back to make your documents accessible with relative ease, which is not true of other formats.

Alternative Text

When Coombs (2010) and course design standards call for alternative text or text equivalents, they mean adding descriptions of the images, photos, tables, graphs, and other nonnarrative elements. If an image does not load or a student cannot see it, a screen reader can read these descriptions aloud. Sometimes students without visual disabilities also prefer to use settings that skip image viewing and use only the alternative text description so they can move through content more quickly. Exhibit 7.3 explains ways to make images accessible.

Exhibit 7.3. How to Make Images Accessible

ALTERNATIVE TEXT FOR IMAGES

Add an "Alt Tag" or "Alt Text" for images. Typically, you can right-click on an image and choose "Format Image" to see the pop-up with "Alt Tag" or "Alt Text" listed. For other visuals, when you right-click, you may see "Format Object." A pop-up window will give you space for a "Title" and "Description." A title can be useful, but the screen reader reads what you enter in the "Description" area. Keep the description short but meaningful. For purely decorative images, enter something like "Decorative Blue Line," or enter the following term with *no space* between the quotes to signal the screen reader to skip the description: alt="".

LONG DESCRIPTION FOR COMPLEX IMAGES

Long descriptions sometimes help both sighted and nonsighted students interpret complex images such as charts, diagrams, and maps. For example, for a bar chart, you might need to explain data, relationships, or time periods. When you think a long description is needed, create it, but do not enter it in the "Alt Tag" or "Alt Text" area. You can provide the long description above, below, or adjacent to an image or in a link to a separate site. For the "Alt Text," simply use the "Description" area to tell the student where to find the long description.

Clark (2002c) recommends you write what you actually see—for example, "bright red earphones half the size of a grapefruit" (Chapter 6, ¶40). However, if you display the image of the teaching assistant in a course, you could enter something like "Portrait of _____, Teaching Assistant," omitting details unless relevant for understanding content, or choose the path of conversational engagement by describing the person's curly hair, bright smile, and flannel shirt (Clark, 2002c, ¶40). Exhibit 7.4 provides a sample long description for a mathematical diagram.

Exhibit 7.4: Long Description for a Math Diagram

Greg's feet are at point G. The mirror is 8 feet to his right at point M. The base of the flagpole is 24 feet to the right of point M and labeled point F. The distance from point G, Greg's feet, to his eye is 5 feet. This is the vertical leg of a right triangle. The hypotenuse connects Greg's eye to point M, the mirror on the ground. A similar triangle is formed from point M, the mirror, to point F, the base of the flagpole. The distance from point M to point F is 24 feet. The height of the flagpole is labeled H. This is the vertical leg of the second right triangle. The hypotenuse connects the top of the flagpole to point M, the mirror on the ground.

Source: National Center for Accessible Media (2009).

Tables and Graphic Representations

Instructors often use a tabular format for layout even though the content within the table can easily be provided in a narrative or list form. Instructors also often make densely complex tables or graphic displays of data that cause students cognitive overload, especially multilevel displays. Therefore, use tables and graphic data only when really needed to show data relationships, and keep them as simple as they can be.

More complex tables generally can be broken down into several simpler tables (Coombs, 2010; National Center for Accessible Media, 2009) so that data become easier for all students to interpret. Also, adding an explanation about a table's format and the type of information the data are intended to show can help blind or low-vision students make sense of the table layout (Coombs, 2010). For true tabular data, Excel often is a better choice because you can tag the headers, rows, and columns. Since instructors tend to make data representations more complex than they need to be, we include the following exhibits to show alternate accessible ways of expressing data. Even in these presentations, students can still be asked to reorder and interpret the data.

- Exhibit 7.5 shows sample data in a bar chart and the same data in a simple table format.
- Exhibit 7.6 shows an example of an alternate description for a bar chart with data placed into a list format.
- Exhibit 7.7 shows examples of two alternate descriptions for a Venn diagram, one brief and easy to understand and the other long and superfluous.

Exhibit 7.5: Bar Chart Followed by Alternate Simple Table Format

BAR CHART

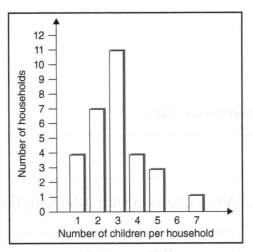

Source: University of Surrey, n.d.

ALTERNATE DESCRIPTION OF THE BAR CHART IN A SIMPLE TABLE FORMAT

Number of Children	Number of Households
1	4
2	7
3	11
4	4
5	3
6	0
7	1
Total	30

Exhibit 7.6. A List Format with an Introduction to Explain Some Sample Data from a Bar Chart

The bar chart is titled, "How People Who Are Deaf, Hard-of-Hearing, Blind, or Low-Vision Are Alerted to Emergencies."

The first number in the list below indicates responses from those who are deaf or hard of hearing; the second number indicates responses for those who are blind or have low vision. Responses for each method are approximate.

- Don't Know: 70, 79
- Friend: 59, 62
- Family: 65, 64
- Coworker: 33, 38
- TV: 102, 65
- Radio: 30, 80

Source: National Center for Accessible Media (2009).

Exhibit 7.7: Venn Diagram with Alternate Descriptions

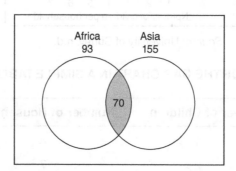

In a survey of 250 European travelers, 93 have traveled to Africa, 155 have traveled to Asia, and 70 have traveled to both of these continents, as illustrated in the Venn diagram above.

ALTERNATE DESCRIPTIONS FOR THE VENN DIAGRAM

Brief and Easy to Understand Description:
    The Venn diagram shows two intersecting circles, one labeled Africa 93 and the other labeled Asia 155. The area of intersection is labeled 70.
    Long and Superfluous Description:
    The figure is a Venn diagram and shows two intersecting circles inside a large rectangle. The circles do not touch the rectangle. The circle on the left is labeled Africa and the number 93 is under Africa and above the circle. The circle on the right is labeled Asia and the number 155 is under Asia and above the circle. The intersection of the 2 circles is shaded and has the number 70 in the shaded region.
Source: National Center for Accessible Media (2009).

Mathematical Equations

You can make equations accessible in several ways:

- Mark up math equations with MathML so students can use a reading system to interpret them or an equation editor such as Design Science's MathType (Design Science, 2016; National Center for Accessible Media, 2009).
- Use MathSpeak to convert complex equations and formulas to Nemeth Code, which can represent math in Braille (2004 MathSpeak Initiative).
- Use LaTeX, an open-source typesetting program that transmits to a Braille display. You can locate several LaTeX tutorials with a simple word search such as "LaTeX tutorial" or "Introduction to LaTeX."

Signposts and Tips

Course files can include useful signposts and tips that you may not yet have considered. For example, the placement of a URL for a link to a website, a table of contents, structure and style treatments for text and headings, and the ways you save files and create forms can help or hinder a student's accessibility to course content.

URL Placement and Screen Tips

Instead of placing a full URL within the narrative, you can embed it as a hyperlink within a title or key words of the source, allowing the narrative to maintain coherence. Another signpost you might not have noticed is the option to add a "screen tip" or "tool tip" for the hyperlink. This tip should appear in the pop-up panel when inserting a URL to a title. When you select "Screen Tip," you can enter the text you want to use. For example, you might write a tip to advise students of what to do when they reach the website, such as: "Look for heading 'Image Description, Examples, and Explanations.'" Exhibit 7.8 shows the URL placement and the added screen tip.

Exhibit 7.8: URL Placement for Narrative Flow Online and Screen Tip

The National Center for Accessible Media (2009) provides examples of how to describe complex graphic displays of data.

URL Placement with Poor Narrative Flow	Embedded URL for Better Readability with Screen Tip
The National Center for Accessible Media at http://ncam.wgbh.org/experience_learn /educational_media/describing-images-for-enhanced/professional-development-for-e provides examples of how to describe complex graphic displays of data.	Look for heading "Image Description, Examples, and Explanations." *Screen tip shows only when hovering over link* The National Center for Accessible Media provides examples of how to describe complex graphic displays of data.

Source: National Center for Accessible Media (2009).

Structure and Hidden Characters

You can even add signposts in your course documents, such as a Word file. A simple example from Coombs (2010, p. 36) illustrates the big difference that attention to design detail can make for readers. The left-hand column list of states and cities in exhibit 7.9 has accurate information, but nothing to tell us the state-versus-city relationships. In the list shown in the right-hand column, the relationships become clearer by printing the states in bolded CAPS.

Exhibit 7.9. Using Font Treatment to Signal Relationships

List 1: No Signal of Relationships	List 2: Visual Signal of Relationships
New York	**NEW YORK**
Albany	Albany
Buffalo	Buffalo
Washington	**WASHINGTON**
Spokane	Spokane
Seattle	Seattle

Yet while such treatment may help the reader who has no visual impairment, the bold and capitalization treatment will not be enough for all readers: labels are missing to signal the "state" level, and a read-aloud device is not likely to detect the bold unless you tag it with an underlying style. With this in mind, Goodson and Surface (2016a) explain that when you type on a typewriter or enter text on a computer screen, what you see is generally what you get visually. However, when you input information on a computer, nonprinting characters also become part of the file, even if you cannot see them. Coombs (2010) calls these "under the hood" characters (p. 58). When someone uses a screen reader or other device to read a file aloud, the device will also read those nonprint characters. For example, a screen reader might read "tab, tab, tab, tab" if the tab key manually created the spacing. Students face even more difficulty when using an electronic reading device for an unformatted table. Without clear signals provided by style sets, the screen reader can go off to never-never land and lose the student.

An unstyled narrative document may be readable, but the structure is clearer when you use the tools within Word to apply styles (Coombs, 2010; Goodson & Surface, 2016a). The need for styles becomes apparent when you see the hidden characters. The example of a course schedule from an unstyled syllabus in exhibit 7.10 shows a couple of features that undermine readability. (The hidden characters are not shown.) You can see how the use of two columns creates a problem for both the sighted and unsighted reader: reading across in the wrong order of Unit 1, then Unit 5, rather than in order of Unit 1, Unit 2, and so on. The rollover of the word *Insurance* under Unit 3, instead of Unit 7, muddies readability even more. A second problem for sighted readers is the underlining of "Course Schedule" because in our electronic files, such underlining typically signals a web link, where in this example none is intended.

Exhibit 7.10: Unformatted Section from a Course Syllabus

Course Schedule:

Unit 1: Introduction to Financial Literacy   Unit 5: Savings and Investment

Unit 2: Career Exploration   Unit 6: Credit and Debt

Unit 3: Paychecks and Income   Unit 7: Risk Management & Insurance

Unit 4: Planning and Money Management

A third problem arises when the hidden characters are shown, as in Exhibit 7.11. To reveal them, you can use the Microsoft paragraph symbol (¶) located on the Home ribbon or menu. In the "show" mode, you can see the number of tabs used to manually create the spacing. A student using a read-aloud device such as a screen reader would have to endure not only confusing organization caused by the layout but also hearing "tab" every time the tab mark appeared.

Exhibit 7.11: Syllabus Section with Hidden Characters Revealed

Course Schedule: ¶

Unit 1: Introduction to Financial Literacy→   →Unit 5: Savings and Investment¶

Unit 2: Career Exploration →   →   →   →   →Unit 6: Credit and Debt¶

Unit 3: Paychecks and Income →   →   →   →Unit 7: Risk Management & Insurance¶

Unit 4: Planning and Money Management¶

Avoiding such manual typewriter treatments along with using the styles tool in Word works around this problem and improves the document's appearance for all students. The result is the kind of readable presentation shown in Exhibit 7.12: a heading style applied to "Course Schedule," the removal of excess nonprint characters, and a clear sequence of topics.

Exhibit 7.12: Syllabus Section with Styles Instead of Nonprint Characters

Course Schedule

Unit 1: Introduction to Financial Literacy

Unit 2: Career Exploration

Unit 3: Paychecks and Income

Unit 4: Planning and Money Management

Unit 5: Savings and Investment

Unit 6: Credit and Debt

Unit 7: Risk Management and Insurance

Style Sets

Exhibit 7.13 provides guidelines for how to use style sets built into your LMS and Word (or a similar word processing program). Even without practice, you should find it easy to apply styles to any document.

Exhibit 7.13. Style Sets for Course Materials

Style Sets in Your LMS and Word (or Similar Program).

- In your LMS, the text editor (content editor) should allow you to identify text as a Heading, Subheading, or Paragraph, and to format a list.
- In Microsoft Word, you can find Style Sets at the Home tab. These allow you to identify headings, subheadings, normal paragraphs, and lists. You can use any of the styles, or modify them (right click, choose modify), keeping in mind the standards for accessibility (font style, size, color, contrast, and spacing).

These are the basic steps for using a style set:

- Choose a style set.
- Place the cursor over or highlight the word(s) in the text to which you want to apply one of the "quick styles."
- From the list in the style set, click the quick-style name you want to apply (e.g., Title, Heading 1, Heading 2, Heading 3, List, Emphasis).

If a "look" you want is not in the list of style names, you can make a new style by highlighting the word or phrase where you want the new treatment, add the treatment you want, and while highlighted save it as a new style name. For example, Goodson and Surface (2016a) created the "Week Heading" style for the schedule in the syllabus because they wanted a border around it, as shown in Exhibit 7.14. Although they used the style name "Week Heading," they also indicated within the Style Set that it was based on heading level 5.

Exhibit 7.14: Customized Style Based on Heading Level 5

The syllabus has a narrative format in the "Course Schedule" SECTION.

Week 1: [Insert beginning and ending dates.] **Topic:** [Insert topic.]
- List required reading or other preparation to do during the week.
- List activities and assignments for the week—add DUE dates.

Week 2: [Insert beginning and ending dates.] **Topic:** [Insert topic.]
- List required reading or other preparation to do during the week.
- List activities and assignments for the week—add DUE dates.

In addition to heading levels (such as Heading 1, Heading 2, and so on), they wanted style names that were meaningful for faculty within a syllabus, such as SECTIONS, TOPICS, Topic Paragraphs, and Lists. The syllabus style set also can be used with other course files. You can access the IPFW Syllabus Template at http://ipfw.edu/offices/celt/online-teaching/index.html.

Table of Contents

For longer documents, you may want to create a table of contents within Word. This can help students find content within a file, which is especially useful when a student wishes to review course content. If you have applied styles, the steps are simple and you can find Word tutorials to give more information:

- Create a blank line where you want the table of contents to appear and leave your cursor there.
- Find "Table of Contents" on the Word ribbon and choose the table of contents style that you want to use.

Saving a Word Document

Instructors generally save a Word document as Word.doc or .docx, and often also as a PDF because PDFs are faster and easier for students to open at an online course site. Some instructors upload both the Word and the Adobe PDF formats because students can add notes to the Word file.

When saving to a PDF, keep the styles and structure tags in the file. Doing this correctly requires a few simple basic steps, which exhibit 7.15 shows using screen shots. (Layouts vary with different versions of Word, but steps are essentially the same.)

1. Begin with a document that already has styles added because they create the "document structure." Without the style treatment, the PDF copy will provide "flawed" or "weak" accessibility (Karlen Communications, 2013).
2. Do not choose the "print to PDF" or "save as PDF" shortcuts. Instead, first select "Save As," and then choose PDF from the pull-down list of file choices, as shown in exhibit 7.15. After that, select "Options" and choose to show "Bookmarks, Tags, and Structure" when you save the file. These options allow a screen reader to "see" the structure of the file (such as Title, Heading 1, Heading 2, and so on), and for a student to easily move around in the document.
3. When posting files at the online course site, also add the file format to the title, such as "Class Schedule DOCX" or "Class Schedule PDF." Your LMS should signal the file size, but if not, do add it because size information may be useful to your students.

Exhibit 7.15: How to Save a Word Document as a PDF with Correct Options

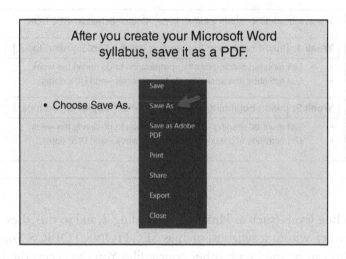

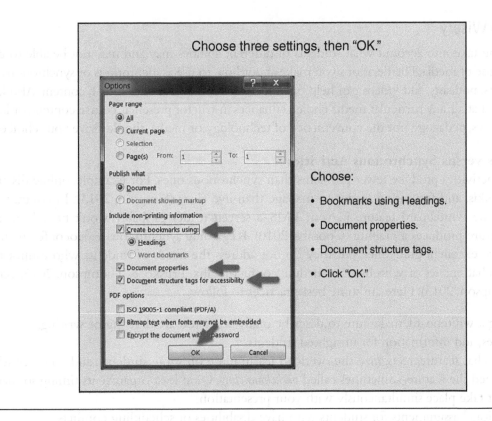

Fixing Existing PDF files

If you have PDF files that already have been created without saved styles, you can add markups to fix them with tools in Adobe Acrobat Pro or other resources listed in appendix B of this book. Another option is to transform a PDF file to a Word format, apply styles, and resave the file correctly as a PDF.

Accessible Forms

Adobe Acrobat Pro allows you to create forms so that they will be easy for all students to complete. Washington State University provides steps for "Creating Accessible PDF Forms Using Adobe Acrobat Pro" (http://www.washington.edu/accessibility/documents/pdf-forms/).

Checking Accessibility

To check color treatments, print out a sample page in gray scale to see if the contrast is strong enough. Keep in mind that almost no one has trouble seeing blue, but many people cannot distinguish red and green (Clark, 2002d, ¶24). For PDFs, you can use the read-aloud function and listen to see if the audio makes sense. If you have access, you also can also check with a screen reader; some campuses have this tool installed at computer labs. Ask for help with checking from your information technology services team or from the disabilities services office. The University of Washington provides an Online Course Accessibility Checklist for syllabi, documents, Excel workbooks, PowerPoint presentations, video, and audio (https://depts.washington.edu/uwdrs/faculty/online-course-accessibility-checklist/).

Using Media Wisely

In general, if you take into account what students of different abilities may and may not be able to do, you can make wise use of media. The decisions you make about how to use asynchronous or synchronous activities, PowerPoints, podcasts, and videos can help or hinder a student's access to course content. Also keep in mind how well, if at all, any particular media choice enhances instructor presence, course content, or learning activities. As always, pedagogy, not the convenience of technology or media, should drive your choices.

Asynchronous versus Synchronous Activities

Asynchronous activities produce fewer problems than synchronous ones. For example, online discussions, tweets, blogs, wikis, and forums are easier to manage than live chats (Simpson, 2013). In contrast, if you choose to use the whiteboard feature in your LMS, a screen reader probably won't be able to read it because this feature produces a graphic (Coombs, 2010). Regarding synchronous videoconferencing, several authors give excellent guidelines, but they do not address the needs of students who cannot rapidly enter and read chat entries or who have a schedule conflict (Calix, Prusko, & Thompson, 2015; Gautreau et al., 2012; Simpson, 2013). Here are some best practices to follow:

- When using a whiteboard, make sure to describe orally what you are drawing or writing.
- If using slides, add information for unsighted students.
- If using the chat feature, recognize the overload it can place on some students, and consider whether you really need the feature, sometimes called *backchanneling*. Or at least organize its timing so that chatting will not take place simultaneously with your presentation.
- Provide optional assignments for students who have disabilities or scheduling conflicts.
- Record the session so that all students can access it for future study and review.

To take into account these multiple factors in his online communication courses, Dircksen (2010) offers alternative days and times for a synchronous session, alternative assignments for those who do not participate, and archived recordings of the sessions to allow students to access and review them. In this way, he provides equal opportunity and avoids calling out any student who may have a disability that makes participation difficult.

Multimodal Feedback

Dircksen also provides varied forms of feedback on the more substantial papers in his courses (A. Dircksen, personal communication, September 15, 2016):

- Students have access to the scoring rubric in the Blackboard grade book where they see both quantitative and qualitative feedback.
- Students are e-mailed their papers with comments in the margins and the rubric copied at the bottom of each paper.
- Students are e-mailed a three- to four-minute video recording of Dircksen talking through their papers and giving suggestions on the most important areas he sees.

PowerPoint

We have previously mentioned in this chapter some common pitfalls in how instructors use PowerPoint presentations in online courses. Here we address specific production issues to consider when creating an accessible PowerPoint.

Adding Audio

While on the surface it seems like a good practice to add audio to each slide in a PowerPoint presentation (and generally it is), when you think through how a screen reader works, you can foresee some difficulties: a student who uses a screen reader will be hearing any text information on the slide simultaneously with the audio recorded for the slide. As you might imagine, making sense out of these competing audio tracks is difficult. You can still add audio, but the workaround is for the student to turn off the screen reader or for you to also provide a version with NOTES only and no sound. This latter strategy works well only if your NOTES are complete. Use the NOTES section to enter what you would say if you were making the presentation in person to ensure that you thoroughly summarize the slide's content (Coombs, 2010). Then when you print the PowerPoint with NOTES, you will have your script for recording.

Superfluous Text

Too often, PowerPoint presentations are loaded with long strings of text. If that is the case with your own slides, reconsider the need for that PowerPoint. Would an easy-to-read and appropriately styled Word file converted to PDF work as well? Some online instructors use Word with a simple table layout to add attractive images and narrative, and the product looks as good as or better than a slide. We mention this alternative not to dismiss PowerPoint but to help you make better use of this presentation format.

Visual Design

Create your PowerPoint presentations following good visual design basics for online courses:

- Choose a slide design with simple organization and good contrast of letters and background.
- Use the prebuilt placeholders to enter text information. Do not add any more text boxes because screen readers cannot read them.
- Avoid animations because they tend to interrupt the flow of the presentation and the animations you add can sometimes cause a seizure.
- Avoid auto-timing because the pace you set may not match a student's pace of processing information.
- Use the default font size or one slightly larger to allow clear readability.
- Write a complete phrase or sentence in the title area of each slide, and create a new phrase or sentence for each succeeding slide. This practice forces you to give a clear content core for each slide and helps you focus your students' attention.
- Add ALT Tags or ALT Text behind images. If you need to add a long description for an image, consider putting it inside the placeholder's text area first and matching the font color to the background or making the image large enough to cover over your description. In this way, a sighted person will not be distracted by the description and an unsighted person will be able to hear it with a reading device.
- When adding a multimedia presentation within a PowerPoint, set up the slide to have the presentation play automatically.

Saving and Converting PowerPoints

Many instructors save their PowerPoint presentations as a PDF as well as a presentation. PowerPoints can also be saved as flash files or in other formats. Check with your information technology services for best practices for converting PowerPoints.

Podcasts

Podcasts work well in courses such as linguistics or language, and they can add a personal voice to any course. You may create your own or find many excellent ones through a web search. Of course, you will also find poor ones, but you can easily sort the good from the bad.

When making your own, check with technical support on your campus for recommendations and, if needed, the use of equipment for recording and editing. You also need to know your campus guidelines for storing, uploading, and streaming. Consult with your information technology unit, instructional designers, online or distance learning team, or library as appropriate for your campus. Good practices in using podcasts include these:

- Make sure each podcast has a meaningful title.
- Keep your recording within brief time limits of seven to eight minutes maximum.
- Prepare a script, and rehearse before recording.
- Record in a space with low or no competing noise.
- Edit out gaps, pauses, and filler sounds.
- Provide a transcript for your students.
- Make sure students have the option to turn off the audio.
- Store and post audio according to your campus protocols.

Videos

When you create your own videos, you add a personal touch to your online course, but you also can find many good videos through a web search. Your LMS may be set up with a "mashup" tool that facilitates your web search and shows how the video link will appear at your course site. As with podcasts, check with your technical support team on protocols for recording, storing, and uploading videos. We recommend the following practices:

- Begin with a plan, such as a shooting script or storyboard for the videos you make yourself, and as noted in previous chapters, plan to keep them short (six to eighteen minutes). Reserve longer videos you select for those that are critical or strongly engaging (such as an engaging TED talk, a historical documentary, or the demonstration of steps in a procedure or movement).
- Record in a space with good lighting and low or no background noise. Low lighting may introduce flicker into your final video.
- Audio and visual elements do not speak for themselves. Provide spoken content for the visual elements and subtitles or captioning for the audio elements.
- Keep audio and visual content aligned with each other. This may seem like a no-brainer, but the alignment can slip when you edit the video. In addition, when you add captions, make sure the words match the visuals.
- If you cannot add captioning, provide a transcript. Even for students who do not have hearing problems, captioning and transcripts help in focusing on and reviewing content (Linder, 2016). Your campus may have designated captioning providers. For your own videos, you can follow certain procedures for adding captions, and if you start your preproduction with a script (a good practice anyway), you should find it fairly easy to add the captions.

Appendix B to this book provides additional resources for captioning.

HTML in Your LMS

If you are familiar with HTML (hypertext markup language) in web page design, you know the virtues of this platform-independent format. When you enter text in your LMS, it is in HTML, but the LMS hides the markup language so you will not be distracted by it. Most instructors do not notice it because the text editor is a WYSIWYG, pronounced "wiz-ee-wig" and meaning "what you see is what you get." As you enter content in the LMS, you can see the look of your finished product while the system itself adds the HTML coding "under the hood." You can see the markup language behind your text by selecting "HTML" on the text editor menu. The HTML may look daunting at first, but knowing some codes can help you to make sense of what you see and, more important, fix some text sections when the WYSIWYG does not work properly:

- The symbols < > contain the instruction on how something has been coded. For example, <b> indicates that bold font will appear on the word or phrase that follows; <i> indicates italics; <p> indicates a new paragraph; <ul> indicates an unordered list; <li> indicates a listed item.
- The symbols </> signal where a code ends. For example, </b> indicates where the bold ends; </i> where the italics ends; </li> where an item ends; </ul> where the unordered list ends.
- The symbol <br> adds an extra line space. You do not have to add </br> to signal the end of the line break.

ADDITIONAL RESOURCES AND ADVICE

Dell et al. (2015, p. 175) provide the following steps toward universal design of online courses:

Presentation

- Create content first; then design.
- Provide simple and consistent navigation.
- Include an accommodation statement.
- Use color with care.
- Choose fonts carefully.

Action and Expression

- Model and teach good discussion board etiquette.

Engagement and Interaction

- Choose content management system (CMS) tools carefully.
- Provide accessible document formats.
- Convert PowerPoint to HTML.
- If the content is auditory; make it visual.
- If the content is visual; make it auditory.

Appendix B lists dozens of additional resources that you may wish to use or discuss with your technical support team.

Here are some ways to reduce your workload as you build your online course:

- Look for course materials among the electronic resources of your campus library. You probably will find resources in accessible formats and for which copyright issues have already been addressed for course use.
- Search for accessible open educational resources (OERs; see chapter 3) to use as course materials. Piña (2016) reports that using more OERs for online courses also improves learning—most likely because

focusing on how well the OERs align with learning outcomes shifts the attention away from alignment with textbook chapters.

- Add scanned documents with correct settings for readability (OCR, optical character recognition). Otherwise the screen reader will "see" the text as an unreadable graphic and will not be able to read the text aloud to the student.
- Search for videos that already have the closed captioning (CC) feature.
- When preparing your own podcasts, voice-overs, or videos, write a script beforehand or as you go to save you time in writing a transcript later.
- Format for accessibility when initially developing documents and presentations.
- When selecting a textbook, look for one that is available in digital and print format because using print alone requires scanning all the pages for conversion to a readable format for a student who has low or no vision.

Reflections

For Instructors

- What is the accessibility policy for online courses on your campus?
- Who provides accessibility support for online courses on your campus? What kinds of services or resources do they provide? What technology support is available to you?
- How do your course materials measure up against these accessibility criteria? What would you want to improve?
- What resources or consultations with others on campus could support you in making needed changes or transformations?
- If you work with or plan to use publisher supplemental resources, how well can you answer the following questions? Do not take a publisher's word that supplemental materials or an e-book are accessible and easy to navigate. Check out such claims.
  - Video and audio materials: Are there transcriptions? Are the videos captioned or subtitled? If not, find out how the publisher will provide the transcriptions and captioned/subtitled editions.
  - Text with images: Can the text materials be read aloud with assistive technology, including alternative text descriptions for the images? If possible, check the accessibility on your own or with assistance from your information technology support or disabilities services.
  - E-book: If you are considering an e-book, check to see if there is a Document Accessibility Profile (DAP) with information about its accessibility features (http://stepp.gatech.edu/dap.php).
  - Supplemental or e-book materials: Find out how students can use the navigation tools.

For Instructional Designers

- What can you do to support faculty in accessibility design for the following types of online course materials?
  - Microsoft Word
  - PDFs
  - Excel
  - PowerPoints
  - Podcasts

- Videos
- Forms
- Tables
- Complex graphics
- Making files ready for Braille
- Other
- How can you support faculty in providing guidance to students about assistive technology or other useful applications?
- What course site features and tools will support students who have disabilities? What will interfere?
- How can you support the posting of course files so that their titles convey their use and their different formats?
- Where can you go on your campus to gain support for accessibility design? What kind of support can you expect?
  - Disabilities office
  - Faculty development center
  - Other instructional designers
  - Distance education unit
  - Library
  - Office of institutional equity or other similar entity
  - Other
- What resource files could be created and preloaded at different campus websites or in course templates to inform faculty and students about accessibility support resources?

For Administrators

- Who has completed an evaluation of accessibility design practices for online courses on your campus? If no one, what group could you establish for this purpose? How can you involve all stakeholders? What other resources might give you this information, such as a faculty development center, the student disabilities office, faculty who teach online, librarians, and information technology specialists?
- How can you develop greater collaboration and cooperation among the partners on your campus who support accessibility design for online courses?
- How can different campus offices collaborate to create and preload resources at different campus websites or in course templates to share accessibility support resources?

■ REFERENCES

2004 MathSpeak Initiative. (n.d.). [website]. Retrieved from http://www.gh-mathspeak.com/

Accessibility at Blackboard. (n.d.). [website]. Retrieved from http://www.blackboard.com/accessibility.aspx

ADA: What is the Americans with Disabilities Act? (n.d.). [website]. Retrieved from https://adata.org/learn-about-ada

Angel Learning. [website]. Retrieved from http://www.angellearning.com/products/lms/accessibility.html

Bastedo, K., Sugar, A., Swenson, N., & Vargas, J. (2013). Programmatic, systematic, automatic: An online course accessibility support model. *Journal of Asynchronous Learning Networks*, 17(3), 87–102. Retrieved from http://files.eric.ed.gov/fulltext/EJ1018300.pdf

Bozarth, J. (2015, July 7). Nuts and bolts: It's not just about "compliance": Accessibility in learning. *Learning Solutions Magazine*. Retrieved from http://www.learningsolutionsmag.com/articles/1737/nuts-and-bolts-its-not-just-about-compliance-accessibility-in-elearning

Calix, L. P., Prusko, P. T., & Thompson, J. (2015). Building community through synchronous sessions. In *Proceedings of the 31st Annual Conference on Distance Teaching and Learning*. Retrieved from https://dtlconference.wisc.edu/wp-content/uploads/2015/08/Proceedings-2015.pdf

Campus announces restriction of public access to educational content. (2017, March 2). *Daily Californian*. Retrieved from http://www.dailycal.org/2017/03/02/campus-announces-restriction-public-access-educational-content/

CAST. (2008). *Universal design for learning: Version 1.0*. Wakefield, MA: Author. Retrieved from http://www.uvm.edu/~cdci/universaldesign/about-us/events/images/udlpdf/UDL_Guidelines_v1.0.pdf

CAST. (n.d.). *Accessibility and policy*. Retrieved from http://udloncampus.cast.org/page/policy_landing

Chickering, A. W., & Ehrmann, S. C. (1996). Implementing the seven principles: Technology as lever. *AAHE Bulletin, 49*(2), 3–7. Retrieved from https://www.aahea.org/articles/sevenprinciples.htm

Chickering, A. W., & Gamson, Z. F. (1987, March). Seven principles for good practice in undergraduate education. *AAHE Bulletin*, 3–7.

Chisholm, W., & May, M. (2008, September 17). *Universal design for web applications*. Web 2.0 Expo. Retrieved from http://cdn.oreillystatic.com/en/assets/1/event/16/Universal%20Design%20for%20Web%20Applications%20Presentation.pdf

Cielo24. (2017). *UC Berkeley will remove public access to online content—and replace it with new accessible content*. Retrieved from https://cielo24.com/2017/03/uc-berkeley-will-remove-public-access-to-online-content/

Clark, J. (2002a). Why bother? *Building accessible websites*. Retrieved from http://joeclark.org/book/sashay/serialization/Chapter02.html

Clark, J. (2002b). What is media access? *Building accessible websites*. Retrieved from http://joeclark.org/book/sashay/serialization/Chapter04.html

Clark, J. (2002c). The image problem. *Building accessible websites*. Retrieved from http://joeclark.org/book/sashay/serialization/Chapter06.html

Clark, J. (2002d). The image problem. *Building accessible websites*. Retrieved from http://joeclark.org/book/sashay/serialization/Chapter09.html

Color blind: Which are your blind colors? (2009). [website]. Retrieved from http://www.color-blindness.com/2009/03/15/color-blind-which-are-your-blind-colors/

Coombs, N. (2010). *Making online teaching accessible: Inclusive course design for students with disabilities*. San Francisco, CA: Wiley.

D2L. (n.d.). [website]. Retrieved from https://www.d2l.com/accessibility/

Dell, C. A., Dell, T. F., & Blackwell, T. L. (2015). Applying universal design for learning in online courses: Pedagogical and practical considerations. *Journal of Educators Online-JEO, 13*(2), 166-192.

Design Science: How science communicates. (2016). [website]. Retrieved from https://www.dessci.com/en/

Dircksen, A. (2010). General description of online courses taught and descriptions of the innovative online teaching approaches utilized. Retrieved from https://www.ipfw.edu/dotAsset/13702cb7-dba0-48b3-b006-3ae90392a523.pdf

Dolhansky. B., & Paire, P. (2016, November). *A journey to accessibility—How Temple University is implementing an accessible information and technology initiative university wide*. Lecture given at the 19th Annual Conference on Accessing Higher Ground: Accessible Media, Web, and Technology. Westminster, CO. Retrieved from http://accessinghigherground.org/wp/wp-content/uploads/2013/04/A-journey-to-accessibility-Final.pptx

Frey, B. A., Kearns, L. R., & King, D. K. (2012). *Quality Matters: Template for an accessibility policy for online courses.* Retrieved from https://www.qualitymatters.org/accessibility-policy-template/download/QM%20Accessibility%20Policy%20Final.pdf

Gautreau, C., Glaeser, B. C., Renold, L. C., Ahmed, S., Lee, J., Carter-Wells, J., . . . Schools, J. (2012). Video conferencing guidelines for faculty and students in graduate online courses. *Journal of Online Learning and Teaching, 8*(4). Retrieved from http://jolt.merlot.org/vol8no4/gautreau_1212.htm

Goetze, L. (2016). *Legal costs can be big to defend inaccessible web content in postsecondary education.* Retrieved from http://www.ncdae.org/resources/articles/legalcosts.php

Goodson, L., & Surface, K. (2016a). Jumpstart syllabus session for new faculty at Purdue University Fort Wayne.

Goodson, L., & Surface, K. (2016b). *Learner-centered design: Best practices.* Retrieved from http://guides.library.ipfw.edu/learnercentered

Grasgreen, A. (2014, April 2). Dropping the ball on disabilities. *Inside Higher Ed.* Retrieved from https://www.insidehighered.com/news/2014/04/02/students-disabilities-frustrated-ignorance-and-lack-services

GRCC Distance Learning Standards. (2015). Retrieved from http://www.grcc.edu/sites/default/files/attachments/GRCCDLStandards.pdf

HHS.gov: Section 508 of the Rehabilitation Act. (n.d.). [website]. Retrieved from https://www.section508.gov/section-508-of-the-rehabilitation-act

HHS.gov: What is section 504 and how does it relate to section 508? (n.d.). [website]. Retrieved from http://www.hhs.gov/web/section-508/what-is-section-504/

Ingeno, L. (2013, June 24). Online accessibility a faculty duty. *Inside Higher Ed.* Retrieved from https://www.insidehighered.com/news/2013/06/24/faculty-responsible-making-online-materials-accessible-disabled-students

IPFW Online Course Design Standards. (2016). Retrieved from http://www.ipfw.edu/dotAsset/d405f15e-760b-46bb-b7a6-b2c9eb5fbbb8.pdf

Karlen Communications. (2013). Accessible PDF documents. (n.d.). [website]. Retrieved from http://www.karlencommunications.com/AccessiblePDF.html

Leavitt, N. O., & Schneiderman, B. (2006). *Research-based web design and usability guidelines.* US Department of Health and Rehabilitative Services. Retrieved from https://www.usability.gov/sites/default/files/documents/guidelines_book.pdf

Lee, I. (2016). *Winning in college: A guide for students with disabilities.* Retrieved from http://www.edsmart.org/students-with-disabilities-college-guide/

Linder, K. (2016, November). *How does closed caption use impact student learning?* Session given at the 41st Annual Conference of the Professional and Organizational Development Network, Louisville, KY.

Microsoft Office compatibility pack for Word, Excel, and PowerPoint file formats. Retrieved from https://www.microsoft.com/en-us/download/details.aspx?id=3

Moodle: Accessibility. (n.d.). [website]. Retrieved from https://docs.moodle.org/28/en/Accessibility

National Center for Accessible Media. (2009). *Effective practices for description of science content within digital talking books.* Retrieved from http://ncam.wgbh.org/experience_learn/educational_media/stemdx/intro

National Center on Disability and Access to Education. (2016). *Tips and tools: Content management systems and accessibility.* [website]. Retrieved from http://ncdae.org/resources/factsheets/cms.php

National Center on Universal Design for Learning. (2014). The three principles of UDL. [website]. Retrieved from http://www.udlcenter.org/aboutudl/whatisudl/3principles

O'Rourke, T. (2013). *Access to technology ADA compliance.* Retrieved from http://www.temple.edu/cfo/resources/documents/ADApresentation1-21-13.pdf

Portland Community College. (n.d.). *Who's responsible for accessibility of online courses?* [website] Retrieved from https://www.pcc.edu/resources/instructional-support/access/documents/a11y-responsibilites-final-web.pdf

Piña, A. (2016, October). *Effects of open education resources on students, faculty, and instructional designers.* Presentation at the Association for Educational Communications and Technology International Convention, Las Vegas, NV.

Public Affairs, UC Berkeley. (2016, September 13). *A statement on online course content and accessibility.* Retrieved from http://news.berkeley.edu/2016/09/13/a-statement-on-online-course-content-and-accessibility/

Quality Matters. (2014). *Rubric standards 2011–2013 edition with assigned point values.* Retrieved from http://www.elo.iastate.edu/files/2014/03/Quality_Matters_Rubric.pdf

Quality Online Course Initiative: Complete rubric. (n.d.). Retrieved from http://www.ion.uillinois.edu/initiatives/qoci/docs/QOCIRubric.rtf

Quality Online Learning and Teaching (QOLT) instrument. (n.d.). Retrieved from https://drive.google.com/file/d/0BxN4M6qCVbDPOEl0d1dKWmFXOEk/view

Ralabate, P. K. (2011). Universal design for learning: Meeting the needs of all students. *ASHA Leader, 16,* 14–17.

Resolution Agreement, University of Phoenix. (2015). Retrieved from http://www2.ed.gov/about/offices/list/ocr/docs/investigations/more/08152040-b.pdf

Rodgers, B. (2015, April 28). *Hidden disabilities diagnoses up but some students remain unreported at Iowa colleges, universities.* Iowa Watch.org. Retrieved from http://iowawatch.org/2015/04/28/hidden-disabilities-diagnoses-up-but-some-students-still-go-unreported-at-iowa-colleges-universities/

Section 508.gov. (n.d.). [website]. Retrieved from https://www.section508.gov

Section 508.gov. (n.d.). Quick reference guide to Section 508 requirements [website]. Retrieved from http://www.section508.gov/content/learn/standards/quick-reference-guide#1194.22

Settlement between Penn State University and National Federation of the Blind. (n.d.). [website]. Retrieved from http://accessibility.psu.edu/nfbpsusettlement/

Simpson, E. (2013, February 19). Clearing up accessibility for distance education administrators: Accommodating the new students. *Evolllution.* Retrieved from http://evolllution.com/opinions/clearing-up-accessibility-for-distance-education-administrators-accommodating-the-new-students/

Stachowiak, J. R. (2009). Technology tools for implementing universal design for learning in postsecondary settings. *Accessibility in Action, 1*(2). Retrieved from http://education.jhu.edu/PD/newhorizons/Journals/spring2010/universaldesignforlearning/

Sutton, J. (2002). *A guide to making documents accessible to people who are blind or visually impaired.* Retrieved from http://www.sabeusa.org/wp-content/uploads/2014/02/A-Guide-to-Making-Documents-Accessible-to-People-Who-are-Blind-or-Visually-Impaired.pdf

UDL guidelines—Version 2.0. [website]. Retrieved from http://www.udlcenter.org/aboutudl/udlguidelines

University Business. (2016, January). *Web accessibility: A campuswide approach—Developing a comprehensive strategy to meet the needs of students with disabilities.* Retrieved from https://www.universitybusiness.com/article/web-accessibility-campuswide-approach

University of Surrey. (n.d.). Chapter 2 tables and charts. [website]. Retrieved from http://libweb.surrey.ac.uk/library/skills/Working%20with%20charts%20and%20graphs%201/MU120_4M5_section5.html

University of Washington. (2016). Legal cases by issue [website]. Retrieved from http://www.washington.edu/accessibility/requirements/legal-cases-by-issue/

University of Washington: Accessible Technology. (n.d.). Resolution agreements and lawsuits. [website]. Retrieved from http://www.washington.edu/accessibility/requirements/accessibility-cases-and-settlement-agreements/

US Department of Education, Office of Civil Rights. (2016). *Reading room.* [website]. Retrieved from http://www2 .ed.gov/about/offices/list/ocr/frontpage/faq/readingroom.html

US Department of Justice, Civil Rights Division. (2016, August 30). *The United States' findings and conclusions based on its investigation under Title II of the Americans with Disabilities Act of the University of California at Berkeley.* (DJ No. 204-11-309). Retrieved from https://news.berkeley.edu/wp-content/uploads/2016/09/2016-08-30-UC-Berkeley-LOF.pdf

Vasquez, L., & Johnson, J. (2016). *Online education and accessibility for students with disabilities* [PowerPoint presentation]. Retrieved from http://www.asccc.org/sites/default/files/2016%20Online%20Education%20and%20Accessibility %20for%20Students%20with%20Disabilities_0.ppt

W3C®Web Accessibility Initiative. (n.d.). [website]. Retrieved from https://www.w3.org/WAI/

WebAIM Canvas certification. (2015). [website]. Retrieved from http://webaim.org/services/certification /canvas?utm_content=buffer29dd7&utm_medium=social&utm_source=plus.google.com&utm_campaign=buffer

WebAIM Fonts WebAim. [website]. Retrieved from http://webaim.org/techniques/fonts/#blink

Web Learning @ Penn State: Penn State quality assurance e-learning standards. (2016). Retrieved from https:// weblearning.psu.edu/resources/penn-state-online-resources/qualityassurance/

Wentz, B., Jaeger, P.T., & Lazar, J. (2011). Retrofitting accessibility: The legal inequality of after-the-fact online access for persons with disabilities in the United States. *First Monday, 16*(11). Retrieved from https://nfb.org/images/nfb /publications/bm/bm12/bm1205/bm120504.htm

CHAPTER 8

Creating a Supportive Culture for Online Teaching

College and university administrators, instructional design teams, teaching center staffs, and online-teaching faculty themselves can ignite the development of programs and activities needed to create a supportive culture for online teaching. This kind of culture prepares confident instructors who can design and teach top-quality online courses that satisfy students, reduce the number of dropouts, and improve retention. However, many disincentives stand in the way, so institutional leaders must ensure that the strategic plan, policies, programs, organizational structure, and resources are in place to develop the skills and competencies faculty need. Most important are the professional development initiatives. They require a strong conceptual design and research-based practices. Because faculty do the actual frontline teaching, their professional development must take into account their perceptions, concerns, and needs. We present the features of successful development programs as well as three different model programs.

If high-quality online courses and programs are a priority for universities, then instructors must be qualified, motivated, and satisfied with teaching online.

—D. Dietrich (2015)

■ THE IMPORTANCE OF QUALITY IN ONLINE COURSES

We now know that students can learn as much or more from online courses as from traditional ones (Swan, 2014; US Department of Education, 2010). We also know that faculty with experience teaching online view online learning more favorably than those without online teaching experience. They also improve

195

their classroom as well as online teaching, make better use of multimedia content, and, with good use of technology tools, can apply instructional strategies in their online classes similar to those in their face-to-face ones (Chiasson, Terras, & Smart, 2015; Hunt et al., 2014; Straumsheim, 2016). However, not all courses measure up or have the same outcomes. Many lack the high-quality features needed for success. These features more often appear in courses designed and taught by knowledgeable instructors who gain professional satisfaction in online teaching.

Chaloux and Miller (2014, p. 10) lay out the role of leadership and faculty in creating quality:

> Ensuring quality in this area means that leaders must involve their organization in a variety of functions, from instructional design to faculty development, assessment, and retention, and other factors that reflect learning outcomes.

> Faculty satisfaction means broad acceptance by faculty for the use of technology and online pedagogical strategies that enhance the teaching and learning environment. More specifically, it addresses the need for faculty to find value in their online learning experiences and be assured that the quality is sound and that the technology helps them to meet learning objectives.

In addition, administrative leaders—presidents, chancellors, vice chancellors, directors, and senior campus leaders and faculty—need to connect online learning to the institution's mission, priorities, and strategic plan (Chaloux & Miller, 2014). They also need to invest in professional development because it directly strengthens online program quality, student satisfaction, and student retention (Gregory & Martindale, 2016). Courses that are designed and taught by well-trained online instructors tend to meet quality standards, have more productive student interactions and better instructional materials, and facilitate student achievement of course learning outcomes (Sun & de la Rosa, 2015). In contrast, courses taught by faculty without adequate training leave students feeling disengaged (Alexiou-Ray & Bentley, 2015). A poor online learning experience can close off students' future learning, whereas an excellent one can "foster a lifelong learning relationship between the learner and the institution" (Ragan & Schroeder, 2014, ¶19). When only half of our institutions seem to give adequate support for creating and teaching online courses (Straumsheim, 2016), we may be only half as likely to achieve those excellent experiences and lifelong relationships.

Online course and program quality can strengthen an institution's reputation and thereby its potential value to future students. Many institutions, including Penn State World Campus, Rio Salado College, University of Illinois at Springfield, Empire State College, and American Public University System, measure the success of their online programs by their enrollment numbers and revenue (Chaloux & Miller, 2014). This success emanates from the vision of online programming held by leaders of these institutions, even though their responsibilities vary. For example, at Rio Salado College, faculty chairs carry the load for implementing and evaluating online courses, while at Penn State, the academic unit and their World Campus unit share decision making. Yet all the leaders have prioritized online learning and have actively shaped policy to support their online programs.

Beyond enrollments and revenues, some leaders measure success using these indicators as well (Swan, 2014, ¶49):

- Course grades/success
- Satisfaction
- Retention
- Achievement
- Proficiencies

To excel on these measures, leaders must share the research about what makes online programs successful (Chaloux & Miller, 2014; Schroeder, 2014) and ensure it informs strategic decisions and professional development.

Leaders can begin with the major meta-analysis comparing online to traditional courses by the US Department of Education (2010). This review documents the efficacy of online learning and the instructional strategies associated with effectiveness. Another important knowledge base is the National Survey of Student Engagement (NSSE, 2009, 2013; Swan, 2014). The 2009 NSSE survey found that technology and online learning lead to multiple gains in student engagement, with both students and faculty actively using technology for course announcements, assignments, readings, lecture notes and slides, and grade books. The 2013 survey reports that students who take their course work online use more effective learning strategies and spend more time studying, reading, and writing. Although students taking all their courses online collaborated less and interacted less with faculty, they considered the quality of their interactions better than that of the classroom students (NSSE, 2013).

The best training and support come early in instructors' online teaching careers and address faculty concerns about student learning, not just the use of technology or technical online operations (Horvitz, Beach, Anderson, & Xia, 2015). Some early adopters simply have more online teaching experience and can more easily combine it with technology innovations. Others tended to work with instructional designers in a more self-directed way (Ragan & Schroeder, 2014). These faculty are usually younger, familiar with technology tools, and comfortable with risk (Hixon, Buckenmeyer, Barczyk, Feldman, & Zamojski, 2012). Those with more teaching experience and familiarity with web search tools, social media, and other computer technologies are in the best position to launch into online teaching.

Later adopters tend to be older, less familiar with computers, and more skeptical of innovations, and most faculty fall into this category. They are more likely to struggle with learning the technology, conceptualizing their course design for the online context, and setting aside the time needed to make the appropriate and timely transformation of course content and instructional strategies. Although face-to-face teaching experience initially informs online teaching (McQuiggan, 2012), too little competent guidance and support leave faculty spending more time just trying to figure out how to do basic tasks online.

Many faculty actually gain satisfaction from their online teaching and want to continue doing it (Bolliger & Wasilik, 2009). Some even prefer teaching online, especially those who have more teaching experience and technology skills and value the flexibility it gives them to work on their research (Roby, Ashe, Singh, & Clark, 2013). They see the ways that online instruction can promote best teaching practices, such as providing students with prompt feedback, extending their time on task, and upholding high expectations (Chickering & Gamson, 1987; Roby et al., 2013). In addition, many instructors report making positive changes in their face-to-face classes—for example, tightening course design, instituting more active learning and reflection, and better communicating with students—because of their online teaching experiences (McQuiggan, 2012; Straumshein, 2016).

■ FACULTY CHALLENGES IN TRANSITIONING TO ONLINE TEACHING

Faculty encounter new demands and adjustments when they transition to online teaching. Many approach this transition with deep skepticism about the quality of online learning and their own skills using the learning management system (LMS), teaching online, fostering student engagement, and creating a sense of community online (Lin, Dyer, & Guo, 2012). They are also apprehensive about the shortage of opportunities for them to acquire online teaching expertise and their loss of face-to-face interaction with students (Horvitz et al., 2015). Here we examine the faculty's major disincentives for teaching online.

Lack of Institutional Support and Rewards

The absence of strong leadership, institutional commitment and support, encouragement, and rewards (recognition, money, and credit toward tenure and promotion) discourages faculty from teaching online (Cook, Ley, Crawford, & Warner, 2009; Howell, Saba, Lindsay, & Williams, 2004; Hunt et al., 2014; Lloyd, Byrne, & McCoy, 2012; Taylor & McQuiggan, 2008). Many instructors also express concerns about the lack of clear policies and standards for online courses at their institutions (Lloyd et al., 2012). All too common is the administrative failure to involve faculty in course decision making, appropriately limit online enrollments, and give release time for course design and development (Cook et al., 2009; Gregory & Martindale, 2016; Howell et al., 2004; Lloyd et al., 2012; Marek, 2009).

Unreliable Technology

Faculty report obsolete and unreliable technology and rapidly changing software or delivery systems as major disincentives to teaching online. They also worry about students who lack DSL/fast access on their computers and the technical skills for learning well online (Hunt et al., 2014; Lloyd et al., 2012; Tabata & Johnsrud, 2008).

Absent or Poor Technical Support

Faculty lose motivation to teach online when the campus lacks sufficient technical support for them and their students (Cook et al., 2009; Green, Alejandro, & Brown, 2009; Tabata & Johnsrud, 2008), and they fear having to handle unfamiliar technology on their own (Ragan & Schroeder, 2014). In any LMS, they are likely to confront plenty of unfamiliar course areas, terminology, tools, links, checkboxes, setting options, and multiple methods and places for uploading content.

Absent or Inadequate Training

Faculty express concerns about the lack or inadequacy of training on their campuses to prepare them for online course design and teaching (Cook et al., 2009; Howell et al., 2004; Hunt et al., 2014; Lloyd et al., 2012; Tabata & Johnsrud, 2008; Samuel, 2016; Taylor & McQuiggan, 2008). Lack of training breeds doubts about the value of online learning and fear of the unknown, especially among instructors who also lack pedagogical training (Ray, 2009). Many faculty are not even aware of the professional development opportunities at their institutions (Taylor & McQuiggan, 2008) and are left with learning by trial and error (Schmidt, Hodge, & Tschida, 2013).

Proactive education and the practical strategies for high-quality online courses can preempt many faculty concerns. This is important because until faculty experience online teaching, they have trouble conceptualizing it (Ragan & Schroeder, 2009). They cannot simply structure content for asynchronous online learning the same way as for face-to-face classes (Chiasson et al., 2015; Fish & Wickersham, 2009; Ray, 2009; Smidt, McDyre, Bunk, Li, & Gatenby, 2014).

Faculty must reconceptualize not only the classroom but also classroom dynamics (McQuiggan, 2012; Ragan & Schroeder, 2014; Ray, 2009). They are accustomed to communicating with students face-to-face and expect a certain type of student participation and social dynamic between them and a class. But in online classes, technology mediates all communication, participation, and social relationships.

Without training and at least some successful experiences with online technology, the transition to online teaching can be a slow, bumpy ride. Faculty may prefer to be either released from online teaching or rescued by experts (Northcote, Gosselin, Reynaud, Kilgour, & Anderson, 2015).

Concerns about Workload

Some faculty fear the effort needed to build and teach an online course—specifically, about not having enough time to learn the new technologies (Chiasson et al., 2015), prepare and revise a course, monitor and maintain it, and grade and give feedback (Hunt et al., 2014; Lloyd et al., 2012). Indeed, planning and developing an online course does require considerable upfront time, while a face-to-face class allows stretching its development well into the term (McQuiggan, 2012). Once developed, however, an online course shifts instructor time almost completely to teaching and assessing rather than preparing course materials.

Concerns about Quality

While experienced online faculty report that their online students take more responsibility for learning than their classroom students do (Chiasson et al., 2015; Scagnoli, Buki, & Johnson, 2009), those without this experience question the quality of online courses and tend to oppose or resist online teaching (Gregory & Martindale, 2016; Tabata & Johnsrud, 2008). Their concerns about quality take various forms. Some faculty—55 percent in one study (Vivolo cited in Ubell, 2016)—fear losing touch with their students. They think of the online context as impersonal, in part because it removes the visual cues that help them respond best to students and can limit student-to-student interactions (Hunt et al., 2014; Lloyd et al., 2012). Some faculty have more concerns about online accessibility of students with disabilities (see chapter 7; Hunt et al., 2014), and many of these prioritize getting technical support to develop accessible materials (Roby et al., 2013). Others fear that online courses make cheating and plagiarizing too easy and likely (Hunt et al., 2014; Lloyd et al., 2012; Straumshein, 2016).

Fears about quality escalate with added concerns about online pedagogical skills (Hunt et al., 2014; Lloyd et al., 2012). Some faculty even worry that the requirements of the online format may reflect badly on their personal standards of teaching (Ragan & Schroeder, 2014). They may feel that they are stepping into a bog of skepticism even when their administrators believe strongly in the efficacy of online education (Straumshein, 2015). In particular, junior faculty on tenure track may fear that lower student ratings or higher dropout rates could muddy their tenure progress. These concerns undermine the motivation to teach online (Tabata & Johnsrud, 2008), underscoring the need for campus leaders to disseminate research-based knowledge about online learning successes, along with furnishing encouragement, training, and support.

Because of the overall lower retention rates in online courses and residual skepticism about the quality of online teaching, online courses more often are reviewed and evaluated against a set of course design standards (see chapter 3). Institutions face increasing pressure, much of it from accreditation agencies, to evaluate the quality of not only the courses but also the professional training to prepare faculty for online teaching (Gregory & Martindale, 2016). Relatedly, others can easily view and evaluate the online course design and teaching strategies for a whole semester. Even a faculty member's content expertise comes up for review because online content is visible, stored, and updated (Major, 2015). While online course design standards do not examine content expertise per se, they do require a review of course materials for alignment with outcomes and content accuracy, relevance, and comprehensiveness.

Approaches to course review vary across institutions, ranging from collegial quality-improvement feedback to evaluation and scoring by external evaluators. For example, California State University, Chico (2016), makes its Quality Online Learning and Teaching (QOLT) rubric available as a guide for course design, redesign, self-evaluation, and recognition of exemplary courses. Purdue University Fort Wayne uses a collegial quality-improvement peer review process with a "met" or "not yet met" rating and action plan for improvement (IPFW Online Course Design Standards, 2016). Many campuses use an external review process through Quality Matters that yields a quantitative score on discrete standards as rated by multiple reviewers (Quality Matters Higher Education Program, 2016; Swan, 2014). Other institutions require or invite online instructors to complete certification training designed to meet accreditation requirements (e.g., Texas State Distance Learning, n.d.).

■ FACULTY INCENTIVES AND SUPPORT FOR ONLINE TEACHING

Faculty satisfaction with online teaching derives from a constellation of incentives, and the sections that follow address each one. Concomitantly, support for online course design and teaching requires a constellation of resources, infrastructure, and central and departmental leadership (McCarthy & Samors, 2009). No single incentive, resource, training program, or type of support will do the job, and faculty need opportunities to make choices that fit with their schedules, needs, and interests (Cook et al., 2009). Not all instructors need a financial incentive to teach online, though it stands to reason that they would not turn it down. Some need no incentive at all (Taylor & McQuiggan, 2008).

Despite differences across instructors, these incentives create a favorable culture for cultivating faculty interest and expectations for success (Cook et al., 2009; Howell et al., 2004; McArthur, Parker, & Giersch, 2003; Roby et al., 2013; Tabata & Johnsrud, 2008; Travis & Rutherford, 2013):

- Training in online pedagogy and technology
- Stable technical and design support in developing and teaching an online course
- Stable hardware and software, including a reliable and accessible LMS
- Receipt of a university-sponsored certificate of achievement
- Release time to develop or deliver an online course
- Stipends while developing new online courses during the summer
- Additional pay
- Credit toward promotion and tenure

The later adopters of online teaching and those with less teaching experience tend to be more motivated by incentives such as merit pay, stipends, release time, royalties, and tenure considerations (Cook et al., 2009; Hunt et al., 2014). Still, the most potent motivator across faculty is research-backed evidence that online teaching benefits students and improves their learning (Dahlstrom, 2015).

Leadership

Faculty are more likely to be motivated to teach online when their administration demonstrates commitment, management, and encouragement of online teaching accomplishments (Cook et al., 2009; McArthur et al., 2003; Howell et al., 2004; Tabata & Johnsrud, 2008; Travis & Rutherford, 2013). Faculty also want clear policies and standards for online courses (Lloyd et al., 2012)—guidelines that will improve students' experiences and keep the institution competitive on quality (Kane, Shaw, Pang, Salley, & Snider, 2016; McCarthy & Samors, 2009; Roby et al., 2013). These policies, which can come only from campus leaders, should reflect the priorities of accrediting agencies, national education associations, professional associations, and e-learning organizations (Chaloux, 2014).

Strong central leadership can facilitate the faculty's transition to online teaching in three ways. First, it can publicize the pedagogical value of technology and online education effectively by anchoring its claims in scholarly research (Jones, Lindner, Murphy, & Dooley, 2002). Second, it can remove the disincentives for teaching online, such as a lack of training, support, release time, and encouragement (Cook et al., 2009; Howell et al., 2004) and offer the incentives that faculty actually want. Third, it can create a supportive culture by ensuring that faculty and staff feel comfortable and confident using online technologies. Only high-quality technical support, consulting, and training in technological, course design, and online teaching skills can provide this comfort and confidence.

Administrators from several universities have shared their successful strategies to increase faculty satisfaction (Dahlstrom, 2015):

- Recognize that support starts with a commitment to lead.
- Keep the impact on students and the quality of teaching and learning in the forefront.
- Foster a faculty and staff culture of group collaboration, creative problem solving, innovation, experimentation, and sharing of best practices.
- Promote ongoing collaboration and regularly scheduled meetings of deans, faculty, and leaders to discuss best practices.
- Encourage the partnership between faculty and instructional designers and technologists.
- Give faculty access to qualified, competent, active, and approachable technical and instructional design support.
- Foster collaboration between instructional technology and academic units.
- Furnish multiple training opportunities in multiple modalities, some intensive, to meet pressing needs.
- Supply reliable technology and wireless access.
- Provide incentives and opportunities for faculty to conduct research on their pedagogical uses of technology and to publicize their projects and findings at conferences and in publications.
- Publicly recognize faculty accomplishments.

Based on an early literature review, Howell et al. (2004) proposed seven basic strategies that resonate with more recent studies:

- Help colleges and departments accept more responsibility for online course activities.
- Supply faculty with information about online education programs and activities.
- Urge faculty to use technology in their traditional classrooms.
- Institute strong incentives to teach online.
- Improve instructional training and support for online faculty.
- Build a strong online faculty community.
- Encourage faculty to conduct research on online learning.

Leaders can provide further support by creating or working with standing committees and task forces to continually examine technology and professional development needs, program scope, financing, quality assessment, and improvement of online courses (Chaloux & Miller, 2014). For instance, the Center for the Enhancement of Learning and Teaching (CELT, 2016) at Purdue University Fort Wayne coordinates the Committee for the Advancement of Scholarly Teaching and Learning Excellence (CASTLE), the Online Course Design and Review Team, and a standing advisory board to give guidance for program development.

Stable Technology

A foundation for using technology well begins with a stable instructional technology infrastructure, available and accessible equipment, and reliable online student services (Bolliger & Wasilik, 2009; Cook et al., 2009; Dahlstrom, 2015; McArthur et al., 2003; Travis & Rutherford, 2013). Building on this foundation, faculty want to have confidence that the technology they will be using to design and teach online will work the way they expect. Strong technical support can relieve the anxiety faculty feel when they have few technical skills of their own (Northcote et al., 2015).

High-Quality Professional Development

Faculty want and need training in both technology and online pedagogy before they teach online (Lackey, 2011; Meyer & Murrell, 2014; Udell, 2012). Even their motivation to learn more about best online teaching practices can improve student learning (Merillat & Scheibmeir, 2016). Proactive professional development boosts faculty satisfaction by reassuring them that they are receiving well-designed training and can improve student learning. In turn, their satisfaction improves the quality of their online teaching, their students' satisfaction, and their students' achievement of learning outcomes (Dietrich, 2015). Except for the technology component, these markers for satisfaction parallel those for faculty in general (Sabagh & Saroyan, 2014). The kind of support matters too. Faculty must feel confident and comfortable seeking guidance (Dahlstrom, 2015).

The training that most faculty get moves too quickly and focuses too much on technology. (Those who design and develop courses as part of a team with an instructional designer or educational technologist may not need to know as much.) This training also suffers from too little emphasis on course design and other bedrock teaching principles (Lane, 2013; Northcote et al., 2015). Good teaching actually transcends the environment, so it makes sense to put pedagogy ahead of technology. In addition, the training must integrate pedagogy and technology (Benson & Ward, 2013; Major, 2015). With more emphasis on teaching, faculty should be able to design courses that achieve the same or better outcomes as the face-to-face versions, which we know is possible (see chapter 1).

In addition, faculty attitudes shift when their training focuses on pedagogical purposes of technologies and the wide range of options (Northcote et al., 2015). Fear and suspicion transform into interest and enthusiasm, concerns into confidence, and frustration into appreciation for technology and its role in active and personalized online learning. Faculty enjoy the chance to reach new audiences, the intellectual challenge, and the new possibilities and technology, as long as disincentives are removed (Cook et al., 2009).

Release Time and Workload Management Advice

Faculty not only want but need release time to design or redesign their online courses. In fact, release time is a top motivator (Cook et al., 2009; Dahlstrom, 2015; Gregory & Martindale, 2016; Marek, 2009; Tabata & Johnsrud, 2008). Strategic management matters a great deal. A department can schedule online courses way ahead of teaching time (Ragan & Schroeder, 2014) and be flexible about reassigning duties while faculty work on developing new online courses (Roby et al., 2013).

Faculty also need reassurance and guidance about the actual time and effort commitments required of online teaching. How much effort depends on how we look at the data. In a survey of faculty by the Association of Public and Land-Grant Universities, 64 percent reported that online courses take more effort than classroom ones, which also means that 36 percent did not report added effort (McCarthy & Samors, 2009, p. 19).

Jones (2012) suggests that the reported added effort derives from the demands of creating a higher-quality course than required for face-to-face classes. Or perhaps it is the shift from teacher-centered instruction to student-centered learning or the pressure to meet quality standards for online courses (McQuiggan, 2012). Or it may be the feeling that one must be more accessible in an online course than a classroom one.

Perhaps those who did not report more effort received strong support or were already savvy in using technology. Perhaps they knew that they should set time limits as to when they will communicate in the course. We cannot be sure (Gregory & Martindale, 2016). Nor do we know how many surveyed faculty counted developing their course materials as part of their online teaching time. It is no wonder that Ragan and Schroeder (2014) present mixed empirical results as to whether the time demands are actually the same, higher, or lower.

A review of studies by Conceição and Lehman (2011) suggests that the issue is not the amount of time but the instructor's allocation of time. A study by Mandernach, Hudson, and Wise (2013) found that online faculty spend over half their teaching time on grading papers and assignments, a pattern similar to classroom teaching. If instructors grade the same assignments as in a face-to-face class, why would grading take more time? Others report that time goes to facilitating and grading discussion threads, but some faculty create their own time sinks by making the grading criteria far more complex than for a campus-based class. Because we do not grade students for every word they utter in a classroom, why would we give so much time to grading discussions online? Where is the pedagogical merit? This is not to say that we should not award points for discussions, but a more holistic scoring strategy across multiple discussions has merit. In fact, some online instructors do not grade discussions at all.

Similarly, some faculty see communicating with online students as a major time demand. Indeed, there tend to be more interactions in an online class than in a face-to-face one. However, careful course management can improve efficiency. Faculty need to know that they can set up a virtual office to reduce the stockpile of student e-mails. They also need to know that although interaction can enhance student learning and satisfaction, numerous mechanistic interactions help neither students nor instructors and can actually hurt. Unbridled e-mails, chats, blogs, phone contacts, tweets, Facebook posts, and other social media communications can explode beyond control (see chapter 6). When this happens, instructors become overwhelmed with the workload.

In fact, hundreds of communication exchanges in a semester may not signify quality interactions. They may indicate confusion or ambiguity requiring frequent clarifications, a symptom of poor course design. Quality management and strategic planning for interactions, rather than unharnessed communication, actually increase faculty satisfaction and offer the best return on investment of time (Dietrich, 2015). Other tried-and-true course management strategies also can help beginning online instructors save time (Ragan & Schroeder, 2014, ¶28):

> Over a period of offerings, many online instructors have developed their own strategies for gaining efficiencies when teaching online. Many of these strategies—for example, the use of weekly discussion forum summaries or creating a course operation checklist and grading rubrics—can be shared with novice online instructors as a way to become more efficient when teaching online.

Several faculty development programs and resources address effective course management, including allocation of time—for example:

- Time Management Strategies for Online Instructors (University of Wisconsin, Stout): https://www2 .uwstout.edu/content/profdev/rubrics/time_management.html
- Online Course Facilitation and Time Management (Johns Hopkins University, videos of instructors speaking about time management): https://ep.jhu.edu/faculty/learning-roadmap-for-new-online -instructors/online-course-facilitation-and-time-management
- Many practical ways to gain efficiency with course management strategies: Conceição and Lehman (2011).

Resources

Faculty identify an array of valuable resources for designing, developing, and teaching their online courses:

Pedagogical Support

- Instructional design support to help them integrate technology into teaching and learning (Dahlstrom, 2015; Grover, Walters, & Turner, 2016; Northcote et al., 2015; Roby et al., 2013)
- A faculty teaching center that provides expertise on information technology (Dahlstrom, 2015)
- Training and support that reduce the time and effort needed to adapt or develop new teaching strategies (Sibley & Whitaker, 2015)
- Interaction with colleagues who have experience teaching online (Taylor & McQuiggan, 2008)
- Mentors and structured mentoring programs (Barczyk, Buckenmeyer, Feldman, & Hixon, 2011; Marek, 2009; Samuel, 2016; Williams, Layne, & Ice, 2014)

Technical Support

- A designated instructional technology center available to all faculty (Dahlstrom, 2015)
- Technical help in implementing the technologies of their choice (Dahlstrom, 2015; Roby et al., 2013)
- Ongoing technical support (Cook et al., 2009; Travis & Rutherford, 2013)
- Opportunities to experiment with emerging learning technologies (Dahlstrom, 2015)
- Online resources with how-to instructions (Grover et al., 2016)
- Copyright and licensing information and assistance (Roby et al., 2013)

Course Models and Examples

- Course templates (Northcote et al., 2015)
- Models of good practice (Meyer & Murrell, 2014)
- Opportunities to view exemplary courses (Elliott, Rhoades, Jackson, & Mandernach, 2015; Northcote et al., 2015)

Course Materials Resources

- Access to helpful librarians (Roby et al., 2013)
- Assistance locating electronic or web-based materials (Roby et al., 2013)
- Online materials from publishers (Roby et al., 2013)

Course Review and Feedback

- Constructive feedback on course design and teaching (Williams, Layne, & Ice, 2014)
- Peer review of courses (Grover et al., 2016)
- A rubric, such as a set of online course design standards, to guide and evaluate course development (Northcote et al., 2015)

Recognition

Faculty want encouragement and recognition for their online teaching efforts from their colleagues and administrators (Cook et al., 2009), as well as grants and awards for developing innovative uses of instructional technology (Dahlstrom, 2015). They also respond more favorably to a sense of excitement about online learning—such as appeals to their curiosity, their desire to develop new skills, and their chance to innovate—than to institutional pressures to teach more online courses (Bunk, Li, Smidt, Bidetti, & Malize, 2015; Dahlstrom, 2015; Sibley & Whitaker, 2015). In addition, they value recognition toward promotion and tenure, formal rewards such as showcases, university-sponsored certificates of achievement, and other types of professional advancement (Cook et al., 2009; Dahlstrom, 2015; Lloyd et al., 2012; Northcote et al., 2015; Sibley & Whitaker, 2015; Taylor & McQuiggan, 2008).

Research Funding

Not all faculty seek financial incentives (McQuiggan, 2008; Taylor & McQuiggan, 2008), but funding for their research to advance the quality of online teaching can be a potent motivator, especially when they receive rewards for presenting or publishing that research. Such initiatives thrive in faculty communities of inquiry, practice, and learning that promote the scholarship of teaching and learning (SoTL) (Dahlstrom, 2015; Northcote et al., 2015; Sibley & Whitaker, 2015). This funding can extend to cover the travel expenses to attend professional conferences on online learning, both to disseminate their results and to learn more (Northcote et al., 2015).

Research funding simultaneously meets the faculty's needs to acquire online teaching expertise and conduct research without increasing their workload. Vaughn (2016, ¶1) explains:

> Faculty members in higher education are often overwhelmed with the competing demands on their time in the areas of teaching, research, and service. In order to overcome this issue, there has been a growing trend in faculty development to focus on the scholarship of teaching and learning (SoTL) through a community of inquiry (CoI) approach. SoTL attempts to integrate teaching, research, and service through a process of scholarly inquiry into student learning, which advances the practice of teaching by making the findings of the inquiry public. Rather than undertaking this inquiry process in isolation, faculty members are being encouraged to participate in CoIs, which

are composed of other faculty, students, and staff. These CoIs engage in active and collaborative research projects that investigate student learning across the disciplines.

■ DESIGNING EFFECTIVE PROFESSIONAL DEVELOPMENT

Because professional development plays such a crucial role in motivating and preparing faculty to teach online, it deserves additional treatment.

Themes and Topics

Faculty seek out and participate in an array of development initiatives, especially those that meet their immediate needs and interests. New online instructors benefit more from a somewhat limited topical focus; they do not need to know all the features of an LMS all at once (Ragan & Schroeder, 2014). At Texas State University, instructors begin with foundational training and later move to more advanced levels (Texas State Distance Learning, n.d.). Initial training might be limited to benefits for students, methods for interactions in an online course (see chapter 6), and simple, easy-to-implement course management strategies (Horvitz et al., 2015). Other campuses focus on assessing learning, creating online communities, training in various technological tools, and online instructional design models (Northcote et al., 2015). Therefore, a smorgasbord of themes and topics can serve faculty well (Elliott et al., 2009). Exhibit 8.1 lists examples of such themes and topics.

Exhibit 8.1: Professional Development Themes and Topics for Online Faculty

ONLINE CONTEXT

- Metrics and standards for quality of online learning and teaching (Ragan & Schroeder, 2014)
- Characteristics of online students (Ragan & Schroeder, 2009)
- Adult learning theory and strategies (McQuiggan, 2012; Ragan & Schroeder, 2014)
- Classroom dynamics in online courses (Ragan & Schroeder, 2009)
- How to shift to student-centered instruction (McQuiggan, 2012)
- How to design effective learning activities for students (Northcote et al., 2015)
- How to engage online students in learning activities (Ragan & Schroeder, 2014)
- How to use cooperative, experiential, reflective, and coaching strategies (Lewis & Wang, 2015)

TECHNOLOGY

- How to use LMS tools and areas (Ragan & Schroeder, 2009)
- Other technologies for online courses (Taylor & McQuiggan, 2008)
- How to use technology in pedagogically sound ways (Northcote et al., 2015; Ray, 2009)
- Technical and pedagogical skills for developing student-content, student-student, student-instructor, and student-interface interactions in online courses (Travis & Rutherford, 2013)

COURSE DEVELOPMENT

- How to develop an online course with a design team (Ragan & Schroeder, 2009)
- How to manage the legalities of online education (Ragan & Schroeder, 2009)

- How to convert or select online course materials (Taylor & McQuiggan, 2008)
- How to build in accessibility (Ragan & Schroeder, 2009)
- When and how to create video clips (Taylor & McQuiggan, 2008)
- How to connect students with support resources (Ragan & Schroeder, 2014)

STUDENT ASSESSMENTS

- How to assess student progress (Taylor & McQuiggan, 2008)
- How to create effective online assessments (Northcote et al., 2015; Taylor & McQuiggan, 2008)

TEACHING

- Organization, facilitation, and time management skills for teaching online (Lewis & Wang, 2015; Ragan & Schroeder, 2014; Taylor & McQuiggan, 2008)
- Classroom management skills such as explaining expectations, setting up routines, and addressing disruptive online behavior (Horvitz et al., 2015)
- How to establish and maintain a teaching presence beyond just posting course outlines and resources (McQuiggan, 2012; Ragan & Schroeder, 2014; Northcote et al., 2015)
- How to be active, visible, and engaged while guiding students in their learning (McQuiggan, 2012; Ragan & Schroeder, 2014; Northcote et al., 2015)
- How to construct online discussion activities (Ragan & Schroeder, 2014)
- How to design online activities as core learning experiences (McQuiggan, 2012; Ragan & Schroeder, 2014; Northcote et al., 2015)

INTERACTION

- How to get to know students and help them get to know each other (Ragan & Schroeder, 2014)
- How to interact meaningfully with online students (Ragan & Schroeder, 2014)
- How to develop an online learning community (Ragan & Schroeder, 2014)
- How to build faculty-student relationships (Taylor & McQuiggan, 2008)

COURSE COMMUNICATION AND FEEDBACK

- Online communication strategies (Northcote et al., 2015)
- How to launch and facilitate active online discussions (Northcote at al., 2015; Ragan & Schroeder, 2014; Taylor & McQuiggan, 2008)
- How to use social media for communicating with online students (Ragan & Schroeder, 2014)
- How to facilitate web-conferencing sessions (Taylor & McQuiggan, 2008)
- How to provide meaningful feedback on assignments (Taylor & McQuiggan, 2008)

Strategies for Professional Development

The institutional infrastructure, such as enrollment systems and technical support, affects the speed and ease of faculty transitions to online teaching (Northcote et al., 2015). When a sound infrastructure is in place, faculty development programs can be successful. They can be formal, informal, voluntary, or required and may include coaching, mentoring, workshops, and seminars (Kane et al., 2016).

Currently, few universities and colleges provide reflective, well-designed faculty development programs (McQuiggan, 2012), and many offer no training at all for beginning online instructors. Some institutions operate with a hands-off policy (Ray, 2009). In the absence of a faculty development program, instructors can turn to training produced by external sources such as Magna Publications, the Online Learning Consortium (formerly known as the Sloan Consortium), Coursera, edX, Instructure, Udemy, other universities, and outside consultants.

Whatever the format and mode of delivery, faculty must have a need for and interest in the topics. Frequently this interest arises from practical, hands-on, and problem-solving opportunities with follow-up support. Aside from relevant and easy-to-access information, faculty want connections to their colleagues, so they benefit from having a mentor as one piece of ongoing, multifaceted training (Lewis & Wang, 2014; Northcote et al., 2015).

Required or Voluntary

Although some institutions require training, a flexible and diverse program that allows self-selection and self-paced scheduling will better accommodate the disparate professional needs and interests of faculty (Gregory & Martindale, 2016). This may include just-in-time support for immediate needs (Northcote et al., 2015).

Format Preferences

Faculty value a range of formats for their professional development (Taylor & McQuiggan, 2008). Therefore, development initiatives should incorporate a variety of face-to-face experiences whenever possible: workshops, seminars, minicourses, tutorials, panel discussions, showcases, one-on-one training and consultations, short sessions in a series, hands-on training, one-time training, mentoring sessions, brown bag lunches, and informal meetings. Effective training may also take the form of self-paced online courses, webinars, and teleconferences (Elliott et al., 2015; Gregory & Martindale, 2016; Herman, 2012; Meyer & Murrell, 2014). Faculty appreciate online programs that demonstrate and model online technologies, pedagogies, and communities of practice (Northcote et al., 2015). Some institutions use an "each one teach one" arrangement where faculty who learn online teaching skills then teach or coach other faculty (Elliott et al., 2015). Northcote et al. (2015) recommend replacing just-in-case blanket workshops with just-in-time instruction in the skills and knowledge needed at different times in the semester.

Activities that fit with a faculty member's own pace, needs, and schedule attract participation. For example, new instructors profit from an orientation to online learning, while a brown bag seminar may appeal more to experienced faculty. However, those coming late into online teaching value more structure and support (Hixon et al., 2012). All online faculty appreciate anytime-access websites with FAQs and practical tips.

Duration

According to Taylor and McQuiggan (2008), the optimal length of time faculty are willing to spend in professional development for online teaching ranges between a series of short (less than one day) workshops over several weeks to a single, one-day workshop and self-paced materials that can be accessed as needed. For instance, the Center for the Enhancement of Teaching and Learning at Purdue University Fort Wayne provides a three-week online program at the start of the summer session and has enjoyed robust enrollment, active participation, and a high rate of completion (X. Jia, personal communication, December 7, 2016). Within this program, faculty take on the role of online learners, but they also identify some elements they would like to integrate into their own online courses.

In one of the program's major activities, faculty work in small groups to use the university's online course design evaluation standards to assess the quality of an exemplary course. They can choose from several courses that experienced online faculty have made available as teaching models. By reviewing these exemplary models, faculty become familiar with the university's standards and the kinds of learning activities that work well in an online course. The university uses a similar strategy in its face-to-face seminars to familiarize faculty with the standards.

MarylandOnline's interinstitutional Certificate for Online Adjunct Teachers (COAT) program runs for nine weeks and also places faculty in the role of online students (Shattuck, Dubins, & Zilberman, 2011). It covers these topics: online learning; skills in technology and learning management; basic principles of instructional design, pedagogy, and andragogy; social presence; ways to manage assessment; and legal issues and institutional policies.

The Texas State Office of Distance and Extended Learning offers a two- to five-week training program in the foundations of online learning and an advanced training program in online course design and development over a full semester (Texas State Distance Learning, n.d.). The Office also makes available a menu of alternative courses through Quality Matters and the Online Learning Consortium, varying from two to ten weeks in length.

Sandboxes and Examples

Faculty benefit from opportunities to experiment with the LMS and the tools in it (Taylor & McQuiggan, 2008). Giving them a "sandbox" site allows them to create and revise components of their online course before copying them over to their live course site. Some institutions provide templates to give faculty a time-saving kick start, facilitate their designing a coherent and well-aligned course, and guide them in using different course areas and online tools (Goodson, 2014; Northcote et al., 2015). Faculty also profit from reviewing and evaluating online courses and teaching practices against online course standards (Elliott et al., 2015; Northcote et al., 2015; X. Jia, personal communication, December 7, 2016).

Design Teams

Some institutions provide design teams. Composition varies depending on the resources available in a department or on campus. In addition to the instructor, the team may include program managers, instructional designers, technologists, librarians, media technologists, or others with specialized expertise appropriate for a particular course. Whether the design team has only two or ten members, everyone must have expertise in some skill required to create an excellent online course. Otherwise these teams are no better than a single instructor at the same level (Jones, 2012). Collaborative or faculty-driven course design can work or fail equally well.

Faculty Community

Faculty value opportunities to share their experiences with colleagues (Taylor & McQuiggan, 2008), and informal collegial networks embody an unofficial yet robust way of exchanging information about online teaching. Orientations for faculty new to online teaching and ongoing workshops, seminars, and programs can help build these informal networks. A few formal methods can complement the informal, such as the "each one teach one" format and internal conferences on online course design and teaching.

■ MODELS FOR A PROFESSIONAL DEVELOPMENT PROGRAM

Effective professional development programs use a variety of methods to furnish faculty with technology experiences and incentives to design and teach online:

Methods

- One-on-one coaching to meet the faculty's just-in-time course design and teaching needs (Picciano, 2015)
- Design modules to allow faculty skills to build systematically (Picciano, 2015; Teräs & Herrington, 2014)
- Expert instructional design teams (Picciano, 2015)
- Faculty involvement in planning programs to meet their needs and interests (Elliott et al., 2015; Grover, Walters, & Turner, 2016; McQuiggan, 2012; Teräs & Herrington, 2014; Tobin, Mandernach, & Taylor, 2015)
- Demonstration of sound teaching and learning principles (e.g., social construction of knowledge, student interaction, instructor responsiveness; Picciano, 2015)

Technology

- Faculty access to appropriate software and equipment, especially laptops (Picciano, 2015)
- Room for faculty choice of technology tools (Teräs & Herrington, 2014)
- Hands-on activities so faculty can learn to use and experiment with the equipment (Picciano, 2015)

Incentives

- Incentives for faculty to invest the time and effort to develop an effective online course (Picciano, 2015)
- Within the department, course release, peer mentors ("each one teach one"), content-specific assistance, and skilled student assistants (Marek, 2009; Picciano, 2015)
- Within the institution, infrastructure investments, clear policies on online courses, instructional design support, information technology workshops, one-on-one technical training, and faculty reward systems (Marek, 2009)
- Funds for external continuing education (e.g., conferences, college courses, and commercial training; Marek, 2009)

Faculty choice of technologies deserves elaboration because it represents authentic e-learning and pairs well with learning while working on a course, collegial sharing, and reflecting on one's progress (Teräs & Herrington, 2014). It also enhances student satisfaction. According to a recent *Educause* report (Dahlstrom, 2015, p. 10), "At institutions that provide support for faculty to use the technologies *the faculty chooses to implement*, students are more positive about their instructors' integrated use of technology."

The next three sections describe three models of professional development, the last two created for Penn State but different in details. All three follow research-based practices.

University of Illinois Online

This exemplary faculty development program started with Sloan Foundation and university funds as part of the effort to establish multidisciplinary online programs across three campuses. In the beginning, the Springfield campus initiated the Office of Technology Enhanced Learning to help instructors teaching hybrid and online courses. This office has evolved into the Center for Online Learning, Research, and Service, which provides faculty support for teaching, scholarship, and service. In addition, it offers faculty incentive funds to adapt their classroom-based courses to the online environment and grants for conducting and disseminating research. The center's funding comes from a combination of online course fees, grants, contracts, and the state. Online faculty development includes multiple venues (Ragan & Schroeder, 2014):

- More than a dozen eight-week online classes
- Weekly campus sessions with simultaneous online streaming
- More than one hundred ten-day online workshops offered through the Online Learning Consortium (formerly the Sloan Foundation)
- Monthly webinars for multiple campuses
- Community practice sessions with national speakers offered four times a year

Penn State's World Campus Model 1

This program offers a range of delivery formats, including individual online training, independent study, cohort online learning, and face-to-face workshops. Faculty receive a certificate for completing the training. The program focuses on the learning outcomes, which are distributed across separate minicourse sessions, shown in exhibit 8.2.

Exhibit 8.2: Mini-Courses with Their Learning Outcomes in Penn State's World Campus Program

Orientation to Online Teaching—1.5 Hour Face-to-Face Workshop

- Illustrate the unique characteristics of online teaching and learning including class dynamics, time management, and basic technology interface.
- Introduce and explain the structure of the World Campus as a delivery system and its relationship with the academic unit or department.

Accessibility—Self-Paced Independent Study

- Identify the appropriate resources available to assist in managing accessibility accommodations.
- Describe commonly experienced student accessibility issues and the impact on online learners.
- Post and reinforce in the course the common protocols that can benefit students both with and without disabilities.

ProveIT!—Self-Paced Independent Study

- Demonstrate competencies in using the most common tools and features of the LMS.
- Apply policies concerning syllabus requirements, the Family Educational Rights and Privacy Act, academic integrity, and student behavioral expectations in the online classroom (e.g., netiquette guidelines).

Effective Online Instruction—Cohort-Based Four-Week Course Facilitated by an Experienced Online Instructor

- Identify and perform essential preparation tasks before teaching the course.
- Articulate an instructor's role in an online learning environment.
- Develop appropriate active learning strategies.
- Recognize learner characteristics and differences.
- Apply appropriate strategies for monitoring and facilitating online learning.
- Apply effective strategies for facilitating and assessing online discussions.
- Manage time, workload, and administrative issues related to teaching effectively online.

Teaching Presence—Cohort-Based Three-Week Course Facilitated by an Experienced Online Instructor

- Apply strategies to establish a teaching presence that fits your instructor persona and online courses.
- Articulate the role that teaching presence plays in students' social and cognitive presence for learning online.
- Apply strategies to maintain an effective and efficient instructor-student relationship during an online course.
- Set up a schedule for feedback to students on their learning in an online course.

Source: Ragan et al. (2012, pp. 78–79).

This program is also mapped to expected teaching behaviors and pedagogical competencies that the Penn State Online Coordinating Council Subcommittee for Faculty Engagement uses to develop the faculty online readiness self-assessment rubric (Ragan, Bigatel, Kennan, & Dillon, 2012).

Penn State's World Campus Model 2

This second Penn State program for developing online teaching competencies borrows elements from the following fourteen models. The first seven received the Sloan-C Excellence in Faculty Development for Online Teaching Award:

- State University of New York Learning Network
- Illinois Online Network's Making the Virtual Classroom a Reality
- University of Central Florida's IDL6543
- University of Nebraska Lincoln's Summer Institute for Online Teaching
- University of Massachusetts Lowell's Online Teaching Institute
- University of Maryland University College's CTLA201 Teaching with WebTycho
- University of West Florida's Studio

- University of Wisconsin–Madison's Distance Education Certificate Program
- Penn State's World Campus OL2000
- Louisiana State University's Professional Development Model for Online Course Development
- University of Calgary's Institute
- Sloan-C's Online Teaching Certificate
- Conceptual: Four Quadrant Model for Professional Development (individual and public reflection and performance)
- Conceptual: Adult Learning Model for Faculty Development (adult learning theory)

From these programs, McQuiggan (2015) selected seven features to include in the model online professional development course she built:

- Recognition of faculty needs, concerns, and goals, such as honoring their personal learning objectives
- Individualized planning, such as meeting with faculty in advance to discuss and polish their online course project proposals
- Use of faculty experiences by having participants share ideas, successes, concerns, and insights
- Creation of a supportive learning environment with year-long personal and community support featuring faculty discussions, face-to-face meetings, and individual consultations with a multimedia instructional designer
- Opportunities for faculty reflection on the fit of existing teaching strategies with the online environment
- Observations of existing online courses
- Ongoing support for a year, along with new training opportunities each semester

The course has the following structure:

- "Pre-Interviews" includes the precourse information of a "Getting Started" folder with topics of "Read Me First," "How to Participate in a Threaded Discussion," and "Netiquette." This same folder has a "Technical Support," an "I Don't Understand," and a "Let's Get to Know Each Other" discussion forum; a private reflection journal space for each participant; and a two-hour face-to-face group discussion in the computer lab. Instructors enter their private journal reflections at the close of each module. Their expressed interests and needs guide the selection of additional resources and the subsequent modules. Prompts for journal entries suggest reflection on these kinds of topics (McQuiggan, 2015, pp. 43–45):
  - How did you become a teacher, and what events and experiences have made you the kind of teacher you are today?
  - What new insights do you have about your teaching and redesigning your classroom courses for hybrid delivery?
  - What has been the most significant learning for you? Any surprises?
  - Post your action plan progress. What is done, and what still needs to happen?
  - Group e-mails remind participants to post in the journals and add new information related to the module topic.
  - Individual consultations give hands-on guidance for using technology tools and writing clear directions for students.

- Module 1: "Reflection and Conceptualization" begins with an overview, objectives, and activities, followed by readings, a discussion forum, group e-mails, and individual consultations.
- Module 2: "Student Interaction and Collaboration in Your Online Course" follows a similar structure with new readings, a folder of resources for interaction and collaboration, and a synchronous web conference.
- Module 3: "Learning Activities and Assessments in Your Online Course" has new readings and a folder of resources for learning activities and assessments.
- Module 4: "Teaching and Managing Your Online Course" follows the same structure as previous modules with folders of resources for these topics: the LMS, course planning tools, course quality, discussion resources, games and simulations, learning object repositories, open courseware, synchronous meetings/communication, the TEACH Act (copyright information), technology tools, and other course resources.
- Both the "Classroom Observations" and "Post Interviews" probe faculty to identify changes, if any, in their assumptions and beliefs about teaching and assessment with questions like these:

  How have you prepared to teach online?
  What have you found most helpful in this course? Any suggestions for its next offering?
  What are your thoughts on the reflective journal?

McQuiggan (2015) has published her action research from this course. Her data reveal changes in the participants' teaching practices, assumptions, and beliefs that reflect these themes:

- The effectiveness of the reflective writing, collegial discussions, and reviews of existing online course for forging changes in thinking about teaching
- The strong impact of professional development in online teaching on classroom teaching practices
- The close relationship between the amount of time and engagement faculty invest in professional development activities and their movement toward transformative learning and new teaching practices

Ironically, training in online teaching can be among the most powerful strategies for motivating faculty to improve their classroom teaching.

■ SUMMARY

A positive culture for online teaching starts with leadership commitment. Although we have presented examples of model programs, the campus culture must shape the design of professional development initiatives if they are to be successful. However, faculty across institutions want practical strategies, the opportunity to experiment with and ease into technology, time to learn online teaching strategies, the ability to customize the pace of training, templates and course examples, and the benefits of teaching online, such as flexible scheduling for disciplinary research and the scholarship of teaching and learning. Incremental innovation and use of technology stand a greater chance of success when faculty and program leaders have a hand in choosing their design and implementation.

Reflections

For Instructors

- What teaching strategies do you find to be most effective in your current teaching practices?
- What topics for online teaching do you want to learn more about?
- What technology applications do you want to be able to use in your online courses?
- Where are some of your trouble spots in organizing and planning your online courses?
- What time sinks do you experience in your teaching and grading?
- What resources can you turn to for more guidance or training?
- From whom can you request training or consultation about your LMS, course design, or teaching strategies?
- What grants might support your technology innovations for your teaching and research?
- Where can you find examples of exemplary online courses to review?
- What resources does your campus library offer to guide your online course design and teaching?
- What web-based open-enrollment courses (from Canvas or Coursera, for example) can you find to learn more about online course design and teaching?
- What external sources (e.g., the Online Learning Consortium) offer courses you may want to complete?
- What impact has your online teaching experience had on your classroom teaching practices, and vice versa?

For Instructional Designers

- How can you identify the needs and interests of the faculty with whom you consult or collaborate about course design?
- What are those needs and interests?
- What do you know about the formats and duration of training programs that faculty want? How might you change these features to better meet faculty preferences?
- What topics are important to instructors? How can your training programs and consultations address these topics more fully?
- If faculty are not following best practices, what strategies can you incorporate into training events to encourage them to do so?
- Which instructors who are already experienced with online teaching can you recruit as training collaborators?
- What inhibits faculty from participating in and completing training?
- What incentives do you think would encourage faculty to obtain more training?

For Administrators

Chaloux and Miller (2012) developed these questions to help participants prepare for a Pennsylvania State University and Sloan Consortium Leadership Program. Administrators should know the answers to these knowledge questions before addressing the reflection questions that follow them:

- What is your institution's vision for online learning? How does it fit with its overall mission and goals?
- Where is the online learning unit located within your institution? What is its relationship with academic units and faculty who teach in other learning environments?
- What is your governance structure?

- What is the reporting line from you to the president/chancellor/chief administrative officer?
- Who sits on the online learning unit's internal leadership team? If the unit has an institution-wide governing, steering, or advisory committee, who sits on this?
- How are the unit's costs and expenses recovered? What happens to after-cost revenue?
- How are the various support functions—technology, student support, faculty support, registration, and so on—organized? What functions are organized within a central online learning unit? Which are distributed to individual academic units?
- Where is policy about online learning made and approved? How are policy issues resolved?
- What is the organizational culture in which the online learning initiative functions at your institution? Is it similar to or different from the organizational culture in other parts of the institution? Do the differences or similarities matter? How?
- What are the most significant leadership arenas for online learning at your institution: administrative (e.g., organization, finance), academic (e.g., program approval, faculty relations), technology, or other?

Now reflect on these questions:

- How reluctant are your faculty to teach online? If certain groups are resisting, why do you think that occurs?
- What have you done to ensure that your institution's technology is stable and reliable? Can you do more?
- What have you done to ensure that faculty receive well-designed professional development and adequate support services in both teaching and technology? Can you do more?
- What other incentives can you institute to attract faculty to online teaching, such as release time to prepare new online courses, workload management advice, research-based knowledge about the effectiveness of online learning, collegial support programs, and research funding?
- What have you done to ensure that faculty who teach online courses receive meaningful recognition and rewards for excellence in online course design, teaching, and assessment? Can you do more?

▪ REFERENCES

Alexiou-Ray, J., & Bentley, C. C. (2015). Faculty professional development for quality online teaching. *Online Journal of Distance Learning Administration, 18*(4), 1–6.

Barczyk, C., Buckenmeyer, J., Feldman, L., & Hixon, E. (2011). Assessment of a university-based distance education mentoring program from a quality management perspective. *Mentoring and Tutoring: Partnership in Learning, 19*(1), 5–24.

Benson, S.N.K., & Ward, C. L. (2013). Teaching with technology: Using TPACK to understand teaching expertise in online higher education. *Journal of Educational Computing Research, 48*(2), 153–172.

Bolliger, D. U., & Wasilik, O. (2009). Factors influencing faculty satisfaction with online teaching and learning in higher education. *Distance Education, 30*(1), 103–116.

Bunk, J., Li, R., Smidt, E., Bidetti, C., & Malize, B. (2015). Understanding faculty attitudes about distance education: The importance of excitement and fear. *Online Learning, 19*(4). Retrieved from https://olj.onlinelearningconsortium .org/index.php/olj/article/view/559

California State University, Chico. (2016). *Using the QOLT instrument*. [website]. Retrieved from http://www.csuchico.edu/eoi/chicofaculty/usingtherubric.shtml

CELT. (2016). [website]. Retrieved from http://ipfw.edu/celt

Chaloux, B. (2014). Policy leadership in e-learning. In G. Miller, M. Benke, B. Chaloux, L. C. Ragan, R. Schroeder, W. Smutz, & K. Swan (Eds.), *Leading the e-learning transformation of higher education* (pp. 177–199). Sterling, VA: Stylus.

Chaloux, B., & Miller, G. E. (2014). E-learning and the transformation of higher education. In G. Miller, M. Benke, B. Chaloux, L. C. Ragan, R. Schroeder, W. Smutz, & K. Swan (Eds.), *Leading the e-learning transformation of higher education* (pp. 3–22). Sterling, VA: Stylus.

Chiasson, K., Terras, K., & Smart, K. (2015). Faculty perceptions of moving a face-to-face course to online instruction. *Journal of College Teaching and Learning*, *12*(3), 231–240.

Conceição, S.C.O., & Lehman, R. M. (2011). *Managing online instructor workload: Strategies for finding balance and success*. San Francisco, CA: Jossey-Bass.

Cook, R. G., Ley, K., Crawford, C., & Warner, A. (2009). Motivators and inhibitors for university faculty in distance and e-learning. *British Journal of Educational Technology*, *40*(1), 149–163.

Dahlstrom, E. (2015). *Educational technology and faculty development in higher education* (Research Report). Louisville, CO: ECAR. Retrieved from https://library.educause.edu/~/media/files/library/2015/6/ers1507-pdf.pdf

Dietrich, D. (2015, February). Why instructor satisfaction cannot be ignored. *eLearn Magazine*. Retrieved from http://elearnmag.acm.org/featured.cfm?aid=2735931

Elliott, M., Rhoades, N., Jackson, C. M., & Mandernach, B. J. (2015). Professional development: Designing initiatives to meet the needs of online faculty. *Journal of Educators Online*, *12*(1), 160–188.

Fish, W. W., & Wickersham, L. E. (2009). Best practices for online instructors: Reminders. *Quarterly Review of Distance Education*, *10*(3), 279–284.

Goodson, L. A. (2014, November). *Re-fillable faculty templates for online course design*. Session given at the Annual International Convention of the Association for Educational Communications and Technology, Jacksonville, FL.

Green, T., Alejandro, J., & Brown, A. H. (2009, June). The retention of experienced faculty in online distance education programs: Understanding factors that impact their involvement. *International Review of Research in Open and Distance Learning*, *10*(3). Retrieved from https://archive.org/stream/ERIC_EJ847784/ERIC_EJ847784_djvu.txt

Gregory, R., & Martindale, T. (2016, October). *Faculty development for online instruction in higher education*. Paper presented at the Association for Educational Communications and Technology Convention, Las Vegas, NV. Retrieved from http://tinyurl.com/aect16-gregory

Grover, K. S., Walters, S., & Turner, R. C. (2016). Exploring faculty preferences for mode of delivery for professional development initiatives. *Online Journal of Distance Learning Administration*, *19*(1), 1–12.

Herman, J. H. (2012). Faculty development programs: The frequency and variety of professional development programs available to online instructors. *Journal of Asynchronous Learning Networks*, *16*(5), 87–106.

Hixon, E., Buckenmeyer, J., Barczyk, C., Feldman, L., & Zamojski, H. (2012). Beyond the early adopters of online instruction: Motivating the reluctant majority. *Internet and Higher Education*, *15*(2), 102–107. doi:10.1016/j.iheduc.2011.11.005

Horvitz, B., Beach, A., Anderson, M., & Xia, J. (2015). Examination of faculty self-efficacy related to online teaching. *Innovative Higher Education*, *40*(4), 305–316. doi:10.1007/s10755–014–9316–1

Howell, S. L., Saba, F., Lindsay, N., Williams, P. B. (2004). Seven strategies for enabling faculty success in distance education. *Internet and Higher Education*, *7*(1), 33–49.

Hunt, H. D., Davies, K., Richardson, D., Hammock, G., Akins, M., Russ, L. (2014). It is (more) about the students: Faculty motivations and concerns regarding teaching online. *Online Journal of Distance Learning Administration*, *17*(2). Retrieved from http://www.westga.edu/~distance/ojdla/summer172/Hunt_Davies_Richardson_Hammock _Akins_Russ172.html

IPFW Online Course Design Standards. (2016). Retrieved from http://www.ipfw.edu/dotAsset/d405f15e-760b -46bb-b7a6-b2c9eb5fbbb8.pdf

Jones, D. (2012, December 14). *Beyond the early adopters of online instruction: Motivating the reluctant majority*. [weblog]. Retrieved from https://davidtjones.wordpress.com/2012/12/14/beyond-the-early-adopters-of-online-instruction -motivating-the-reluctant-majority/

Jones, E. T., Lindner, J. R., Murphy, T. H., & Dooley, K. E. (2002, Spring). Faculty philosophical position towards distance education: Competency, value, and educational technology support. *Online Journal of Distance Learning Administration*, *5*(1). Retrieved from http://www.westga.edu/~distance/ojdla/spring51/jones51.html

Kane, R. T., Shaw, M., Pang, S., Salley, W., & Snider, J. B. (2016). Faculty professional development and student satisfaction in online higher education. *Online Journal of Distance Learning Administration*, *19*(2). Retrieved from http://www .westga.edu/~distance/ojdla/summer192/kane_shaw_pang_salley_snider192.html

Lackey, K. (2011). Faculty development: An analysis of current and effective training strategies for preparing faculty to teach online. *Online Journal of Distance Learning Administration*, *14*(4), 8.

Lane, L. M. (2013). An open, online class to prepare faculty to teach online. *Journal of Educators Online*, *10*(1). Retrieved from http://files.eric.ed.gov/fulltext/EJ1004897.pdf

Lewis, E., & Wang, C. (2015). Using an online curriculum design and a cooperative instructional approach to orientate adjunct faculty to the online learning environment. *Journal of Continuing Higher Education*, *63*, 109–118.

Lin, H., Dyer, K., & Guo, Y. (2012). Exploring online teaching: A three-year composite journal of concerns and strategies from online instructors. *Online Journal of Distance Learning Administrators*, *15*(3). Retrieved from http://www .westga.edu/~distance/ojdla/fall153/lin_dyer_guo153.html

Lloyd, S. A., Byrne, M. M., & McCoy, T. S. (2012). Faculty-perceived barriers of online education. *MERLOT Journal of Online Learning and Teaching*, *8*(1), 1–12.

Major, C. H. (2015). *Teaching online: A guide to theory, research, and practice*. Baltimore, MD: Johns Hopkins University Press.

Mandernach, B. J., Hudson, S., & Wise, S. (2013, July). Where has the time gone? Faculty activities and time commitments in the online classroom. *Journal of Educators Online*, *10*(2). Retrieved from http://connection.ebscohost .com/c/articles/90564640/where-has-time-gone-faculty-activities-time-commitments-online-classroom

Marek, K. (2009). Learning to teach online: Creating a culture of support for faculty. *Journal of Education for Library and Information Science*, *50*(4), 275–292.

McArthur, D., Parker, A., & Giersch, S. (2003). Why plan for e-learning? *Planning for Higher Education*, *31*(4), 20–28.

McCarthy, S. A., & Samors, R. J. (2009, August). *Online learning as a strategic asset: Vol. 1. A resource for campus leaders*. Washington, DC: Association of Public and Land-grant Universities. Retrieved from http://www.onlinelearningsurvey .com/reports/APLU_online_strategic_asset_vol1.pdf

McQuiggan, C. A. (2012). Faculty development for online teaching as a catalyst for change. *Journal of Asynchronous Learning Networks*, *16*(2), 22–35. Retrieved from http://files.eric.ed.gov/fulltext/EJ971044.pdf

Merillat, L., & Scheibmeir, M. (2016). Developing a quality improvement process to optimize faculty success. *Online Learning*, *20*(3), 159–172.

Meyer, K. A., & Murrell, V. S. (2014). A national study of theories and their importance for faculty development for online teaching. *Online Journal of Distance Learning Administration, 17*(2), 1–15.

National Survey of Student Engagement. (2009). *Assessment for improvement: Tracking student engagement over time— Annual results 2009.* Bloomington: Indiana University Center for Postsecondary Research.

National Survey of Student Engagement. (2013). *A fresh look at student engagement: Annual results 2013.* Bloomington: Indiana University Center for Postsecondary Research.

Northcote, M., Gosselin, K. P., Reynaud, D., Kilgour, P., & Anderson, M. (2015). Navigating learning journeys of online teachers: Threshold concepts and self-efficacy. *Issues in Educational Research, 25*(3), 319–344.

Picciano, A. G. (2015). Planning for online education: A systems model. *Online Learning, 19*(5). Retrieved from https://olj.onlinelearningconsortium.org/index.php/olj/article/download/548/187

Quality Matters Higher Education Program. (2016). [website]. Retrieved from https://www.qualitymatters.org/reviews-certifications

Ragan, L. C., Bigatel, P. M., Kennan, S. S., & Dillon, J. M. (2012). From research to practice: Towards the development of an integrated and comprehensive faculty development program. *Journal of Asynchronous Learning Networks, 16*(5), 71–86. Retrieved from http://files.eric.ed.gov/fulltext/EJ1000092.pdf

Ragan, L. C., & Schroeder, R. (2014). Supporting faculty success in online learning: Requirements for individual and institutional leadership. *Leading the e-learning transformation of higher education* (pp. 108–131). Sterling, VA: Stylus.

Ray, J. (2009, June). Faculty perspective: Training and course development for the online classroom. *MERLOT Journal of Online Learning and Teaching, 5*(2), 263–276. Retrieved from http://jolt.merlot.org/vol5no2/ray_0609.pdf

Roby, T., Ashe, S., Singh, N., & Clark, C. (2013). Shaping the online experience: How administrators can influence student and instructor perceptions through policy and practice. *Internet and Higher Education, 17*, 29–37. Retrieved from http://faculty.washington.edu/rvanderp/DLData/RobyAshe2012.pdf

Sabagh, Z., & Saroyan, A. (2014). Professors' perceived barriers and incentives for teaching improvement. *International Education Research, 2*(3), 18–40.

Samuel, A. (2016). Online faculty development: What works? In *Proceedings of the Adult Education Research Conference.* Charlotte, NC. Retrieved from http://newprairiepress.org/cgi/viewcontent.cgi?article=1069&context=aerc

Scagnoli, N. I., Buki, L. P., & Johnson, S. D. (2009). The influence on online teaching on face-to-face teaching practices. *Journal of Asynchronous Learning, 13*(2), 115–128.

Schmidt, S. W., Hodge, E. M., & Tschida, C. M. (2013). How university faculty members developed their online teaching skills. *Quarterly Review of Distance Education, 14*(3), 131–140.

Schroeder, R. (2014). Operational leadership in a strategic context. In G. Miller, M. Benke, B. Chaloux, L. C. Ragan, R. Schroeder, W. Smutz, & K. Swan (Eds.), *Leading the e-learning transformation of higher education* (pp. 162–173). Sterling, VA: Stylus.

Shattuck, J., Dubins, B., & Zilberman, D. (2011). MarylandOnline's interinstitutional project to train higher education adjunct faculty to teach online. *International Review of Research in Open and Distance Learning, 12*(2), 40–61.

Sibley, K., & Whitaker, R. (2015). Engaging faculty in online education. *Educause Review.* Retrieved from http://er.educause.edu/articles/2015/3/engaging-faculty-in-online-education

Smidt, E., McDyre, B., Bunk, J., Li, R., & Gatenby, T. (2014) Faculty attitudes about distance education. *IAFOR Journal of Education, 2*(2), 181–209.

Straumsheim, C. (2016, October 24). Doubts about data: 2016 survey of faculty attitudes on technology. *Inside Higher Ed.* Retrieved from https://www.insidehighered.com/news/survey/doubts-about-data-2016-survey-faculty-attitudes-technology

Sun, J., & de la Rosa, R. (2015). Faculty training and student perceptions: Does quality matter? *Internet Learning, 4*(1). Retrieved from http://digitalcommons.apus.edu/cgi/viewcontent.cgi?article=1048&context=internetlearning

Swan, K. (2014). Enhancing e-learning effectiveness. In G. Miller, M. Benke, B. Chaloux, L. C. Ragan, R. Schroeder, W. Smutz, & K. Swan (Eds.), *Leading the e-learning transformation of higher education* (pp. 77–107). Sterling, VA: Stylus.

Tabata, L. N., & Johnsrud, L. K. (2008). The impact of faculty attitudes toward technology, distance education, and innovation. *Research in Higher Education, 49*(7), 625–646.

Taylor, A., & McQuiggan, C. (2008). Faculty development programming: If we build it, will they come? *Educause Quarterly, 3*. Retrieved from http://er.educause.edu/~/media/files/article-downloads/eqm0835.pdf

Teräs, H., & Herrington, J. (2014). Neither the frying pan nor the fire: In search of a balanced authentic e-learning design through an educational design research process. *International Review of Research in Open and Distance Learning, 15*(2), 232–253. Retrieved from http://www.irrodl.org/index.php/irrodl/article/view/1705/2835

Texas State Distance Learning. (n.d.). [website]. Retrieved from http://www.distancelearning.txstate.edu/faculty/online-teaching-certification.html

Tobin, T. J., Mandernach, J., & Taylor, A. H. (2015). *Evaluating online teaching: Implementing best practices.* San Francisco, CA: Jossey-Bass.

Travis J. E., & Rutherford, G. (2013). Administrative support of faculty preparation and interactivity in online teaching: Factors in student success. *National Forum of Educational Administration and Supervision Journal, 30*(1), 30–44.

Ubell, R. (2016, December 13). Why faculty still don't want to teach online. *Inside Higher Ed.* Retrieved from https://www.insidehighered.com/advice/2016/12/13/advice-faculty-members-about-overcoming-resistance-teaching-online-essay

Udell, C. (2012). *Learning everywhere: How mobile content strategies are transforming training.* Pembroke Pines, FL: Rock-Bench Publishing.

US Department of Education. (2010). *Evaluation of evidence-based practices in online learning: A meta-analysis and review of online learning studies.* Washington, DC: Author. Retrieved from http://www2.ed.gov/rschstat/eval/tech/evidence-based-practices/finalreport.pdf

Vaughn, N. (2016). Faculty development. *ELI: 7 things you should know about . . .* Retrieved from https://library.educause.edu/~/media/files/library/2016/2/eli7129pdf.pdf

Williams, T., Layne, M., & Ice, P. (2014). Online faculty perceptions on effective faculty mentoring: A qualitative study. *Online Journal of Distance Learning Administration, 17*(2), 86–102.

Online Course Development Checklist

Quality instruction involves many complex tasks, so looking at each one individually can make the challenge a little easier. The following sections examine some best teaching practices, including those uniquely important in online courses. You can use these topics as a checklist to guide your course design and development and get your course ready to launch. Also, acquaint yourself with any existing templates or models of online courses. Ask to view exemplary courses to get ideas on how to use online course tools.

■ COURSE BEGINNINGS

Course Identification

Make sure that the top of the opening page of your course clearly shows the course ID and title, followed by your name and credentials. You can make a course banner or add an item that identifies the course in an attractive way. Consider adding an image such as the cover of a required textbook or images that express the focus of the course—for example, health care images for a nursing course, a picture of a saxophone player for a jazz history course, or a photo of lab activities for a chemistry course.

Fonts, Colors, and Styles

Choose a clean, sans serif font, such as Arial or Calibri. Most learning management systems (LMSs) give a choice of color schemes, but not all of them are effective, so choose carefully. Keep in mind that the best color combinations provide high contrast among text, images, and background. High contrast does not mean red because students with color blindness will see red as gray. You can still use color—white or yellow font on a dark blue background is an excellent option—but use type size and style along with color to give emphasis. For example, you might assume that a hyperlink to a website is obvious because it has a slightly different color from the rest of the text, but some students may find this difference hard to detect. Add underlining if this does not automatically appear with your link. Add bold or italics to make a link stand out more vividly, or place the word LINK in front of the title, like this: LINK: IPFW Web Site, where the hyperlink is embedded in the title [http://www.ipfw.edu].

Navigation

Use brief, clear names and labels for your course areas, and organize them in a logical and consistent way. Keep the same structure across each week or module of study. For example, start every week with the focus of study and a checklist of activities to be completed—content changes but structure remains the same.

Syllabus

Most LMSs have an area for inserting the syllabus or allow you to create a link to the syllabus on the course menu. You also may want to link it to your Welcome or Start-Here tips. Because the syllabus is your blueprint for your course, students should be able to access it easily from multiple locations. To ensure they read your syllabus, consider giving a graded "scavenger hunt" quiz over the document and orientation information (see below). Some instructors require a perfect score on this type of quiz (over multiple attempts) before allowing students to view the other course materials.

Welcome

Add a recorded welcome message to students with a personal introduction, an image or video, and background information on yourself. Also introduce those who support your course, such as a co-instructor, teaching assistant, or librarian, or have them create their own introductions.

Start-Here Tips

Prepare a friendly e-mail to send out to students before the course starts to welcome them and advise them of what to do first. At the course site, include a visible signal for where to start. This could be a "Start Here" folder or you might simply start with "Week 1." Either approach works well. Place navigation tips early to help students know where and how to begin. Insert the syllabus accompanied by:

- Links to major online resources used in the course
- Descriptions of and links to student support services
- The course schedule

Outcomes

Clearly list or, better yet, sequence and flowchart your learning outcomes into an outcomes map that will show the learning process by which students will achieve those outcomes. Explain how the outcomes will benefit them in the future. Even if you are given preset outcomes, you can add clarity with a "Focus of Learning" paragraph or list at the top of each week. Briefly review the kinds of assessment students can expect for the outcomes even if you already do this in the syllabus. If you do not do this in the syllabus, provide fuller descriptions at the top of each week.

Orientation

Orient students to your course by providing a text, audio, graphic, or video walk-through of the syllabus. Emphasize this information:

- The purpose of the course
- Its alignment with licensure or accreditation standards
- Its organization
- The course schedule
- Important course policies
- Technical requirements

Communication

Use multiple ways to communicate with students, such as an online office, e-mail, phone, and social media.

- Explain online communication and courtesy expectations. You can call it netiquette or network etiquette, but it boils down to professional courtesy. Use institutional policies, web resources, and your own personal statement to make your expectations clear. Several institutions have created guidelines, such as *Core Rules of Netiquette* (Colorado State University: http://learning.colostate.edu/guides/guide.cfm?guideid=4).
- Explain your availability and when students should expect your response to their e-mails and online messages, the return of assignments, and the posting of grades (such as within forty-eight hours for e-mails, within one week for assignments). Announce times when you must be away that might cause delays. Advise students if you will be available by instant messenger or social media. If you use social media, comply with Family Educational Rights and Privacy Act requirements by not discussing grades or suggesting assessment of a student's work in any other way. Student records must remain private.
- Use the tools within the LMS to give students informative, targeted feedback on assignments as well as grades. For example, you may make electronic notes or circle key strengths or weaknesses in a paper and add comments to explain your notations. Some instructors provide brief audio or video feedback.

Academic Integrity Expectations

Give the links to relevant campus policies, and explain how they apply in your course assignments and tests. Place the positive expectations and code of ethics ahead of the consequences for cheating and plagiarism.

Directions for Getting Help

Throughout the course, remind students of the resources that they can turn to when they need help, such as the writing center, the academic success center, online technology tutorials, electronic library services, and other support services (e.g., advising, registration, counseling, and services for disabled, military, minority, and international students). Include links and contact information. Remember: "Tell 'em, tell 'em again, and tell 'em what you told 'em." Use a just-in-time strategy rather than trying to frontload everything you feel they need to know.

■ TECHNOLOGY

Technical Information

Communicate technical expectations and resources:

- Tell students when and how to turn to campus information technology for support and when to turn to you.
- Provide a link to information about browsers, computers, and technical requirements for your LMS and other software you use. Add phone numbers, e-mail, and hours of available technical support.
- Add a link to a student online readiness survey, if your institution has one. Many such self-assessments are available (e.g., on the websites for Purdue University Fort Wayne and California State University, Stanislaus). For a thorough readiness survey, consider Georgia OnMyLine's *Online Education Readiness Assessment* (http://goml.readi.info/).

LMS Tools

Become familiar with the LMS tools that support your teaching strategies as well as the technology tutorials, training courses, and support available through your institution. But don't dig deeply into a tool unless you are planning to use it. Have a solid purpose for every tool you choose, and do not use more than one tool for the same purpose. Tools may include these:

- Course-building options such as adding a content folder or module, document file, item, web link, or media
- Menu-building options such as content areas, tools, and course links
- E-mail, message, and announcement tools
- A calendar for posting key activities, assignments, and dates
- Glossary-building area
- Group-building options such as your own manual or random grouping of your students
- Discussion areas where you create discussion forums and threads (sometimes called a bulletin board)
- Journal areas where students can enter private information that only you can see
- Assessment tools such as assignment submission areas, sometimes called a dropbox, and areas for building test item pools, quizzes, whole tests, and surveys
- The grade center or grade book
- Evaluation/participation data and reports
- Other tools such as wikis, chats, and blogs

Other Technology Choices

Use alternative or additional technologies only if they have no institutional restrictions (e.g., Zoom, GoogleDocs) and facilitate your students' achievement of your course outcomes:

- Incorporate a technology only if you thoroughly know how to use it and explain it to students.
- Avoid technology with a steep learning curve and high technical requirements.
- Avoid unreliable or unneeded technology.

- Consider adding tools that allow your students to assess themselves, such as StudyMate for making flash cards or crossword puzzles.
- Find out if your institution has a license for a tool where you can build test items rapidly and then upload them to the LMS. Sometimes you can take an existing test prepared in Word and upload it to the LMS. You also can upload publisher test files.
- If you use a publisher's database of test items, choose those that match your course outcomes, and add or change items when you identify gaps in alignment.
- Find out how to use your LMS assessment tools to curtail opportunities for cheating, how to review log-in and log-out data to detect patterns of cheating, and what other tools may support detection.

Student Technology Choices

Give students the option of choosing a technology type or format for assignments. You can describe your content expectations in a rubric and allow students to present the content in a paper, a video, a slide presentation, a podcast, a website, or a combination of these when appropriate.

User-Friendly Tools and Materials

Prepare course materials in formats that are user friendly for all students. Information technology specialists or instructional designers can advise you.

- When creating Word documents, use a consistent text format and organization, clear fonts and short labels, explicit headings and subheadings, style sets, and embedded hyperlinks. Write concise alternative descriptions (alt text/alt tag) for images.
- When creating videos, write out the script to post online or, if you post your video on YouTube, upload your script to generate closed captioning. Then students can select the YouTube "CC" option to read the words rather than only listen to the audio. Instead of trying to post videos on your own, use your institution's media streaming system for uploading videos that you can then link to your course site. Course sites generally have space limits, and streaming saves space.

Other Adjustments for Students with Disabilities

These adjustments include extended time on an exam or alternative forms of the content. Students with different disabilities require different adjustments. Consult the unit in your institution that provides services for students with disabilities on what adjustments to make for any individual student. Aside from including your campus policies and resources on disabilities or accessibility, add your personal encouragement. It can make a difference in how comfortable students feel in self-identifying their needs and seeking support.

■ ASSESSMENTS AND GRADING

Rubrics and Examples

Prepare rubrics for scoring graded assignments and distribute them to students when you give them instructions for assignments and essay tests. In addition, give students examples of excellent and poor work of similar assignments to help them understand your expectations.

Assessments

Use a variety of periodic assessments. Make sure they clearly align with your course outcomes and show student progress toward achieving them:

- Take advantage of the ways that you can build question sets with test-item pools. Build in random sampling and sequencing so that each student receives a different test. If randomizing item choices, avoid using "all of the above," "none of the above," "both a and b," and similar constructions. When you want multiple answers, use the multiple-answer/true-false format instead.
- If you use a plagiarism detection tool, find out what databases it checks because students may use other databases. Ask your librarian or information technology specialist for details.
- Design unique, personally relevant assignments that students cannot purchase online, and entertain alternatives to papers.

Instructor Feedback

You need to continually monitor your students' participation and progress in your online course. LMS tools generally make it easy to view student activity in different course areas:

- Plan to give periodic feedback to students on their progress with an emphasis on how they can improve.
- Time management presents challenges in online courses without a fixed meeting schedule, so actively encourage your students to stay on task. Preplan reminders to send out to students each week about the progress they should be making or due dates for upcoming assignments.
- Early in the course, use the LMS to check who has and has not been online, and urge any latecomers to get on board.
- After the first academic discussion, send an e-mail to each student to affirm that she or he is on track and should continue with the same quality, or explain how a discussion post fell short and what the student can do in future discussions to hit the mark.

Final Course Grades

Make clear how discussions (the quantity and quality of participation), peer reviews, assignments, and tests contribute to the final grade. Following the official grading scheme of your program or institution, match the ranges of points or percentages to course letter grades from A to F. Clearly describe how you will deal with late work and emergencies, and give the link to "My Grades" so that they can check their progress at any time.

Student Feedback

An underlying assumption in online course design standards is that you care how students perceive the course and think it can be improved. So make sure to periodically ask students for their opinions:

- Create discussion forums with the titles "How Is It Going?," "Most Useful Things," "Muddiest Points," and "Ask the Prof."
- Send a survey to students with questions about aspects of your course, such as how well a publisher's resources are working for them, what challenges they are having with technology, or what material has proven most helpful to their learning.

- If you give an objective test in which most students do not do well, be prepared to conduct an item analysis to identify the troublesome items. Your LMS may furnish the item analysis so you can see what questions produced the most wrong answers and what distracters many students chose. For classroom tests, you can find step-by-step directions for item analysis at:
  - *Classroom Assessment: Selected Response* (Pinellas School District and University of South Florida): https://fcit.usf.edu/assessment/selected/responsec.html
  - *Item Analysis* (University of Kansas): http://www.specialconnections.ku.edu/?q=assessment/quality_test_construction/teacher_tools/item_analysis
  - *Item Analysis of Classroom Tests: Aims and Simplified Procedures* (Linda S. Gottfredson, University of Delaware): http://www.udel.edu/educ/gottfredson/451/unit9-guidance.htm
  - Also consider asking students what created the difficulties
- At the end of the course, give a wrap-up assignment in which students can reflect on their learning and compare what they could do at the beginning of the course to what they can do after completing it.

COURSE MATERIALS

Organization

Use logical organization for facilitating your own and your students' course navigation, and make that organization visible. Avoid long scrolling. Use a chronological scheme in which one folder for each week or module contains all the materials students will need to study. This approach will simplify the organization for the students and reduce their chances of getting lost in the course layout.

Content Materials

Ensure that your content materials are comprehensive enough to help students achieve your course outcomes:

- Sequence and structure your course content to help students see the relationships among topics. Prepare a graphic syllabus to display these connections.
- Label the materials that are required versus optional and state how to access them.
- Make the purpose and value of the materials explicit, especially if a title fails to convey the content or topic.

Learning Activities

Make sure that each activity has a purpose that clearly aligns with one or more outcomes and that you communicate this purpose to students:

- Effective activities include discussions, peer review, group work, interactive learning objects, self-assessments, reflections, flash cards, online quizzes, practice exams, and periodic progress reports on larger projects.
- Choose and design activities to give students practice performing the learning outcomes with the goal of their achieving them at a high level. Make most of these practice activities ungraded, and inform students of this.

- To help students learn how the technology works, give some low-stakes or ungraded fun quizzes and assignments early in the course.
- If you teach a mathematical or other problem-solving discipline, prepare process worksheets, worked examples, and partially worked examples to reduce students' cognitive load and scaffold their learning.
- When possible, allow students choices and options to further explore concepts that interest them.

Media Variety

Different kinds of materials should support learning:

- Students often will view a video or listen to a podcast rather than read material. Consider giving them a checklist or set of questions to answer while viewing or listening. Keep in mind that most students attend to no more than six minutes of a video, so record or select several short videos rather than one long one.
- For variety, try to add audio and interactive sites. For example, a number of music-oriented sites allow students to manipulate rhythm and sounds. Some biology videos demonstrate dissection procedures. Some physiology videos show blood flow through the circulatory system. Documentaries and virtual reality dramatize history.

Academic Integrity

Model academic integrity by practicing it in your course documents:

- Cite the sources of all images, videos, audio, and websites, as well as content.
- Make sure your course materials comply with online copyright guidelines. When in doubt, consult your library or institution's general counsel.
- Students need to know your personal expectations for academic integrity in your course. Provide links to relevant campus policies, but also explain what you mean in your own words and give students resources to guide them. Place the positive expectations and code of ethics ahead of the consequences for cheating and plagiarism.

■ STUDENT INTERACTIONS WITH THE CONTENT, INSTRUCTOR, AND PEERS

Students need to interact with the course content, with you, and with each other. Explain your expectations for interactions of each type and their relationship to your course outcomes.

Interactions with the Content

See the "Course Materials" section above. In addition, connect the interactions with the content to real-world problems and issues and require students to apply material and develop higher-level thinking and problem-solving skills.

Interactions with You as Instructor

Never forget the huge influence you have on your students' success:

- Suggest ways that students can succeed in your course: study strategies for your discipline, ways of thinking in it, and tips for overcoming the special time management challenges of online learning.
- Privately guide students who are off track to get back on the right path.
- Plan to put out a motivational message every week or two.

Interactions with Fellow Students

What you do to foster student-to-student interaction should fit with your personal style and the character of the course. Keep in mind that online students in particular have no time to waste, so explain the value of these interactions, even the introductions and group work:

- Dedicate a discussion forum or blog for students to introduce themselves and share information. You might ask them to describe what they want to get out of the course, what tips they have for succeeding online, and how the course fits in with their education or career plans.
- Model what you expect by posting your own introduction to start.
- Ask students to share photos of themselves and their hobbies.
- Invite students to participate in an icebreaker, such as telling two truths and one lie and having other students guess the lie.
- Students can get to know each other and work together more effectively in small groups. Generally four or five members work well.
- The LMS should let you set up groups randomly by the computer or manually by you as soon as students enroll in the course. It should also supply a link where they can see their group members but not the members of other groups. Depending on the LMS, you may need to add yourself and any assistants to each group. You can also let each group review the progress of other groups, even if only making creative use of discuss threads where you designate discussion space for each group.
- On occasion, you may want groups to report out their deliberations or research findings to the whole class, in which case you should set up a class discussion forum for this purpose.

Accessibility Resources

This appendix contains six parts: (1) strategies to make access to course materials easy; (2) ways to make accessible document files, such as a syllabus; (3) ways to design accessible PowerPoint presentations; (4) captioning resources, (5) accessibility checks, and (6) resources for students.

■ STRATEGIES TO MAKE ACCESS TO COURSE MATERIALS EASY

The following resources provide overall strategies and tips for creating accessible course materials and organizing your course.

Creating Access Strategies

From Educational Institutions

- About Universal Design for Learning (University of Vermont): http://www.uvm.edu/~cdci /universaldesign/?Page=about-udl/guidelines-principles.php&SM=about-udl/submenu.html
- Tutorials (documents, captioning, and PowerPoints from North Carolina State University): https://oit .ncsu.edu/help-support/it-accessibility/tutorials/
- Birbeck for All: Joined up Thinking on Accessibility (Birbeck University of London): http://app1.its .bbk.ac.uk/xerte2/play.php?template_id=468#page1section1
- Accessibility (audit course content, video captions, Microsoft Office, and Adobe PDF from Penn State University): http://accessibility.psu.edu/
- CalPoly Accessibility (checklist from California Polytechnic University): http://www.accessibility .calpoly.edu/content/instmaterials/fac_checklist

231

- E-learning Faculty Modules: Accessibility (Kansas State University): http://elearningfacultymodules.org/index.php/Accessibility
- Universal Design and Accessibility for Online Learning (Blackboard short course, Illinois Online Network): https://www.coursesites.com/webapps/Bb-sites-course-creation-BBLEARN/courseHomepage.htmlx?course_id=_1263_1
- Web Design (course design, colors for the color blind, and style guide): http://www.ion.uillinois.edu/resources/tutorials/webdesign/index.asp
- Fast Facts (guided notes, accessible documents, different disabilities, and writing from Ohio State University): https://ada.osu.edu/resources/fastfacts/
- IT Services Accessibility (quick guides for Word, Excel, Adobe, and dotCMS from Indiana University-Purdue University Fort Wayne [IPFW]): http://www.ipfw.edu/training/accessibility.html
- Accessibility Checklist (Office of Institutional Equity, IPFW): https://www.ipfw.edu/offices/hr-oie/ethics-compliance/web-accessibility

From Government and Accessibility Organizations

- Worldwide Access: Accessible Web Design (DO-IT): http://www.washington.edu/doit/world-wide-access-accessible-web-design
- Tips on Designing for Web Accessibility (The Worldwide Web Consortium [W3C], Web Accessibility Initiative): https://www.w3.org/WAI/gettingstarted/tips/designing
- How Can You Make Resources Accessible for Those with Disabilities? (Jisc): https://www.jisc.ac.uk/blog/how-can-you-make-resources-accessible-for-those-with-disabilities-13-jul-2015
- Best Practice Library (Section508.gov): https://www.section508.gov/best-practices
- How to Meet WCAG 2.0 (guidelines with examples of failures): https://www.w3.org/WAI/WCAG20/quickref/
- Section 508 Checklist: http://webaim.org/standards/508/checklist
- Equal Access to Software and Information (EASI) (webinars listed by month): http://easi.cc/clinic.htm
- Free Learning Tools (for UDL from the Center for Applied Special Technology [CAST]): http://www.cast.org/our-work/learning-tools.html#.WPPpjVPytAY

From Commercial Organizations

- Microsoft Accessibility (guides for accessibility in Microsoft products): http://www.microsoft.com/enable/default.aspx
- Organizing Your Course Accessibly (Desire2Learn): https://d2l.sdbor.edu/shared/sdsu/instructor/le/accessibility/organizing_your_course_accessibly.htm
- Getting Started with Creating Accessible Course Content (Blackboard): http://ondemand.blackboard.com/r91/documents/getting_started_with_accessible_content.pdf

Creating Access Strategies for Math and Science Courses

- Math & Science Accessibility (Word, PowerPoints, tests, dealing with online publisher content, and links to resources such as MathTrax and Access STEM from Portland Community College): http://www.pcc.edu/resources/instructional-support/access/math.html

- Solutions for the Accessibility Community (Design Science, developer of scientific and technical software, such as MathType, MathFlow, and MathPlayer): https://www.dessci.com/en/solutions/access/
- Texas School for the Blind and Visually Impaired, Math Home Page: http://www.tsbvi.edu/math

Organizing Your Course

- *Blackboard Great Ideas: Organizing Your Course* (Duke University video, 3:09): https://www.youtube.com/watch?v=TIMgU1nj1Vs
- 20 Tips for Teaching an Accessible Online Course (organizing a course, structure, headings, fonts; Disabilities, Opportunities, Internetworking, and Technology [DO-IT]): http://www.washington.edu/doit/20-tips-teaching-accessible-online-course

■ WAYS TO MAKE ACCESSIBLE DOCUMENT FILES

The following sources recommend how to choose fonts, scan documents, create tables and data displays, create an accessible syllabus, add alternative text and tag descriptions for images, create accessible Word and PDF files, make talking book and Braille formats, and create accessible forms.

Improving Readability

- Improving Document Readability (Gonzaga University): http://www.gonzaga.edu/academics/colleges-and-schools/School-of-Business-Administration/undergraduate/SBAWR/IDR.asp
- WebAim: Fonts: http://webaim.org/techniques/fonts/#blink
- Tips on Writing for Accessibility (W3C, Web Accessibility Initiative): https://www.w3.org/WAI/gettingstarted/tips/writing.html

Scanning Documents

- Creating High Quality Scans (University of Washington): http://www.washington.edu/accessibility/documents/scans/

Creating Tables and Data Displays

- Make Your Excel Spreadsheets Accessible (Microsoft): https://support.office.com/en-us/article/Make-your-Excel-spreadsheets-accessible-6cc05fc5–1314–48b5–8eb3–683e49b3e593
- Accessible Tables in MS Word 2010 (John Rizzo, San Diego State University, video, 5:30): https://www.youtube.com/watch?v=d1HxroNvXK8&list=PL-wI_kCeoHEs0I_6U8Ami2HgilzNnXH5C
- Professional Development for Educators (National Center for Accessible Media): http://ncam.wgbh.org/experience_learn/educational_media/describing-images-for-enhanced/professional-development-for-e

Adding Styles

- Using Styles in MS Word 2010 (Jon Rizzo, San Diego State University, video 6:05): https://www.youtube.com/watch?v=xSfRiIi_R_4&list=PL-wI_kCeoHEs0I_6U8Ami2HgilzNnXH5C&index=3

- Creating Accessible Documents in Word (University of Washington): http://www.washington.edu/accessibility/documents/word/
- Creating Accessible PDFs from Microsoft Word (University of Washington): http://www.washington.edu/accessibility/documents/pdf-word

Creating an Accessible Syllabus

- Creating an Accessible Syllabus (GRCC video, 7:12): https://www.youtube.com/watch?v=tHEGtHF7Eq4
- IPFW Syllabus Template with built-in styles: http://ipfw.edu/celt/
- Accessible Syllabus: Using the Accessible Syllabus Template (California State University, Sacramento): http://www.csus.edu/atcs/tools/instructional/syllabus_template_guide.pdf
- Universally Designed Syllabus Materials (University of Colorado, Boulder): http://www.colorado.edu/accessibility/resources/universally-designed-syllabus-materials
- Tips to Reach All Students with a Universally Designed Syllabus (University of Vermont): http://www.uvm.edu/~cdci/universaldesign/files/ud_syll_tips.pdf

Adding AltText and AltTags

- Social Security Administration Guide: Alternate Text for Images (steps and examples): https://www.ssa.gov/accessibility/files/SSA_Alternative_Text_Guide.pdf
- OpenOffice.org Writer (an alternative to Microsoft Office that allows adding altTags to images on a Mac, WebAIM): http://webaim.org/techniques/ooo/

Fixing Existing PDF Files

- Fixing Inaccessible PDFs Using Adobe Acrobat Pro (University of Washington): http://www.washington.edu/accessibility/documents/pdf-acrobat/
- SensusAccess (to convert a number of files into more readable formats; for example, bad PDFs can become readable Word files): http://www.sensusaccess.com/
- Equidox (to convert files to accessible formats): https://equidox.co/

Creating Accessible Files

- Microsoft Word: Principles into Practice for different versions of Microsoft Word (WebAIM): http://webaim.org/techniques/word/
- Making an Accessible Google Doc (University of North Carolina): https://accessibility.unc.edu/making-accessible-google-doc-faculty
- Documents, Presentations, and Spreadsheets (Jisc): https://www.jisc.ac.uk/guides/documents-presentations-and-spreadsheets?f[0]=field_project_topics%3A421&sorting=title%7CASC
- Cheatsheets (Word, PDF, PowerPoint Excel, and captions from the National Center on Disability and Access to Education [NCDAE]): http://ncdae.org/resources/cheatsheets/
- Guidelines for Accessible Word Documents (Arapahoe Community College and Red Rocks Community College): http://www.rrcc.edu/sites/default/files/u172/Guidelines%20for%20Accessible%20Word%20Documents%202013_0.pdf

- 30 Web Accessibility Tips (alt text, headings and PDFs from DO-IT): http://www.washington.edu/accesscomputing/tips/
- Best Practices for Educators & Instructors (Word, PowerPoint, and PDFs from the National Center on Accessible Educational Materials [NCAEM]): http://aem.cast.org/creating/best-practices-educators-instructors.html#.WZ8pcZOGPq0
- Microsoft Word—Creating Accessible Documents (Windows and Mac from WebAIM): http://webaim.org/techniques/word/
- Make Your Word Documents Accessible (Microsoft): https://support.office.com/en-us/article/Make-your-Word-documents-accessible-d9bf3683–87ac-47ea-b91a-78dcacb3c66d
- Make Your PDFs Accessible (Microsoft): https://support.office.com/en-us/article/Create-accessible-PDFs-064625e0–56ea-4e16-ad71–3aa33bb4b7ed
- Incorporating Accessibility and Usability When Using LMS and CMS Systems (images, alt text, hyperlinks, and headings from Drexel University): http://gcpsx.coeps.drexel.edu/tech_resources/pdf/Learn_Access_BestPractices.pdf
- PDF Accessibility Overview (Adobe Systems): http://www.adobe.com/accessibility/pdf/pdf-accessibility-overview.html
- Guidelines for Accessible PDFs (Red Rocks Community College): http://www.rrcc.edu/sites/default/files/u172/Guidelines%20for%20Accessible%20PDF%20files.pdf
- Using Google Drive (University of North Carolina): https://accessibility.unc.edu/using-google-drive-faculty

Creating Accessible Forms

- Creating Accessible Forms: General Form Accessibility (WebAIM): http://webaim.org/techniques/forms/
- Creating Accessible Forms: Accessible Form Controls (WebAIM): http://webaim.org/techniques/forms/controls
- Creating Accessible PDF Forms Using Adobe Acrobat Pro (Washington State University): http://www.washington.edu/accessibility/documents/pdf-forms/

Using Talking Book and Braille Formats

- Creating the Best Way to Read and Publish (ways to save a Word file to a DAISY Digital Talking Book format): http://www.daisy.org/
- Creating Nonvisually Accessible Documents (Word, PowerPoint, PDF, and Braille from the National Federation of the Blind): https://nfb.org/images/nfb/products_technology/creating_accessible_documents.docx
- Robo-Braille: Enhancing Document Accessibility (RoboBraille.org): http://www.visionaware.org/blog/visionaware-blog/robobraille-enhancing-document-accessibility-by-scott-davert-hknc-for-deaf-blind-youths-and-adults/12
- Convert a File: https://www.robobraille.org/
- Word—Top 10 Guidelines for Making Your Documents Braille-Ready (Braille Translation Software, Duxbury Systems): http://www.duxburysystems.com/documentation/dbt11.1/working_with_word/Word_Top_10_guidelines.htm
- American Foundation for the Blind's Commitment to Web Accessibility (how the foundation creates accessible materials): http://www.afb.org/info/programs-and-services/technology-evaluation/creating-accessible-websites/afbs-commitment-to-web-accessibility/1235

■ WAYS TO DESIGN ACCESSIBLE POWERPOINT PRESENTATIONS

Most PowerPoint files require layout adjustments, alternative text, and conversion to another format.

- PowerPoint Accessibility (WebAIM): http://webaim.org/techniques/powerpoint/
- Make Your PowerPoint Presentations Accessible (Microsoft): https://support.office.com/en-us/article/Make-your-PowerPoint-presentations-accessible-6f7772b2–2f33–4bd2–8ca7-dae3b2b3ef25?ui=en-US&rs=en-US&ad=US&fromAR=1
- Seven Steps to Creating an Accessible PowerPoint Slideshow and Saving It to a PDF (California Department of Rehabilitation): http://accessibility.sc.gov/Documents/7-Steps-2-Create-Accessible-PowerPoint-Slideshow.pdf
- LecShare Lite and LecShare Pro (to convert PowerPoint to other formats, including Word or an accessible narrated presentation, from LecShare): http://lecshare-inc.software.informer.com
- Accessible Content with Tools You Know and Use (Coombs and Miranda, EASI): http://easi.cc/archive/office-sept2010/part4/web_data/slides_and_notes.htm

■ CAPTIONING RESOURCES

These websites streamline the process of captioning videos and multimedia productions:

- Sub-titling Text Add-In for Microsoft PowerPoint (STAMP, Microsoft): https://support.office.com/en-us/article/Sub-titling-text-add-in-for-Microsoft-PowerPoint-STAMP-df091537-fb22-4507-898f-2358ddc0df18
- YouTube Tips (Luanne Fose, Cal Poly): http://content-calpoly-edu.s3.amazonaws.com/classtech/1/documents/video_services/YouTube_Tips_Tutorial_%28ADA%29.pdf
- Creating Video and Multimedia Products That Are Accessible to People with Sensory Impairments (captioning from DO-IT): http://www.washington.edu/doit/creating-video-and-multimedia-products-are-accessible-people-sensory-impairments
- Cheatsheets (scroll down for captioning YouTube videos, from National Center on Disability and Access to Education): http://ncdae.org/resources/cheatsheets/#accessibility3
- Adding Closed Captions to YouTube Videos (Tech-Ease, from University of South Florida): http://etc.usf.edu/techease/4all/web-accessibility/adding-closed-captions-to-youtube-videos/
- Archive for the "Accessibility" Category: Video Captioning: DIY Method Using YouTube (Indiana University): http://ittrainingtips.iu.edu/accessibility/video-captioning-diy-method-using-youtube/03/2016/
- Add Your Own Subtitles and Closed Captions (YouTube Help): https://support.google.com/youtube/answer/2734796?hl=en
- Amara Subtitle Editor (add subtitles and volunteer to help others if you are so inclined): https://www.amara.org/en/
- Using the Amara Subtitle Editor (video): https://www.youtube.com/watch?v=-NxoPqYwVwo&list=PLjdLzz0k39ykXZJ91DcSd5IIXrm4YuGgE
- Media Access Generator (MAGpie) (free captioning tool from the National Center for Accessible Media): http://ncam.wgbh.org/invent_build/web_multimedia/tools-guidelines/magpie
- Captions Made Simple (Rev, $1 a minute): https://www.rev.com/caption?gclid=CJDi26aVks8CFdgQgQodaYoPOw